"I'm all about looking for the good because when you do, that is exactly what you see. Blindness has taught me that no matter how dark life seems, there is still goodness and grace all around. That is why I love Bobby Lewis' book! He helps us see beyond the bad news and focus our hearts on hope. I really think he may have the cure for the common headlines right here on these pages! After reading just one chapter, I was reminded that God is good. He is here. There is hope and joy is possible."

Jennifer Rothschild
Author of 14 books including bestsellers
Lessons I Learned in the Dark and *Me, Myself and Lies*

"I enjoyed reading the chapter on Eric Piburn and the day he got our big surprise! It was so touching to hear you describe what everyone was doing and how they were feeling on that day on the other side of the camera, that it brought tears to my eyes. I remember being excited to be talking to Eric via satellite, knowing that it would be a bright spot in his life, with all that he has been though. It was a special moment for all involved, and now it's even more so. Thank you for sharing your story through his eyes. I loved the whole experience!"

Vanna White
Co-host, *Wheel of Fortune*

"The stories are gripping, each one has a way of challenging you in your own journey to look at yourself and ask questions. Bobby has a way of getting to your heart in this book and I have been moved by the ability to find joy in ways I didn't know I could."

Asif Shaikh
Olympic Chaplain

FINDING JOY BEYOND THE HEADLINES

BY BOBBY LEWIS

WESTBOW
PRESS®
A DIVISION OF THOMAS NELSON
& ZONDERVAN

WestBow Press books may be ordered through booksellers or by contacting:

WestBow Press
A Division of Thomas Nelson & Zondervan
1663 Liberty Drive
Bloomington, IN 47403
www.westbowpress.com
1 (866) 928-1240

Bobby Lewis headshot taken by Dennis Hollingsworth/DRH Photography.

ISBN: 978-1-9736-3347-1 (sc)
ISBN: 978-1-9736-3348-8 (hc)
ISBN: 978-1-9736-3346-4 (e)

Library of Congress Control Number: 2018907905

Print information available on the last page.

WestBow Press rev. date: 7/23/2018

To my wife, Juslin. Finding joy is easier with you by my side.

CONTENTS

WHY I'M SEARCHING FOR JOY

"**N**ow, I'm doing something different," I said. "It was a difficult transition for me."

Not necessarily the words you'd expect to hear from someone standing on a perfectly lit stage with a newly-earned, gleaming Emmy award in his hand. But, there I was, dressed in my suit and black bow tie, delivering a somewhat bewildering speech. In front of nearly 1,000 of my peers in the industry, maybe more, I told the crowd of TV-lifers that, basically, I really never wanted to be on that stage that night.

At least, I didn't think that was what I wanted.

Two years earlier, I certainly wasn't thrilled to get the news that my dream of covering sports in my hometown was over. I'd spent the last seven years of my life working to get back home to Tampa Bay. I grew up in nearby Clearwater cheering on the hometown Tampa Bay Rays, Lightning and my USF Bulls. I loved my teams. I still hold a little bit of a grudge over being forced to miss out on the first game in then-Tampa Bay Devil Rays history back in 1998. I was forced to play my own little league game instead.

My dream of playing in the Big Leagues died shortly after that. I ran like a duck. Not an especially fast one, either. But, my dream of being around professional sports wasn't dead at all. I still had a shot to make it to the big-time arenas, albeit as the dorky news boy in a tie wielding a microphone and goofy grin. My smile has always been a little crooked.

I couldn't wipe that grin off my mug after I found out that after five years of tiny-town television experience, in sweltering Louisiana and even-hotter Oklahoma, that I'd be back in Florida doing a job I'd always wanted. My dream job lasted two years before being taken away. Change is inevitable in the TV world. That's what happens in this business. I just

1

didn't want to believe it was happening to me. It tested my faith. It tested my determination, too.

I remember the conversation with my then-news director like it was yesterday. I knew what was coming. His facial expression gave it away. I could read the ensuing bad news in his eyes. He knew how much I loved my gig. Basically, I was told that we didn't need three sports reporters in the current climate of local television. I was the odd man out. Understandable, considering I was the new guy and, subsequently, low man on the totem pole. Understandable, yet surprising. After all, I'd given two Emmy speeches the year before for my local sports reporting. I never thought that they could be my last.

That leads me back to that perfectly lit stage on that elegant December night in Orlando. Same ceremony. Same black suit. Only, I wasn't a sports reporter anymore. I was there on stage accepting an award for my new role as a human interest reporter.

The lights pierced my eyes the way the ones at ballpark used to during live shots. The spotlight partially blinded my view of the crowd. Were they listening? Did they care? Were they playing some game on their iPhone just waiting for me to quit babbling? It was hard to tell. I just wanted to finish my speech before the guy manning the audio booth in the back of the room tried to usher me off the stage with the all-too-common "wrap it up you longwinded know-it-all" music.

"Now that I've gotten a chance to do something different it's really kind of given me a chance to live out something that I appreciate in my own life," I continued.

I'd be lying if I told you I didn't at least rehearse a few lines in my head on the drive over to the gala that evening. I wanted to be prepared to deliver a line to remember if my name was called as a winner.

"It's a verse I read often. It's Colossians 3:17," I said with confidence building in my voice. The sound dude in the back probably had his finger on the "wrap it up" button, but that music would have to wait. I had a line to deliver. "It says, 'In everything that you do, do it as a representative of Jesus Christ, giving thanks to God the Father through Him'. So, I didn't necessarily want to do these stories, but now that I'm on this path, I feel like it's the right path."

From that point, everything was a bit of a blur. There was applause. It may have been gratuitous. Maybe it was genuine. I'll never know. But, I'm sure that the words that preceded the clapping hit the mark with someone out in the audience. It must have. If nothing else, it hit the mark with me.

The direct message of thankfulness from Colossians I shared that night in a room full of strangers has helped me find direction in my life. It's helped me lasso my God-given purpose. In a world full of darkness and chaos, those words have helped me *Find Joy Beyond The Headlines*.

HEADLINES DON'T TELL THE WHOLE STORY

*M*y family was ready for vacation. It had been over a year since we last traveled out of the country to visit my wife's parents. The 1,500-mile trip from Orlando to Cachi, Costa Rica would take the better part of 10 hours. Trust me, with two young kids in tow, that's not always easy. To slice off a little bit of the travel stress, we decided to stay in a hotel a mile from the airport the night before our flight to avoid potentially insurmountable traffic en route to the JetBlue terminal. Our heads hit the pillows with feelings of anticipation. We'd be spending Thanksgiving in the jungle, eating fresh bananas, and enjoying our cups of locally-grown coffee while overlooking distant, puffing volcanoes. We could not wait!

This was the kind of night where not even counting sheep would help. My body naturally woke up every 30 minutes just hoping it was time to leave. It's the same type of predictable restlessness I experience before highly anticipated rounds of golf. The excitement is slumber-suppressing. When my alarm finally did go off, I quickly got dressed and went down to the dining area where the hotel was serving a continental breakfast. A few dozen folks were milling about despite the early hour. It was free, after all. Still a little groggy, I was greeted with a depressing pre-flight headline, courtesy of the TV monitor above the coffee pots:

Murder-suicide investigation from overnight shooting.

What a way to start a vacation. I shook my head as I scooped scrambled eggs onto my plate. I thought I'd left work back at the office but the bad news followed me to the doorstep of my vacation. My food looked delicious but that headline put a bad taste in my mouth before I ever took a single bite. Evil headlines will always find you – even at an airport hotel.

"Good morning!" chirped the bubbly news anchor. But, was it? At

4

6:05 a.m., the first thing I was told that day was that two people were dead. Good morning, indeed. Negative news tends to follow us around. It's hard to escape. Headlines like that murder-suicide are all too common in this fast-paced world. Flip on any television news network and you'll hear dozens within the hour. It's not just TV, either. Radio, newspapers, online – *especially* online – all tend to sell us depressing information. I don't have an appetite for it.

I know the old saying. "If it bleeds, it leads", right? Horrible headlines get all the coverage but it perplexes me as to why. I'm told people crave it. I'm told people want to see the train wrecks. Yet, not a single soul in that entire hotel dining hall was watching the overly-jovial news anchors babble on about those two community deaths. Just me. I was the only person who took the time to look up and absorb the horrid information for longer than a sip of orange juice. As someone who works in the news world, I probably have a higher tolerance for that type of drive-by negativity. After spending over a decade in the business, I've developed an immunity to it by now. It's almost second nature to me. I've been desensitized. What used to shock me doesn't anymore. Maybe you feel the same way.

I sat at the breakfast table with a fork full of eggs and watched the rest of the travelers closely. I was curious to see who would bother viewing the screens. The gentleman two tables over from me glanced up and acknowledged the ugly headline for a split-second before returning to his free Raisin Bran. Soggy cereal was more captivating than the day's first news story. A woman arrived a few moments later and sat down within ten feet of the monitors. The TV anchors handed the story over to a capable field reporter. He stood behind yellow police tape and did a lot of gesturing in the direction of a boring-looking apartment building. The traveler never even burdened her eyes. Her ears were taking the brunt of it since the volume level was turned up exceptionally high with no channel remote in sight. I can't say that I blame those travelers for choosing toast over news headlines.

I hate the type of information this world deems headline-worthy. Reports of death, destruction, and dismay have a way of ruining an otherwise wonderful day. Headlines can be joy killers. They can be fun-suckers. Reports that make us cringe are like rain showers at a picnic. They are like dog poop on our shoes. They are impossibly awful. God didn't put us on this earth to live in fear of what may pop up on the television set at 6 p.m. He created us for joy and love. He created us to seek *good* news, and light over darkness!

Matthew 6:22 (MSG)
"Your eyes are windows into your body. If you open your eyes wide in wonder and belief, your body fills up with light."

There is so much good going on in this world. We never seem to hear about it much. Instead, we get stuck with the story about the child that was abused or the teacher who was suspended for inappropriate behavior. It's constant and it's confounding. I know you are tired of seeing, hearing, and reading the negative headlines. I know you are because I am, too. When's the last time you didn't have to hunt for a positive headline? Let's start with never. Across the globe, on websites, front pages, and news broadcasts, today will be branded as the beginning of our end. The lead story is doom. The second will be gloom. Newspapers, magazines, television, radio – it doesn't matter. The lead story never uplifts. Ever peek at headlines online? Yikes. Here is an actual headline I read from the *New York Post*:

"Turns out this 186-year old tortoise has a gay lover"

I'm not kidding. I sighed so hard I could have extinguished birthday candles. Maybe even 186 of them. What value does that add to anyone's life? In a world where the only thing that seems to matter is seizing as many attentive eyeballs as possible, headlines have spun out of control. They drain our spirits and clutter our consciences. Each new awful report serves as a media uppercut that leaves us gasping for hope. Worse yet, those headlines lull us into a false perspective on life. It can feel like an onslaught. It can feel like there is nothing but evil to broadcast in this world. It can feel defeating. BREAKING NEWS! There is good news beyond the crummy headlines! Trust me. It's my job to find it.

As much as I dislike the headlines that leave us feeling empty and miserable, I totally understand why they exist.

I'm convinced human beings want to believe that this planet is populated by mostly good people who occasionally mess up. We want to believe that most of us are good and those headlines get it all wrong. The Bible teaches otherwise.

Romans 3:23 (NLT)
"For everyone has sinned; we all fall short of God's glorious standard."

Why is there terrible news to report? We live in a broken world full of broken people spiraling out of control and in desperate need of saving. We live on a dark planet urgently seeking light. That's why disgusting news gets all the headlines and *good news* becomes the outlier. Good news is now uncommon. Good news has become an anomaly. It's oxymoronic. It's rare to see good news because, by our very nature, not one of us is good. Yet, it does exist. It exists because God exists and is working in our mess. I don't like the over-saturation of bad news any more than you do, but it sure does make me appreciate the good news.

Without frowns, you can't appreciate smiles.

Without chaos, you'll never understand peace.

Without villains, heroes would never be cheered.

If we learn to see past the negative headlines and embrace the positivity God wants us to uncover each day, we can avoid some of the downfalls that come with living in a broken world. In this modern era of non-stop global information, we simply can't avoid the negative news forever. But, we can certainly praise, uplift, and promote every granule of positive news we find on this earth. That's my mission every morning I pick up a camera and microphone.

I'm tired of the empty feeling that comes with the negative headlines. I have decided it is time to fight back.

As a Christian, I'm desperately searching for the good in the world each day. I search because I know the Source and definition of what good really is and I want others to find Him through my work. I was raised in church, pledged myself to Jesus in fifth grade, and don't apologize for my faith. There is no reason to. While on summer vacation in 2017, I got a tug on my heart. It was barely noticeable. It surely wasn't audible. But, God nudged me. He led me to an idea that I would not have come to on my own. He needed me to write a book about my role in local television news. I needed to write about sharing light in a very dark world.

When God nudges, it's best to move in the direction He's pushing.

In 2015, I transitioned from sports reporting to doing human interest stories. I got my own segment called *On The Road*. It is a collection of daily, feature stories that are uplifting and heart-warming. This new segment marked a pause in my sportscasting career and marked the beginning of what I think God has called me to do. I want viewers to see the way God works and moves in the life of the people I highlight. I want them to realize there is more to life than the junk they hear about at the top of a newscast. I want them to understand that their Creator loves them and is looking out for them through the chaos of the headlines. I want my stories to remind people that there is joy out there, ready to be found. Those stories are way more appealing to me than the stuff we hear first:

A woman gets horribly burned in a highway car wreck.

A baby dies after being left in a hot car for hours at a daycare facility.

A man shoots someone after an argument over a pair of Nikes.

We need good news badly! I have a desire to tell stories that make people smile. I want people to stop what they are doing and look – then keep watching for encouragement. I want people to see good news that penetrates all the way to their hearts. I want to create a personal brand that changes people's minds and opens their eyes to a world beyond the headlines. Basically, I want to do these types of stories:

A young girl races her Soap Box Derby car with a photo of her inspiring grandpa taped inside.

Married couple converts their 1951 Ford farm truck into rolling pizza-mobile.

A musician creates hundreds of mentors for at-risk youth through traveling concerts.

Those are true stories. I shot, edited, and aired all of them for my *On The Road* segment. Good news does exist! When God shows up, I think we need to tell people about it! I want to be the two minutes of "happy" in a newscast full of frowns. Call me crazy, but I think good news belongs in the news. With God's help, I think I'm making it happen, with stories like these:

A local company gives away free air conditioning units to servicemen on Veteran's Day.

Bomb squad officers build beeping Easter eggs for hearing-impaired children's egg hunts.

A 60-year old starts life over with a homemade popsicle business.

Autistic boy finds peace after finding his passion for golf.

Those were mine, too. None of them were the first story of the newscast, but we did air them.

I'm so thankful that God redirected my career. I would have been happy reporting on sports forever, but that would not have made much of a dent in the world. Reaching out and sharing the impact God's influence has on the world is way more important the showing highlights of another homerun or touchdown. I have the opportunity to live out the "be salt and light" command Jesus gave in the most famous sermon ever preached, found in Matthew 5-7. I want positive stories to shine like a bonfire in the woods. I want my uplifting stories to be like a lighthouse in a hurricane. I want the good news I find to be as unavoidable as fireworks in the midnight sky.

My faith has a platform. I am not going to blatantly slam "Jesus stories' in everyone's face every day at 6 p.m., but I know that God's presence needs to be in each newscast. The world is broken, but good news can be the glue we need.

Overwhelming amounts of negative news falsely shapes our reality and gives us a skewed depiction of what the world is truly like. One horrible headline bleeds into the next horrible headline and our emotions begin to get twisted into a frenzy. They gather up and stick to each and leaves us depressed. Headlines pollute and confuse us. Headlines can give us information whiplash. They can cause our spirit to go stale. That's why people change the channel.

Science teaches us that there really is no such thing as darkness. Scientifically speaking, "darkness" is just the absence of light. Similarly, "cold" is defined scientifically as the absence of heat. To me, the same can be said about "evil". I think the world has an absence-of-good problem. That's apparent from the headlines:

"There is so much hate and racism out there!"

"Cops just can't stop shooting innocent people!"

"Teachers everywhere are having sex with students!"

"Did you hear what he said this time?! This President is an idiot!"

"There is just so much awful stuff going on in the world!"

Yes, there is evil in this world. There is also a lot of good. You will find what you're looking for in life. Want joy? It's there. Satisfied with the current headlines? Keep consuming them. I'd rather seek God's goodness in the lives of the people who put their trust in Him:

The third-grader who packs take-home bags full of food for hungry classmates.

The man who has rescued over 200 exotic birds because he's amazed by their beauty.

The senior who made the varsity swim team – with just one leg.

All true. All God. The evidence is there if you just open your eyes and heart.

Romans 1:20 (NLT)

"For ever since the world was created, people have seen the earth and sky. Through everything God made, they can clearly see his invisible qualities – his eternal power and divine nature. So, they have no excuse for not knowing God."

I love thinking about God's "invisible qualities". Just because we can't see God doesn't mean that His work isn't plain to the naked eye. I can attest to that wholeheartedly. How else could I explain what I've seen on the job?

A deaf teenager starring on the high school football team.

A Key West toll booth operator meets his wife in the drive-thru window.

A woman creates glass beads for hospitalized kids in honor of her sister who died as a child.

These are REAL stories and REAL examples of people God has put in my path. They didn't make the headlines, but they made an impact on the world. I never thought I'd get a chance to meet them and share their uplifting stories.

I have broken this book down into seven chapters, each outlining a Biblical principle. God wants us to show ambition, joy, thankfulness, blessing, love, giving, and perseverance. In each section, there are stories of special people who all exemplify how God has come to work in their lives and used them to fight back against the headlines around us. Matching my *On The Road* stories with these principles has opened my eyes to God's goodness even more. I hope it does the same for you.

Maybe you like the headlines. Maybe you want to hear about shootings, terror, and abuse in your newscasts. I understand that sometimes there is an obligation to cover that stuff. But, the devil wants to convince us that the only things happening are doom and gloom. Don't believe it. I'd like to challenge you to seek out joy in your community. It's the challenge I eagerly accept every day. It's out there! I promise you, positive is possible.

With God's help, I'm *Finding Joy Beyond The Headlines.*

AMBITION

*M*y two kids don't know what it means to sleep in past sunrise. I've been known to hit the snooze button for an hour. As weary as I may be, it's nothing compared to my poor wife. Wow, is she a saint! She is a homeschool mom, which means she wakes up at the office, doesn't get vacation days, or a salary. Her commute is short and her days are long. At least I get to put on pants and leave! Dealing with kids comes with its fair share of challenges. My son peed on the bathroom wall the other day. My daughter used nail polish to redecorate her closet. Our latest parenting challenge required patience and persistence. We needed to expel the word "can't" from our home.

That four-letter word is an ambition killer.

My daughter is smart. I mean, *really* smart. Smarter than I was at six years old, I'm sure! Her favorite subjects are science and history. What six-year-old says that? I did well in school. My wife did, too. But, this girl has more than just book smart – she's a problem-solving machine. She is a walking solution. She comes up with workarounds for almost every obstacle. So, I was a bit surprised when she drifted into what I like to call, the "can't gutter".

My wife would ask her to write out a spelling word.

"I can't".

She'd ask her to fold her clothes.

"I can't".

I'd ask her to help put away the dishes.

"I can't".

To me, that word is like manicured fingernails on a chalkboard. Each time she said it, my little angel was quickly re-educated on the expected infrequency of "can't" in our home.

I hate "can't". It is the enemy of ambition. "Can't" is the enemy of effort. If you think I hate the word, imagine what God thinks of "can't". It's not even in His vocabulary. "Can't" will handcuff opportunities waiting to be seized in your life. "Can't" saws your dreams off at the knees. "Can't" is a gateway excuse. If we allow ourselves to foster a "can't" habit when it comes to little things, falling back on "can't" when things get tougher will be far too easy.

Getting rid of that word took a lot of tough love. It took a lot of gentle convincing and nurturing. It required self-esteem boosts and confidence injections. We had to provide our daughter with detailed examples of the times in her past when she'd slain giants. We had to point out that if she toppled roadblocks before, she could easily do it again. It took a while, but eventually "can't" went extinct in our home.

My wife was a trooper through it all. Gradually, our daughter's self-confidence grew. She started diving into school assignments that she was hesitant to try just a few weeks earlier. She was attacking her homework and showing off all that she'd learned. My wife and I were happy to see her blossom into someone who didn't see yellow caution tape everywhere. Our encouragement is all it took to get her to hack up hesitancy and charge on. Expelling "can't" eliminated self-erected roadblocks. Ever build any of those in your life?

The headlines are full of "can't". We can't talk about God in school. They can't have civil political conversations. Teachers can't teach topics that could possibly offend someone.

If all we hear on the news are stories about "can't", where are we going to find the motivation to steer ourselves back towards "can"?

Our Heavenly Father wants Godly children from our marriages. And Godly children are confident children. If you're a parent, don't you want your kids to live life with a bull-by-the-horns attitude? Timidity is one of the devil's tools. It will rob you of ambitious accomplishments. I want to raise fearless kids that have a *CHARGE HADES WITH A WATER PISTOL* attitude. I want them to laugh at giants. I want them to squash problems with their heels and kick future ones in the teeth.

The constant barrage of overwhelmingly sad headlines seems to poke holes in our confidence. Stories of failure become discouraging darts, capable of deflating ambitious attitudes. I've had many good days punctured by the news of a school shooting that killed innocent children.

If you want to be ambitious, you must be willing to risk something.

One of my favorite stories in the Bible is a New Testament account of a bunch of buddies who showed incredible ambition to help a crippled friend. Four men picked up their friend by the corners of his mat and carried him through town to a packed house where Jesus was teaching. There were people everywhere! Picture a mosh pit in your living room. It was a mess. The four men, desperate to help their paralyzed friend, climbed up to the roof and cut a giant hole in a stranger's home before lowering the handicapped guy down through the opening to where Jesus stood preaching! (Read about it in Luke 5:17-25) I'm not sure what the home insurance policies looked like back then, but I hope the guy who owned that house had a good plan. After Jesus amazed everyone by telling the crippled man to get up off the floor and walk, nobody was staring at the sun through the damaged roof anymore. They fixed their eyes squarely on the miraculous healing of a paralyzed man as he danced and praised the Son of God.

It's a remarkable example of a quartet of ambitious men. They risked a lot for their handicapped friend. They risked public ridicule. They risked having to pay for a destroyed house. They risked Jesus deciding not to heal the man. Can you imagine the kind of conversations that were taking place during this impromptu home demolition project? The living room crowd was probably shocked. *"Who are these crazy vandals trying to rob the home through the roof? Are they going to pay for that? Where is the homeowner?"* Meanwhile, the faithful four on the roof was probably encouraging their paralyzed friend. *"Just a few more seconds, man, and you'll be healed! Jesus is down there! You're going to walk today!"* It must have been incredible to witness!

To live with Godly ambition, you must be willing to do something in faith that others may find ridiculous. I can just picture the crowd pointing, laughing, and shouting. *"They're ripping off the roof!"* None of them knew what they were about to witness. Without those four guys risking looking like a bunch of crazy men, tearing mud and branches off the roof, this miracle would never have happened! There was a barrier standing between the crippled man on the mat and the solution to his situation. Jesus was the answer, and the only way to Him was to tear up the roof! The ambition of four courageous men removed that barrier. Had they surveyed the scene, been discouraged by the situation, and left, the crowd of naysayers would have been robbed of witnessing Jesus heal a paralyzed man. It required four men taking a calculated risk. They were desperate for help and executed *Operation: No More Paralysis* to perfection.

I marvel at that kind of ambition. I really like how Paul describes the attitude we should take:

2 Timothy 2:15 (NLT)
"Work hard so you can present yourself to God and receive his approval. Be a good worker, one who does not need to be ashamed and who correctly explains the word of truth".

To become ambitious, you must attack the tasks God has set before you. I have seen so many people succeed because they made the decision to get up and go! We need to stop waiting on something good to find us. The devil prowls around like a hungry lion looking for something to devour. Ask any lion and he'll tell you, it's easier to stalk something that's stationary. We need to chase good news! Today, saddle up and set off in the direction of your biggest goal. Anything less and you're shortchanging yourself.

The opposite of ambition is not laziness. It's timidity. Timidity is 180-degrees off course from God's plan. It will handcuff your progress. Timidity holds you back from running your race. Forget reaching the finish line. You can't finish what you never start. Think of the four friends of the crippled man. They knew Jesus was nearby and had the ability to heal their buddy. What if they had just sat by and done nothing? What if they chose to hesitate? They would have missed out on being part of one of the biggest miracles in history! Their friend could have spent the rest of his life begging for loose change from his ratty, dirty floor mat on the corner of the city street. Lugging their buddy all the way to the feet of Jesus and tearing up a stranger's roof was worth it!

Ambition is the fuel that drives God's purpose in your life.

My favorite types of stories are the ones where longshots accomplish something nobody expects. Those longshots are the ones who embrace challenges. They are the ones who don't accept words like "no", "can't" and "won't". They don't see problems as insurmountable obstacles. They see them as hurdles waiting to be sailed over. They apply ambition.

People think the life of someone on TV is glamorous. It's actually pretty tough. I am what's called a Multimedia Journalist. It's an overly-fancy title that basically means I get no help. It's the way of the world in most TV markets these days. If you can find one person who has the skills of three positions, why wouldn't you just pay one person to do all three jobs? I write, shoot, edit, produce, and plan every one of my stories. I even write what the anchors read on set. There are plenty of reasons to grumble but I've found that choosing to be ambitious eliminates those urges to complain. I have to find my motivation. It's usually rooted in a desire to tell a better story than everyone else that day.

I remember back in 2016, I stumbled across what I thought was going to be a great story. I found a professional underwater photographer named Mark. He had recently been bitten by a blue shark and survived! I was salivating over this story. I just had to meet this guy! The year before I met him, he received a phone call from a buddy who saw a beautiful blue shark near Mark's home. It was quite atypical of a blue shark to be in water that shallow. It was the perfect opportunity to get a big-money shot of a rare animal. Shark videos pay Mark's bills, so he grabbed his camera gear and wetsuit and raced to the shark. Within minutes, he was in the water, just a few inches away from the apex predator.

After a few minutes of shooting, Mark started to get the feeling that the shark was tiring of having a camera in its face. He decided to ignore the warning signs and get a few more frames of video. He kicked his flippers until he pulled even with the shark's dorsal fin. As he zoomed in on the animal, it whipped around and chomped down on Mark's left arm. The damage had been done. The shark disappeared with one swish of its powerful tail.

A friend pulled Mark into the boat and immediately applied pressure to Mark's wound. He was rushed back to land and on to the hospital. On the way, Mark's girlfriend was alerted to how bad the situation was getting. His arm required 58 stitches to seal. Mark nearly died.

Doctors were somehow able to save his arm and he made a full recovery. A month after his run-in with the blue shark, Mark was back in the ocean taking videos for shows that would be seen around the world. This guy sounded like a great comeback story! I wanted to meet him!

But, I could see the upcoming roadblock. It wasn't a small one, either. Interviewing Mark and telling his fascinating survival story would require me to travel over 700 miles. I'd have to meet him in his backyard, the scene of the shark bite, in the lower Florida Keys. Driving that far out of our viewing area is something my station just didn't do, especially for a human interest story. I have worked places where political reporters or investigators travel to state capitols or to Washington, D.C. to interview important politicians. That is a bit different. A feature reporter driving 700 miles and spending all that time interviewing one person about a shark bite? Highly unlikely. The budget at most stations won't allow for that kind of creativity. My segment is designed to be hyper-local. It's all about feel-good stories in our backyard. It's not supposed to be a statewide segment. My station relies on me to be the two-minute bright spot in the news every day. I could feel my faith fading. These kind of ambitious story requests had been turned down in the past. It wasn't in the budget. It wasn't in the cards. On paper, it looked like "can't" would be an appropriate excuse. But remember, ambitious people don't say "can't". They charge on. They bust barriers.

I rolled the dice. I confidently presented my idea to the news director and told him I really wanted to do this. There was passion in my voice, even though I expected a firm "no". But, ambition can be contagious. I was so fired up about possibly telling this remarkable story, my passion ignited an interest in the people around me.

I got the green light, on one condition – I had to find a few other stories from the Keys with a local connection that would make the three-day round trip worthwhile. That was a tough task. It's hard enough to find compelling human interest stories within a few hours of our parking lot. How was I going to find a half-dozen from 700 miles away? I accepted the challenge, knowing it would not be easy to pull off.

After a week of searching and hours of phone calls, I found eight captivating connections to our area that were waiting to be told from the Keys. I presented my ideas to my boss. He smiled as he read them. He loved them all. He loved them enough to sign off on three hotel stays. That's a mini miracle! I gassed up the car and made the nine-hour trip south. I did my interview with Mark. His girlfriend gave such a compelling account of what it was like to hear that her loved one may lose his life. Mark's explanation of why he couldn't quit filming and take some boring desk job was mind-blowingly cool. He said he lived for the rush of being arms-length away from killing machines. A cubicle couldn't offer him that sensation. He was a fascinating dude. He could come face-to-face with great white sharks and hammerheads on any given Tuesday. I could have listened to his adrenaline-pumping stories for hours.

Ambition paid off. I found a gem of a story.

Had I not pushed to tell Mark's story, I would never have gotten the chance to tell other great stories from the Keys, like the one of a muralist who uses cars as canvas. He grew up 20 minutes from our TV station, moved to Key West in 1985, and is practically universally recognized as the top artist in the Keys. I also would never have met the man in the toll booth that leads from Miami to the Keys. He met his wife as she rolled through each morning to pay her $1.00 travel fee. They established a relationship a few seconds at a time each day and it led to their happily ever after. Ambition connected me to those people. Ambition gassed up the possibilities. Ambition made that week one of the best of my career. It was memorable and rewarding. I'm so glad I pushed for something that I expected to get shot down. Timidity could have kept me from adventure and success. Instead, bold ambition triumphed.

In this chapter, you're going to meet four people who all chose to embrace ambition. They vary in age, but have one thing in common: They weren't afraid to go for it. They got up each day and stretched for their goal a little further than they had the day before.

People looked at little Madison Harrison like she was crazy when she explained her dream. Imagine if she would have listened to their low expectations. Her ambitious spirit defied disbelief and taught naysaying adults (like me) a lesson.

The last place Mike Abramowitz probably wanted to spend a free Sunday morning each month was back at his office. He was there all the time for work. But, he and some buddies had an ambitious reason to rearrange the office furniture. They needed to make room for a feeding frenzy to fill bellies and souls!

Sy Schimberg could have slept in every Saturday just like his teenage buddies. Nobody would have blamed him. But, he's no ordinary teenager. Ever since that odd breakfast order at the local diner, a passion was lit inside of him to make a difference in the lives of less fortunate athletes in his neighborhood.

I am positive Donald Nutting is the only 98-year-old riding his bicycle three hours per day. He's not terribly fast, but he is abundantly persistent.

His legs are carrying around almost a century-long workload but that won't keep him from beautifying his home, one tin can at a time.

These are real people with real stories and ambitious attitudes. I want to tell stories like those. They highlight interesting people doing uplifting things in unique ways. Those are God's favorite kinds of stories! He created us to do good works, not to sit back and absorb heinous headlines. Sometimes, the best way to stand out is to stand up. The best way to get where you want to be is to get up, get going, and show a little ambition, even when doubts say it won't be worth it.

#POTUS

*I*f you are a parent, you have fallen prey to the trap of thinking your kid is the greatest mini-human on the planet. We all probably think our kids are the most amazing, beautiful, talented little angels on earth. Little Johnny should be the starting pitcher because he's clearly the best, right? Billy? Obviously, he is the smartest kid in his class. My Jenny should be center stage in the ballet recital because she's so much more graceful than the other girls! How many times have we had these thoughts? I know I have.

Who can blame us? We dream with our kids, encourage our kids, and all want to believe that they are destined for greatness. But, for every hopeful teeter, there is a realistic totter. Parents sometimes live in a fantasy world. We don't want to admit it. Only 536 people have orbited Earth. Only 12 have ever walked on the moon's surface! Odds are, your baby won't become number 13. Joey won't be the all-star starting shortstop for the New York Yankees. No matter how long he practices his music, precious little Chris won't wind up jamming on stage at the Super Bowl.

As adults, deep down, we know most of our kids aren't going to become world-famous superstars. That doesn't mean we should teach them to settle for a mediocre life. We should be aiming them higher. We should spark a confidence in them and a desire to be great. That's one of the many duties of a parent. We are to encourage our kids. We are to build them up and empower them to develop an ambitious spirit. We know the chances of them orbiting Mars, winning a World Series, or playing guitar in the halftime show are slim. So what! We should want our kids to be dreamers. Better yet, doers!

The odds are stacked against us all, but we can't let slim odds deflate our destinies. God wants great things for our children! He wants it more than we do! If you, as an earthly father, have gigantic dreams for your child, imagine the size of the dreams our Heavenly Father has planned for your little one!

Psalm 127:3-5 (NLT)

"³ Children are a gift from the LORD; they are a reward from him.
⁴ Children born to a young man are like arrows in a warrior's hands.
⁵ How joyful is the man whose quiver is full of them! He will not be put to shame when he confronts his accusers at the city gates."

It's our job as parents to point kids in the proper direction. Hopefully, someday, they end up flying down the straight and narrow path. It's my job as a dad to get my kids aimed correctly and fire them out when ready. Part of that difficult task is instructing them to try their best while pursuing the passions of their lives.

I let slim odds impact my expectations when I heard Madison Harrison's dream. I wouldn't say I scoffed at it, but I certainly wouldn't say I had much faith, either. I just couldn't picture a scenario where her dream would come true.

I met Madison, then just eight years old, in a conference room at a local industrial park. She was there snapping photos of her friends' baby dolls. She knew her way around a camera. She was spunky and joyful. I watched for an hour as she clicked her way through hundreds of photos. She told me this was her passion. Imagine that. An eight-year-old who already had a passion. She told me her budding photography business was nothing more than a tune-up for her very grand picture-taking goals. I smiled the smile that most adults do when they hear a child recite their magnificent dreams.

"Sure kid," I thought. "You'll take a photo of the President one day."

I mean, the dream sounded so cute coming out of her mouth. Her smile was bright. Her eyes radiated as much confidence as a third-grader's eyes could radiate. She was genuinely convinced that someday she would graduate from taking photos of her pals' Barbies and get a shot of President Barack Obama in action. There was no wavering from her convictions. It was going to happen! She was confident.

"I also want to take a picture of the President and his family because that would be so awesome!" she said with a smile during our interview. She looked into my camera lens without fear. Talk about ambition!

I spent the better half of the morning in a small, stuffy conference room with Madison and a dozen of her friends. She hung a blueish-white photo backdrop against the wall at the perfect angle so the children's dolls would appear as if they were encased in waves. Many of the kids who had shown up for this photo shoot were dressed identically to their toys. It was kind of a mini-fashion show. All the parents in the room thought *their* child was the cutest, no doubt.

Madison wore her black, Nikon camera strap around her neck and barked out posing commands with the grace of an Army Sergeant. She knew what she wanted and how she wanted it. She directed traffic like cops at a Macy's parade. She got everybody lined up and let loose on the shutter. If her dream was to photograph the President, he had better be ready for some directing.

If you're going to be good at something, you need to be prepared to give it your all. God doesn't honor the dreams of the half-hearted. Madison clearly was all-in on her dream. There was no hesitation in her answers to my questions and the tenacity and poise with which she spoke made me question her birth certificate. She sounded so mature. She surprised me.

Could this child really only be eight years old?

I completed the story after interviewing Madison and her mother and wished her well in her quest to someday take a shot of the President. I also warned her not to use the phrase "shot of the President" too much in public. It could become cause for alarm. I walked away from that encounter thinking Madison was a cute little girl with big goals like many other young students. I knew her ambitious story was one that would make for a great *On The Road* story. All the parents watching the newscast would all think the same thing…

"Aww. What a darling child with such unrealistic goals. I hope she makes it."

And, that'd be it. We never again would give two seconds of thought to whether young Madison would ever get to satisfy her heart's desire. Reaction to my story was exactly as I expected. Our news anchors all commented on the air that Madison was, indeed, darling. She had a bubbly personality that she inherited from her very outgoing mother. She was destined for great things in life – I just wasn't so sure she was destined for the whole picture-of-the-President thing. Any adult could see how ridiculously hard that was going to be.

Madison's mother, Andrea, started sharing my *On The Road* story on Facebook. She started getting clicks. She started getting 'likes'. She posted the story on Madison's photography business website and it started gaining traction. The story was picked up by USA Today and made the rounds across all 50 states. Madison Harrison's wish of taking a photo of President Barack Obama was starting to pick up steam.

There was smoke but not much fire. The Harrisons started using the social media hashtag, #HelpMadisonMeetPOTUS. I asked a buddy of mine, who was working for a local congressman, to make a few calls. He relayed back to me what I already knew. What Madison was asking to do was nearly impossible to pull off. It just wasn't going to happen. He made a call to Washington anyway and was shot down *quickly*. The President's days are scheduled out to the minute. There isn't a lot of space in his planner reserved for 'Make Eight-Year-Old Floridian's Dream a Reality'.

It wasn't going to happen…

The rest of that year passed and I invited Madison back to the TV station to be part of my 30-minute *On The Road* Christmas special. I found her a step ladder and she co-hosted the final segment of the show with me. She was as charismatic as ever and did a great job. She still hadn't met the President, nor did she have any real prospects of making it happen. But, there was hope. The story that we'd done together was out there in the cyber world and the internet never forgets. Even though it was still the longshot of all longshots, I was starting to feel a little more hopeful that her dream *could* happen someday.

Then, someday arrived.

A now nine-year-old Madison was going to Washington, D.C. Someone who had access to the President saw her #HelpMadisonMeetPOTUS campaign online and contacted the Harrison family. Her dream was here! It was going to happen! There were plenty of people who doubted little Madison, but she never let her youth keep her from aiming high.

"I'm pinching myself to make myself believe that I'm really going," she told me. "At first I thought it was a dream."

Madison Harrison with her photo of President Barack Obama

It was a dream that had become a reality. Madison got invited to take photos as a working media member at the United State of Women Summit. It is a gathering of some of the most powerful people in the world who all to speak on issues facing the country. Our TV station helped her with credentials, naming her our official photo ambassador. She would be among 200 media members from around the nation covering the enormous event hosted by then-First Lady, Michelle Obama. Even Oprah was there. Oprah!

I honestly couldn't believe it when I heard the news. I just couldn't wrap my mind around the fact that this little girl was going to stand in the same room as the Commander In Chief and take his photo. Her dream would be realized the moment she hit the button on top of her camera. I was proud of Madison for not giving up.

God loves dreamers. In an age where we look for affirmation more than information, dreamers live counter to convention. Dreamers attack the unattainable. Dreamers ignore critics. Dreamers don't take 'no' for an answer. Dreams are important! Even if people laugh at your dream, it's still important. It provides you with a desired target. It gives you a worthwhile finish line to chase. The ambition required to reach for your dreams, when nobody else thinks you will succeed is even more important than the dream itself. I am so glad I never told Madison that I doubted her. I know as she gets older she'll understand why I would have been inclined to think her hope of photographing the President was a bit out of reach. Turns out, faith like a child is a powerful thing.

Matthew 18:3 (NIV)
"And he said: "Truly I tell you, unless you change and become like little children, you will never enter the kingdom of heaven."

Jesus said these words to demonstrate the attitude that we should all have towards faith. Set a goal and go for it! And, when you go for it, do it with all of your soul. Kids don't have the sense of failure that adults learn over their lifetime. 'Practical' isn't in our vocabularies until we start paying bills. Kids have no reason to believe that 'Dream A' *won't* happen. In their mind, it *has* to happen! It's *their* dream! Shouldn't we all embrace childlike faith? Shouldn't we all have childlike ambition? We'd be happier dreamers, if so.

Madison Harrison's story didn't stop there. She appeared on *The Steve Harvey show*. She took photos of Oprah Winfrey. She was asked to serve as a red carpet photography correspondent for a John Legend movie premiere. She even started taking free photos aboard traveling makeover buses during dress-up events for foster children.

She's developing ambitious new dreams all the time.

God gives us dreams and sits up in the clouds like a proud parent and cheers us on as we chase them down. After we check one off the list, He drops another goal into our hearts. Then, we chase again. Ambition is the fuel. The dream is the destination.

I met with Madison a few months after her big visit to D.C. Her newest dream is to take photos on the red carpet at the Oscars. After photos of President Barack Obama and Oprah, Leonardo DiCaprio should be a piece of cake.

It's another goal that seems out of reach. It's not the first one she's had. Only, this time, I'm not doubting the ambitious photographer with childlike faith.

1 Timothy 4:12 (NIV)

"Don't let anyone look down on you because you are young,
but set an example for the believers in speech, in conduct,
in love, in faith and in purity."

A STICKY FEEDING FRENZY

*I*s there anything tastier than a peanut butter and jelly sandwich?
Many of you out there run screaming from peanuts. I get it. I have family members who can't stomach the lovable legume. They are both delicious and dangerous. For those of you who are allergic, I'm sorry. No, really. I am. Peanuts are so stinking tasty.

For many years, the seemingly simple peanut has been a staple in cuisines worldwide. The National Peanut Board (yes, there is such a thing) claims that the humble peanut probably originated in South America, most likely in either Peru or Brazil. I'd like to think peanuts grew under Adam's toes in the Garden of Eden, but who am I to judge the legitimacy of the National Peanut Board? Peanut-shapes were apparently used as decorations on South American pottery thousands of years ago. The NPB claims that Africans were the first to bring peanuts to North America. For that, we thank you. It seems like the peanut has crisscrossed the globe, entertaining taste buds along the way. Former U.S. Presidents Thomas Jefferson and Jimmy Carter were both peanut farmers! If it's good enough for the White House, it's good enough for me.

I like peanuts roasted, boiled, and smashed into butter. It takes 45 peanuts to make one ounce of peanut butter. I don't discriminate between creamy style and crunchy. I will eat it on bread, in cookies, or even straight out of the jar. Ever eaten a fluffernutter? Seriously, go treat yourself. My favorite childhood movie was Disney's, *Peter Pan*. Ironically, *Peter Pan* is also my peanut butter brand of choice.

One of my favorite stories from my career started with a man's desire to make peanut butter and jelly sandwiches.

My family has a routine on Sundays. We wake up about 8 a.m. and begin the one-hour sprint to the car. There isn't much that needs to be done, but when you have little kids in the house, accomplishing even the smallest task requires a Herculean effort. The duties of dressing, feeding, and ushering kids to the car takes forever. Socks don't always match. Teeth may not always get brushed, but we do our best. It's the only way to get to church on time.

On this particular Sunday, days I typically don't work, we had to rev the get-out-the-door engine into overdrive. I told Mike Abramowitz I would meet him at his office bright and early. He was hosting another one of his monthly "feeding frenzies". The name itself made me wonder what I'd gotten myself into.

I pulled the family car into the lot and started to unpack my camera equipment from the trunk. Young 20-somethings made their way to a little glass door on the side of a drab business plaza. In their hands were heavy-looking cardboard boxes. I rarely take my family with me on story shoots. It's tough to concentrate on my job of asking questions and recording video while keeping at least one eye on a curious child. Not this day. I wanted them there for this one. I had a feeling this story would be something my babies needed to see. My wife piled the kids out of the car and we made our way inside.

One step into Mike's office and I could tell this was indeed going to be a frenzy. At least two dozen folks packed the very small space. The room was lined with eight-foot banquet tables and stacks of bread were piled up in every corner. I still didn't know what a "feeding frenzy" was but I liked the scene. The fire marshal would not have liked this but it sure put a smile on my face.

Mike bounded over with a big grin. He extended his right hand, covered by a plastic glove, and introduced himself with a vigorous handshake.

"Welcome!"

My eyes scanned the room. I saw people of all ages and walks of life. There was a single guy slapping jelly on bread with a plastic spoon. Next to him, a middle-aged woman passed out plastic knives. Across from her, a young woman in yoga pants smeared peanut butter on slices of white bread. It was a conveyor belt of PB&J production.

Mike explained his mission. He was inspired by a national organization whose goal is to feed the homeless with peanut butter and jelly sandwiches.

He decided to start up a local chapter called PB&J For Tampa Bay. A researcher by day, Mike knew all the harrowing statistics about homelessness in his community. It was a major problem in certain sections of town.

"We need some jelly ploppers and some jelly spreaders!" Mike shouted over the crowd in a booming voice. I was beginning to see what he meant by "feeding frenzy".

The sandwiches started to stack up. What began as two empty slices of bread on one end of the table was transformed into a tasty sandwich by the time it reached the other end. Each PB&J passed through the hands of four eager volunteers before being loaded into a box on the floor. My camera was busy. I zipped around the room getting tight shots of sticky fingers and smiling workers. The "feeding frenzy" group didn't have much time. There were only about two hours to make 1,500 sandwiches.

"The hope for humanity is no longer lost," said one man as he slathered strawberry jelly onto a naked slice of bread. "It's amazing to see people just showing up and giving back to the community."

The room got louder as the sandwiches stacked up. Jars of peanut butter began to empty.

"Anybody need a spreader?" Mike shouted above the commotion. He chuckled to himself. "A lot of chaos, I get it."

Fingers furiously finished the frenzy. Mike even ran out of bread at one point and a college kid had to make a run to the store for more. After hitting the 1,500-sandwich mark, the group divvied up the food and loaded up the cars. Half blanketed the southern part of the county. The rest headed north.

I rode with Mike. We cruised towards a park where he'd had prior success finding hungry homeless people. The goal was simple: Return to the office without any food. If Mike emptied his box of sandwiches, bellies would be full. We didn't even make it to the park before pulling up next to a scruffy-looking man standing quietly near a traffic light.

"You hungry, man?" Mike asked as he rolled down the window. He passed a handful of PB&Js to the guy wearing a tattered shirt. His eyes widened as he reached for the food. As the traffic light turned green, Mike sped off towards the park. He smiled as he glanced back in his mirror.

"God Bless. That's what it's all about right there."

Our journey continued downtown where Mike and I found a line of homeless people waiting for a soup kitchen to open. The doors would remain locked for a few more hours, but homeless people were so hungry, they showed up early to get in line. The group mobbed the car after hearing we were packing dozens of freshly-made sandwiches. After that stop, Mike's PB&Js were gone.

"I've got enough," said a homeless man after eagerly accepting the food. "I can eat."

My wife and kids follow in their own car while Mike and I handed out dozens of sandwiches. After distributing all the food, I wished Mike good luck and hopped in the car with my family. We talked about what had just happened. The travel route took us all over town and we ended up being late to church that day. I didn't care. My kids *saw* church that morning and I hope they don't forget what it looked like. The Bible talks about how we are supposed to take care of those who are hurting. Lessons like that are best learned outside of Sunday school classrooms through examples of virtuous living.

<u>Matthew 25:34-40 (NLT)</u>

"Then the King will say to those on his right, 'Come, my Father has blessed you! Inherit the kingdom prepared for you from the creation of the world. I was hungry, and you gave me something to eat. I was thirsty, and you gave me something to drink. I was a stranger, and you took me into your home. I needed clothes, and you gave me something to wear. I was sick, and you took care of me. I was in prison, and you visited me.' "Then the people who have God's approval will reply to him, 'Lord, when did we see you hungry and feed you or see you thirsty and give you something to drink? When did we see you as a stranger and take you into our homes or see you in need of clothes and give you something to wear? When did we see you sick or in prison and visit you?' "The king will answer them, 'I can guarantee this truth: Whatever you did for one of my brothers or sisters, no matter how unimportant they seemed, you did for me."

The headlines in tonight's newscast won't talk about guys like Mike. They may mention something about the homeless population in the city, but only if it caused a problem for the rest of the citizens. Homelessness tends to get swept under the rug. It's not discussed much in the headlines. Call me crazy, but I think what Mike's doing with his feeding frenzies is front page news.

The day I met Mike turned out to be a bit of a milestone. The frenzy effort helped the group of caring volunteers finally surpass the 20,000-sandwich donation mark. It didn't stop there. The frenzy grew with each passing month. A little over a year after I aired that story, Mike's mission to feed the homeless blitzed past 50,000 sandwiches. The ambition required to accomplish a goal that size is off the charts.

The line that jumps off the screen at me from Mike's PB&J for Tampa Bay website is the one that is as obvious as it is serious:

"Everyone deserves to eat."

It seems so simple, yet so profound. Mike's movement is bringing nutrition and hope to the underprivileged and hurting members of his neighborhood. He could have been satisfied with donating 1,000 sandwiches. He could have stopped at 5,000. He could have thrown a big congratulatory party after hitting 20,000. Instead, he set an ambitious new goal. He wants to blow past 100,000.

Has a lack of ambition ever kept you from trying to accomplish something? True ambition never stops. It finds reasons to push forward. As long as a hungry soul exists in Mike's community, his ambition will fuel the frenzies. His website continued:

"Our heart is to reach out and remind those people that they DO matter and that there are still people who care."

The world record for the most peanut butter and jelly sandwiches made in one hour is 49,100. It was accomplished on September 19, 2016 by Temple University's Main Campus Program Board. The record-setting feat required 1,350 volunteers, 4,500 loaves of bread, 4,280 pounds of peanut butter, and 3,551 pounds of jelly. I don't think Mike and his friends will break that record anytime soon, but their monthly sandwich-making commitment is touching lives consistently and profoundly.

God asks us to take care of the hungry and look after the poor. It's not a difficult request when you apply a little ambition. Those sandwiches look simple. It's just peanut butter and jelly smeared on bread. But, if you ask someone on the receiving end of those perfectly paired ingredients, a PB&J

means so much more than a meal. I'm thankful for Mike and his ambitious sandwich makers. God is smiling down on the way they are taking care of His people.

Proverbs 22:9 (NIV)
"The generous will themselves be blessed, for they share their food with the poor."

PANCAKES AND PICKLES

I had a great childhood. I grew up with grass stains on my pants and holes in my socks. I had permanent hat hair and constantly smelled like sunscreen. I practically lived at the baseball field and was never happier than during the hours I spent unsuccessfully flailing at curveballs in a batting cage. Baseball was my first love.

There is something pure about nine people simultaneously working both individually and in unison to accomplish a common goal. The pitcher and catcher start everything in motion and the rhythm continues to their teammates. For the team to succeed, every player must do his part. It's poetry in cleats.

I played at every waking moment. I played in the scorching heat and in the dead of winter, which in Florida meant 70 degrees. I played on all-star teams, AAU teams, and in high school. I cleaned my cleats in the garage after every game. I got addicted to that clickety clack sound metal spikes make on concrete as I walked towards the field from the parking lot. There is a box of my old tee ball photos in my parent's garage near a handful of trophies that have been dented and chipped over time. The game has always been special. I hope that my son grows up and wants to play someday, too.

As much as I care about baseball, I found a pack of kids *On The Road* who love the game even more. The Miracle League is a very special place. It's a league designed to give mentally challenged and physically disabled children and young adults a place to play baseball like any able-bodied person. The league is run entirely by volunteers.

Volunteers like Sy Schimberg.

When you pull up to the field, good luck finding a parking space. On a Saturday morning, the parking lot could easily be confused with a small college football stadium. It's jammed. There are people in colorful ball caps carrying lawn chairs. Dads are rolling drink coolers and moms are passing out bubble gum. After finally finding a place to leave my car, I lugged all my camera equipment towards the field off in the distance. I could hear Sy's voice booming through the loudspeakers.

"Andrew with a big hit! Takes off for first!"

As I got closer, the voice got louder.

"There it is!"

And louder.

"Nice big hit by Jared!"

And louder.

"Lucas will be safe on first!"

When I arrived under the giant, arching Miracle League sign, I finally saw the face that matched the voice. Sy Schimberg wasn't a tall teenager. He wore braces on his teeth and had to continually brush his long, curly, black hair away from his eyes to see the action on the field. He gripped a microphone loosely as he paced the foul line between third base and home plate. Fans were going crazy! Kids were screaming! It was cool to see. For the fourth year in a row, Sy assumed the role of the Miracle League's volunteer play-by-play host.

"*Hard up the middle!*" he yelped as a young boy swung with all his might, managing to dribble a baseball back to the pitcher.

The kids sprinted around the bases with faces full of joy. On this day, the Braves and the Orioles were locked in a friendly battle. Every child got a chance to bat each inning and nobody struck out. Swing and miss eleven times? No problem. Swing a twelfth. If you couldn't hit the pitched ball, a batting tee was waiting. Sy stood ready to announce the action. He wore a black polo shirt with a Miracle League logo on the left chest. He knew every player by his or her face. The player's names were written across the backs of their t-shirts, but Sy didn't need to reference them.

I was enjoying watching the game. I almost forgot I was supposed to record it. I got some shots of kid's hands on bats and cute sneakers stomping on bases. Midway through the second inning, a boy in a wheelchair was escorted to the plate for his chance to swing. After what seemed like 30 whiffs, he finally connected. The ball sailed about ten feet and landed with a thud on the infield turf. Sy erupted as if this was the mighty swat that won the World Series for the Braves.

"Hard the other way!" he shouted. The crowd roared as a volunteer coach wheeled the batter down to first base. Sy's enthusiasm seemed to spread to the players and even to their parents in the bleachers.

Everyone loved Sy. After the game, we went out to right field to chat.

"I never thought I'd say that I enjoy waking up at six in the morning every Saturday morning, especially as a 17-year-old, but I do. I really, really do."

Sy's dad, Barron, is a volunteer coach for the Orioles team. Sy only started helping because his dad dragged him to the complex when he was just ten. Barron's Orioles needed a water boy. What started as a service project turned into an ambitious, weekly regiment. The Miracle League has become woven into the family's schedule. Now, seven years later, there's no dragging Sy away.

There is just one thing wrong with the Miracle League field. It has no stadium lightning. Nearby parks have them. High school fields down the street are illuminated at night. The Miracle League doesn't have enough money to obtain the expensive lights. Without them, the only times games can be played are weekend mornings and afternoons.

Where the league saw a problem, its charismatic teenage announcer saw an opportunity. Sy had been waiting for his chance to give back even more to the Miracle League. His ambitious-side took over and a quirky memory provided an idea.

When Sy was just five, he and Barron went out to eat breakfast not too far from where the Miracle League sits. Sy opted for his favorite – pancakes. Nothing out of the ordinary. Just regular, old pancakes. When the waitress returned with Sy's food, she asked him a very puzzling question:

"Would you like a pickle with your pancakes?"

Is it rude to burst out laughing at the breakfast table? *A pickle? With your pancakes?* What kind of question is that? How about cherries on meatloaf or a jalapeño with my banana split? Sy declined the pickle but the waitress' question provided the topic of conversation with his father during the rest of the meal.

The dialogue led the two Schimberg men to a hilarious idea. What if the two of them co-wrote an alliteration book for children that matched uncommonly paired foods with wacky rhymes? It could be a fun project! They brainstormed alphabet options and came up with page concepts with laugh-inducing themes, like pairing marshmallows with meatballs! They would call the book, appropriately, *Pancakes and Pickles*.

"Mr. Mack mushed marshmallows in his messy mouth," Sy said as he read some of his book to me between Miracle League games. "That's my favorite part."

This impressed me so much. Sy had no obligation to these special kids at the Miracle League, but he wanted to help anyway. He saw a problem and attacked it! He came up with an idea and put it into action.

His hopes for the book are high. Sy wants to sell as many copies of *Pancakes and Pickles* as possible. The money from book sales will go towards purchasing lights for the Miracle League field. So much of the Sy's life has been spent pacing the third base line on that diamond. So many smiles have come because of his uplifting words of encouragement through the stadium speakers. Maybe, thanks to ambitious words on the pages of his book, many more smiles will become a Miracle League reality. Maybe Sy will get the chance to call Miracle League action under the glow of outfield lights on a warm summer evening. Maybe *Pancakes and Pickles* will provide a miracle of its own for the baseball field that has seen so many already.

"Someday there will be lights on this field," he said with confidence.

Ask around and you'll surely get differing ideas on how to find ambition. For Sy, the recipe included a desire to help others. Ambition doesn't have to be selfish. Ambition can thrive when it's based in humility. At just 17, Sy has already learned that lesson.

And to think, it all started with a pickle and some pancakes.

<u>**Philippians 2:3 (NLT)**</u>
"Don't be selfish; don't try to impress others. Be humble, thinking of others as better than yourselves."

THREE-HOUR BIKE RIDES

*I*like to start my days with a good breakfast. I like fruit or eggs. Sometimes I'll make smoothies. A healthy start is a good start, right? No offense to the worldwide burger giant, but starting every morning with a McDonald's breakfast is probably not the key to a long, healthy life. At least, you'd think that'd be the case.

That was exactly what I was thinking as I trailed Donald Nutting's barely-running white Ford hatchback to the restaurant just a quarter-mile from his home. The sun was peeking over the tree line and those golden arches were calling Donald's name again.

It cost him $2.99 to fill up his 98-year-old belly each morning. He always ordered the same kickstarter. The cashier knew he wanted a biscuit, three chocolate chip cookies, and a small, steaming cup of coffee. Not exactly egg whites and a protein shake but who am I to judge? The guy was pushing a century on earth and I get sore just watching golf on TV. As he carried his tray of food away from the register, a group of 'regulars' welcomed Donald to an open booth. It took him about ten minutes to finish his breakfast.

The daily routine had begun.

If you're thinking Donald is a feeble, decrepit geezer, you're mistaken. The WWII veteran is more of a Father Time anomaly than a Florida retiree stereotype.

He really is a remarkable man. His granddaughter, Linda Enders, and I made small talk while Donald milled about on his porch. She told me he enlisted in the Navy out of high school and served four years aboard the USS Mississippi before re-enlisting for five more years when the United States entered WWII. He was on the ground at Normandy on D-Day and received a Bronze Star and two Purple Hearts for his service to the nation.

I watched him closely as he hoisted his garage door and carefully began guiding his bicycle out of the packed space. Sawed-off milk jugs full of aluminum can tabs sat on the ground near the entrance. Donald moved slowly but moved with purpose. I clipped a microphone to his flannel shirt but it wasn't doing much. He went about his work in silence. He wasn't responding to my exploratory questions. I could tell this may be a tricky day to gather soundbites.

At the time I met Donald, in April 2016, he'd just celebrated 78 years of living in St. Petersburg, Fla. He built his house by hand and built a few of the neighboring homes as well. A carpenter by trade, Donald poured hours and hours of blood and sweat into the foundations of those homes. They weren't big, but they were solid. I could tell Donald took pride in his work. He was a dirt-under-the-fingernails type of guy. His skin was leathery from all those years working in the sun. Even now, at nearly a century old, he was still working on his neighborhood.

Donald finally got his bicycle out of the garage and looped a few plastic shopping bags over the handlebars. He gave the kickstand a tap and slowly swung his leg over the seat. He walked his bike down the driveway and pushed on the pedals. Donald carefully steadied himself as he established a left-right-left-right rhythm. Linda smiled as she watched her grandfather wobble down the road. He wouldn't be back for at least three hours. He was off to hunt aluminum cans.

"I think that he started the whole route and can collection on a daily basis probably to escape my grandmother a little bit during the day, initially," she said with a laugh.

The sun was squarely overhead now. Donald pedaled purposefully through the shadows created by the towering oaks that lined the sidewalks. He progressed slowly but surely. His lack of speed was both astonishing and gravity defying. He moved so slowly, it was a wonder he didn't topple over. But, the man was on a mission. Why rush when the treasures you are seeking aren't going anywhere?

Ugly aluminum cans were Donald's prey. He wanted his neighborhood neat and orderly, so he trained his eyes to spot them during his daily three-hour rides. He spotted them on porches, in gutters, and even lying in the grass beside dumpsters. In his earlier years, he'd bend down and scoop up the cans by the hundreds. Lately, his hands seemed further from the ground than ever before. A nail bent into a hook on the end of an old broomstick helped him gather the goods while still seated atop the bike.

Donald did whatever it took to keep his home looking clean and presentable. It was more than just a hobby to keep him active. It was his calling. His ambitious calling.

"This is going to be a good day," he said as he methodically moved down the street. "I'm 98. I was 98 in January. People don't tend to believe it."

Seven days per week, neighbors did double-takes as Donald maneuvered down alleys and up avenues. His determination often netted him a few dozen cans. Remarkably, despite making the rounds each day, he always found new cans each morning. If he found a few that needed crushing, he dragged them over to his bike with his broomstick and pressed his foot down with all of his weight. The flattened can got scooped into one of those plastic bags dangling from his handlebars. The aluminum recyclables jingled as he traveled to his next location. The clinking sound was soothing.

It's not easy to get video of a moving interview subject. Even with a target that moved as slowly as Donald, wheels almost always beat feet. I jogged up ahead of him as he rounded corners. I zoomed in on his feet as they continued to churn. Sweat started to bead on his forehead. His black hat guarded his eyes from the intensifying sun. I put the camera on the ground to get a low angle shot of his worn-out Nikes as he headed for home.

After a few hours in the heat, Donald resorted to half walking, half riding the final few yards to his driveway. The bike was loaded down with cans. The smell from the leftover souring beer droplets in the bottoms of cans was hard to miss as he dumped his catch on the porch. He returned his bike to the garage and sat down next to those sawed-off milk jugs. It was time to pop off the aluminum tabs. Donald explained that he got more money for those at the recycling center if he separated them from the cans. There were thousands waiting to be cashed in.

I was amazed by this ambitious man. Donald did not look like he should be riding a bike for three hours per day. At his age, I would have expected him to be inside enjoying air conditioning and three hours of daytime television. Maybe more. He just couldn't hide his ambition. He couldn't tone down his love for the neighborhood, either. He helped build it and wanted it to remain presentable. It was a big job and he decided he'd be the one to do it!

Linda told me that three years earlier, at the spry age of 95, Donald was hit by a car while crossing a busy intersection on one of his daily bicycle rides. He was taken to a nearby hospital with cuts and scrapes but, remarkably, didn't break any bones. His spirit remained intact, too. At that point, his family sat him down and gently suggested that he retire his tires. He brushed off the notion and reminded everyone that his rides were important to him.

"At that point we did ask him, 'Grandpa, can we get you a three-wheeler so you're a little bit more steady'? " said Linda, who was now standing next to me watching Donald flick the tabs off Bud Light cans. "He's like, 'Nope, that's for old people.' "

He returned to the roads after his body healed. Donald missed a few rides after his wheels disappeared out of his garage one day, but not even a stolen bike could slow him down for too long. A friend from down the street donated one of his old bikes to Donald so he could continue his can searches. A few days later, the original bike was found. Good things come to those who work hard.

After he finished removing all the aluminum tabs, Donald loaded up his white Ford hatchback with all his cans and made the short drive to the recycling center. Linda could not believe the state of Florida renewed his driver's license at the age of 98. But, he manned the steering wheel with steady command. I trailed behind him in Linda's car. Nobody was going to mistake Donald for a NASCAR driver. Slow and steady got the job done, just fine.

"I think he'll do this until the day he dies," she said. "He has a purpose."

The crew at the recycling center knows Donald by name. He walked to the familiar metal compactor and dumped in his cans. The machine rumbled at the push of a button. Donald loved that squeezing sound. A look of satisfaction crept onto his wrinkled face as the crunching sound grew louder. After all the cans were crushed, he wandered over to the cashier's window to collect his pay. The cans netted enough money to buy breakfast next week.

The job was complete. After hours and hours on the roads looking for shiny eyesores, Donald had accomplished his goal. His neighborhood was once again tidy. It may not look as beautiful as the day he laid the foundations, but beautiful nonetheless. He settled back into his lawn chair at dusk and gazed down the street.

It won't be long before the sun returns and Donald can start his routine all over again.

He could have spent his entire life in that lawn chair and nobody would have blamed him. He was pushing 100, you know. That's well past the time when people start pricing caskets. Our expectations lessen with each passing decade, but Donald isn't someone who loves a lighter load. His ambitious spirit was developed in the military and served him well all his life. That life isn't over and neither is his can collecting.

When you sit idly by, life passes you by. Progress isn't made from the porch. No one will ever be able to say that life passed by Donald Nutting. He has a clean neighborhood and dirty tires to prove it.

2 Chronicles 15:7 (ESV)
"But you, take courage! Do not let your hands be weak, for your work shall be rewarded."

CLOSING THOUGHTS ON AMBITION

I was definitely born in a time period that suits me well. Knowing what I know now, I can't imagine living without certain modern conveniences. No running water? No electricity? That was commonplace just a few hundred years ago. It was candle light and well water. No way. I'll take a flashlight and a sturdy faucet, thank you.

It amazes me to think about how humans managed to make life work with far fewer advancements than we have today. The first time indoor plumbing was installed in a home was probably cause for celebration. I can visualize the home owners calling up all their friends to come check out this fancy new invention called the toilet. Or the telephone! Making a long-distance connection on that device for the first time must have been so exhilarating. Think of all the amazing inventions we use each day. Now, imagine getting through your day without them. I know people who would break out in hives if they simply forgot to take their smartphone with them to the bathroom.

Refrigerators, automobiles, airplanes, air conditioning, telephones, light bulbs, internet – all things that were only invented because someone kicked down walls. Alexander Graham Bell was awarded the patent for the first telephone on March 7, 1876. He relayed the words, "Mr. Watson, come here, I want to see you", and stunned the world. All except for the Western Union company, apparently. When Bell tried to sell his patent to them, he was told his invention was essentially useless in their eyes. Western Union thought his device was a cute gimmick that would never make a worldwide impact. That's an obstacle capable of stifling ambition.

The Wright brothers failed at flight for years before putting the first plane in the sky in Kitty Hawk, N.C. on December 17, 1903. That first flight only lasted 12 seconds, reached an altitude of just 20 feet, and covered a distance barely further than home plate to second base. But, they did it! The brothers ignored years of failed flights because they had a hunch and a hope that men could soar. They knew a lot more about the ground than the air up to that point.

The lightbulb? It took Thomas Edison countless missteps before creating a bulb that worked. He told a reporter he never considered his missteps as failures. He simply learned a few thousand ways NOT to make a lightbulb.

"If I had not had so much *ambition* and not tried to do so many things, I probably would have been happier, but less useful," he once said.

Even lesser inventions took incredible ambition to pull off. The makers of WD-40 only gave their solvent that name because it took 40 attempts to get it just right. What if they had given up after 26 tries? We'd have squeaky wheels all over the world.

Eventually someone may have figured out how to fly had the ambitious Wright brothers not stuck with their vision. Someone else would have invented the radio had Guglielmo Marconi not done so in 1895. Someone else would have built an automobile had Henry Ford not built the Model T on October 1, 1908. Someone else would have eventually made the products that the rest of the world would come to rely on. But, those ambitious inventers relentlessly pursued their passions and the result was global change.

We need more ambitious people. The ambitious get remembered! They get rewarded! Ambitious people assess problems and find solutions. In doing so, they demonstrate the attitude God planned for us all. I have interviewed thousands of people, but only the four who showed the most memorable amount of ambition were included in this chapter.

We live in a world of excuse-makers. Too busy to help. Too tired to try. Too small to matter. We live in a world that bails when life gets the least bit hard. Instant gratification through social media and Google contribute to the problem. I say, why not keep trying? Why accept "can't"? Why settle for something less than complete success? God didn't design us to quit.

I chatted with an assistant principal last year at a Tampa K-thru-8 magnet school. I remember listening to her describe her outgoing eighth graders. The group had just completed a summer service project in the

Dominican Republic. This administrator could not mask the pride in her voice as she described every detail from her kid's efforts over summer break. A dozen teens got their hands dirty building an aqueduct that would carry fresh water to residents in a poor, rural village. The people who lived there had never felt the rush of water on their hands before! I can't imagine! It's a modern convenience the students took for granted back home. We all do that. Their service trip was an eye-opening experience for first-world, American kids with iPhones practically permanently fixed to their fingers. Their willingness to go and do something for others, to dig ditches and wells in a foreign country, showed great ambition. There was a payoff, too! They got the joy of seeing a community receive a vital resource due to the work of their hands.

This assistant principal paused after finishing her story. I could see she was mulling over her next words carefully. A wry smile spread over her lips. She delivered a line so obvious, yet profound, that I had to jot it down: *"The distance between dream and reality is action."*

Isn't it, though? We all have dreams. The Wright brothers did. So did Steve Jobs, Bill Gates and Michael Besos. They chased them down with abandon! How many times have you let an outside influence stifle your enthusiasm? How often do we quit when barriers impede progress? I am not immune. I succumb to the sin of complacency. Action tips circumstances in our favor. God is working and fighting right there along with us. More accurately, He's out in front of us like a jungle guide wielding a machete, clearing the path for the people following behind.

A lot of people doubted Madison Harrison's dream of taking a photo of the President. I was the first skeptic in line. Looking back, I feel bad about it. She had a dream and stuck to it! She has a framed shot of Barack Obama on her wall to remind her that she didn't give up when doubt crept in. She was persistent! She was determined! Her ambition, even in the face of naysayers, paid off. Hers is the attitude God wants us to live with.

Mike Abramowitz and his coworkers started off by humbly feeding a few homeless people with a couple dozen PB&Js. That was just the beginning. He applied a little ambition and passed out 50,000 sandwiches within two years. Every time I talk with him, I can hear how proud he is of that accomplishment. I doubt 50,000 was the goal the first time he smeared jelly on rye. I saw the appreciative faces of homeless men and women after they received a free meal. Mike's ambition made God's provision possible in a community. It was a tangible, touchable reminder to the hungry people in his city that somebody cared enough to make a difference. Ambition made unexpected hope a reality.

Sy Schimberg hasn't purchased stadium lights for the Miracle League yet but he has taken a huge first step towards getting them. I checked Amazon. Pancakes and Pickles is selling! People want it and every purchase gets Sy a few bucks closer to his dream of announcing night games. The first pitch under the lights is going to be a spectacle. It will mark the crossing of a finish line that only happened because a teenager had God-sized ambition. He didn't look at the enormous dollar figure standing between him and stadium lights, shrug his shoulders and give up. Sy will find a way to make the money he needs. It may take another year. It may take another decade. He may need a lifetime to raise the $250,000 he needs. It doesn't matter how long it takes. Sy will get his money eventually if he keeps moving forward. I can tell nothing is going to stop that teen from lighting up the Miracle League baseball diamond someday. He doesn't understand "can't" either.

Donald Nutting is a hero of mine. He's a veteran who learned the value of hard work from his military days. He also learned surrendering isn't an option. He learned how valuable ambition is in life. He learned that age is a number that doesn't have to hold you back. I'm sure he's heard the whispers. *"When is he going to slow down? Doesn't he know he's old?"* What if he listened? What if he stopped collecting cans? What if he had given up at the age of 90? He would never have become this great example from the greatest generation. He's proud of his neighborhood and isn't going to sit by and watch it erode. God smiles down on people like Donald Nutting.

Ambition has no expiration date. It is like fuel in your gas tank. It will carry you as far as you want to go. It's up to you to keep your tank full. If you need a jolt, a reminder of why you started chasing your dream in first place, refuel by looking back on what God has already helped you accomplish. Make a list. You'll be surprised how long it gets. Embrace and seek encouragement if you need to. Press on towards your goal! Don't let the potholes of life slow you down. Ambition's sweet reward is waiting at the finish line.

VERSES ON AMBITION

Matthew 6:33 (ESV)
"But seek first the kingdom of God and his righteousness, and all these things will be added to you."

Philippians 2:4 (ESV)
"Let each of you look not only to his own interests, but also to the interests of others."

I Timothy 3:1 (ESV)
"The saying is trustworthy: If anyone aspires to the office of overseer, he desires a noble task."

Psalm 90:17 (NLT)
"And may the Lord our God show us his approval and make our efforts successful. Yes, make our efforts successful!"

Matthew 25:34-40 (NLT)
"Then the king will say to those on his right, 'Come, my Father has blessed you! Inherit the kingdom prepared for you from the creation of the world. I was hungry, and you gave me something to eat. I was thirsty, and you gave me something to drink. I was a stranger, and you took me into your home. I needed clothes, and you gave me something to wear. I was sick, and you took care of me. I was in prison, and you visited me.' "Then the people who have God's approval will reply to him, 'Lord, when did we see

you hungry and feed you or see you thirsty and give you something to drink? When did we see you as a stranger and take you into our homes or see you in need of clothes and give you something to wear? When did we see you sick or in prison and visit you?' "The king will answer them, 'I can guarantee this truth: Whatever you did for one of my brothers or sisters, no matter how unimportant they seemed, you did for me.'

JOY

*W*hen my daughter started homeschool as a kindergartener, my house was a tornado of emotion. There was excitement. There was despair. I had daily conversations with my over-qualified wife where I constantly reminded her that she would not, to borrow her phrase, "mess up my child". Perfectionist and homeschool mom are basically oil and water. They don't mix well.

She was a teacher for a few years before we got married and continued to teach before we had kids. I've seen her do amazing things with kids in the water as a swim coach and equally impressive things in a classroom with children who didn't have much support at home. I have been to visit her classrooms. I was twitching after five minutes. It takes a special person to sign up for that loud, sticky environment.

When we were engaged, she'd call me on the phone at night from Florida. I sat in my tiny apartment in Louisiana listening to her heartbreaking stories of students who showed up to her classroom with nothing but a single, rotten orange in their lunchbox. It was stressful! I was 800 miles away. There wasn't much I could do aside from offer words of encouragement. It was times like those where I did my best to remind her that God wants us to rejoice in the small things. The kids were safe in her room. She provided an environment where she could shower them with love. They could escape the troubles of home for just a few short hours each day just by being around her.

It's easy to smile on sunny days at the beach. Anyone can do that. Sometimes it's hard to find joy in the rainstorm.

But that's what we're called to do. God didn't create us to sit around the couch surfing Facebook all day or looking for the newest fidget spinner on

Amazon. He certainly didn't create us to be fearful news consumers. He created us to live life! To go out and do something for the Kingdom! To get off our rumps and make a difference! To reflect God's light to the world!

To seek joy!

The news can get in the way of that. Joy can feel impossible to find if all we hear are the ugly headlines. News microphones and cameras are there for them all. Networks go live on TV after every shortcoming. Reporters tweet pictures of wrong-doers every night. We dissect tragedies and assign blame immediately. We cover rallies and vigils until we are exhausted, over-stressed, and over-saturated with negative information. Excessive reporting on awful events paints an inaccurate picture of the world. Negative news is a joy killer! If it is terrible, news stations cover it disproportionately. There is more going on out there than just the horrible headlines we hear first. It's possible to find joyful material to cover. I do it every day.

God designed us to be joyful. We don't always follow His blueprint. We rejoice when it's convenient. We pretend we're happy when we're not. Deep down, we're all actors wearing a mask. I understand having days where all you want to do is stay in bed with sweatpants eating Twinkies. We all love the snooze button. Too many of us think tomorrow will be a fine day for accomplishing a goal. But, that's not God's plan for our lives. His plan is to chase joy.

American author Joseph Campbell once wrote, "Find a place inside where there's joy, and the joy will burn out the pain". If there is pain in your life, believe that joy is around the corner. Look for the opportunity to unearth it.

Remember that song from Sunday school? Even if you didn't go to Sunday school, I'm sure you've heard it:

This is the day… (ECHO) this is the day.

That the Lord has made… (ECHO) that the Lord has made.

I will REJOICE… (ECHO) I will REJOICE.

And be glad in it…. (ECHO) And be glad in it.

You know, that's straight out of the Bible. It's Psalm 118:24. Word. For. Word.

And, it's a command. "Let us rejoice and be glad in it." God wants us to rejoice.

I was a sports reporter for six years and I loved it. But, I can honestly say I didn't find joy in the job. It was fun! Be careful not to confuse fun with joy. They are not interchangeable. Fun is finding something that makes you feel good in the moment. Finding joy means finding enduring gladness from an endless source.

Happiness depends on circumstances. Joy does not. Happiness comes from things. Joy does not. The Bible never promises you'll be happy. God promises you'll find joy in Him.

God takes the time to reveal joy to us and it's found in the simplest of places. He hides it in plain sight. We just need to make time to seek it out. When we become too busy, we become too distracted to seek joy. We waste life this way. I just picture God up there expectantly waiting for us to turn the corner and find the gift He's hand-placed for us.

I had a joyful experience in an unexpected place. My family sat on the runway in San Jose, Costa Rica and I could sense the anticipation building at the window seat to my left. My son was beyond giddy. This was the moment he'd been preaching about for days. He told waiters. He told neighbors. He told strangers. He was more excited about the giant steel tube with wings than the tropical jungle all around him on the ground.

The flight attendants gave the obligatory, although almost never necessary, pre-flight safety speech. Like the rest of the passengers, my son could not care less. He was too busy staring out the window. He craned his little two-year-old neck to see the men down on the pavement frantically guiding pilots with red batons. As we taxied to the runway, I could see the twinkle in his eye in the reflection of the window pane. It had only been a few days since his last flight but this one seemed to be even more exciting. Perhaps having experienced it once before amped up the next go-around.

The plane started to gain speed and the passengers sank down into their seats. I always get a little woozy the moment the wheels and ground separate. Sometimes I close my eyes for a moment to just recalibrate my brain and remind myself to breathe. It's not that I'm scared of flying. I just don't love the first few moments of liftoff.

My son? Oh, he does not have that problem. The plane was dead quiet. Quiet, except for my toddler belching out every gleeful adjective he could pull from his developing vocabulary. It started with an, "AHHH!!", followed by a "Wheels go down?". I could see the other passengers all peering over at the loud child in row 13, seat A. "Look at the cars!" he yelped. Then my personal favorite: "We're flying?"

The boy was on cloud nine while literally traveling through clouds. For the other 200-plus people on that JetBlue plane, the magic of flight had faded. Either, they didn't care about the incredible technology that defied gravity or weren't impressed by it. The eyes of a child experienced something we didn't. The little kid on the window seat was having the time of his life. That's the joyful enthusiasm God wants us to have as we travel through life, too.

We take little experiences for granted and forget to jump for joy. We just sit in our seats and close our eyes as the 500-ton plane leaves the ground behind. It's not special anymore. Repetition kills the remarkable. Meanwhile, the innocent eyes of a child are agape and amazed.

For the record, that flight home from Costa Rica was one of the most turbulent I'd ever experienced. As you can guess, that didn't keep my son from gazing longingly at each ray of sun that danced on the edges of the clouds. There was something special going on and he wasn't going to be distracted by a few bumps. I take that approach when I'm working on my news stories. If I can inject a little joy into the world by telling a story that distracts us from life's bumps, I'll call that a win.

God designed us to marvel. Look at what He made and try not to gasp. He gives us incredible gifts each day. We overlook them because we never start looking for them. We see the improbably of creation and shrug it off. Ho hum. The earth spins at 1,000 miles per hour and nobody flies off. A human grows inside a mother's womb for exactly nine months and emerges ready for life. It's astounding! It happens 255 times per minute around the world. God sends a miracle every 4.3 seconds! But, because of its frequency, we write it off as unremarkable. Twice as many people are born each day than die, but when's the last time a birth led a newscast? Embrace the people who understand how precious God's blessings can be.

Jim Peppard, or "Pep" as we called him, was a guy of few words. I gave him a hard time because we sat so close to each other that I could hear him breathe. He was the hub. He was the distributor. He was the grizzled news veteran who knew every back alley, political source, and important community phone number practically by heart. Everybody respected him. He spent a majority of his life in newsrooms and was a leader in mine. From 1964 to 2016, if there was a story out there, Pep was on it. He was serious, yet knew how to be playful when the time was right. He joked, unless it was time to crack the whip. I don't think there was a soul in the room who didn't like the man. The only thing I didn't like about him was his Yankees hat.

The day Pep retired, he did what most folks do when departing a longtime workplace. He sat down at his keyboard and typed out his goodbyes. I expected a short and sweet goodbye note. Instead, I opened my inbox the following morning to one incredible farewell message. It's the only one I've ever saved.

It was a few pages long and worded poetically. The section that stood out to me most was the one that pertained to the *On The Road*-type stories. They get lost in the shuffle of "bigger", "more important" news of the day. The feel-good, uplifting stuff can easily be trumped by Trump or cut out of the news altogether in favor of another neighborhood stabbing. Reading Pep's words renewed my faith in my role in television.

"But it's not just the "Big J" stories that matter," he wrote. "Chronicling the so-called ordinary events, the warm and quirky features, the helping hand we extend – is just as important – in some ways, more so – mirroring life as it is, or ought to be, the tears and tickles, too. You make a difference in the lives of so many people. What a joy, to be part of that."

Notice the last line. "What a JOY, to be part of that."

His goodbye letter is tacked up on the corkboard behind my office computer. Those words stare me in the face. I even highlighted the last line in bright green ink. I read Pep's poignant words whenever I feel like good news is losing the battle. When I'm looking for joy, and the world keeps spitting back fear, hate, and neglect, those highlighted pearls of wisdom reignite my fire. Pep was right. There is joy in being part of something that has the potential to make a difference in the lives of so many people.

Finding joy is not always easy. It's difficult because we are surrounded by negativity at every click of a TV remote. Pep's departing words did not come from a journalism newbie. This was not the observation of some fresh-out-of-community-college kid or a person without knowledge of the "real world". This sendoff statement came from a man who dedicated his life to bringing viewers the most important information of the day. He worked through countless Presidential elections, wars, and the terror of the 9/11 terror attacks. He knew exactly what people cared about and what was most important to them. Yet, he still made a point to write about how the most important moments of the day were often the ones full of "tears and tickles, too".

Jim Peppard died within a year of writing that letter to his colleagues. Brain cancer stole him away too soon. The world lost a little bit of joy that day. I won't throw that letter away. Its lines teem with wisdom. There is so much to learn from it. Wherever this TV life takes me, Pep's letter is riding shotgun.

In life, you find what you're looking for. I try to spend each day looking for joy, and I find that God is always ready to supply more. You'll ready about my favorite joy-filled stories for this chapter. You'll learn a life lesson from Peter Garino, a man who fought for our freedom. Ours was an encounter I won't soon forget. There is a lot of joy in Henry Witherwax's story. He was deeply connected to his favorite animals. I hope you smile when you read about Davis Harkey's attempts to score a basket. He was having too much fun to care if the ball ever made it through the hoop. Finally, imagine what a tough decision it must have been for Abby Vega to give up her successful life in search of ultimate joy. It's a brave choice that really paid off.

Finding joy is important. It won't ever make the headlines but it's not as elusive as you think. Stop closing your eyes. Don't let the bumps of life blind you. Just seek out the "tears and tickles". They will lead you to the joy that God wants you to experience.

"THE SIMPLE PLEASURES"

I like telling veteran's stories. I just do. I am not the most patriotic person ever, but I love meeting down-to-earth vets. They are typically grateful people with a lot to share. I bet I do at least two veteran-related stories per month for my *On The Road* segment. People love to hear positive stories from the men and women in uniform who volunteered to protect us. An Iraqi Freedom fighter jet pilot once described veterans to me as "the one percent who fight for the 99". They are true heroes, in my book.

I had a chance to meet a few of those special men in early 2017. I spent a good portion of my morning at a building where veteran artwork is displayed. I shot video of WWII vets retelling war stories from their service days. A local group of historians wanted those memories recorded for the library of Congress in Washington. It was a way to preserve oral history from a generation that is dying off in larger numbers each year.

That day, I met two memorable men. Bob May was 100 years old but you'd swear by looking at him he wasn't a day over 70. The USAF veteran was sharp as a tack and ready to rumble. He was one of those guys who spoke his mind and didn't care what you thought. I found that out quickly.

"In combat, you feel like your life is worth a nickel," he said. "You'll either come back that morning or you won't. Most of them in my war would do it again because, well, everyone supported it. We felt like we were getting rid of a monster."

I did more listening than speaking with Bob. The other gentleman I met that day was Peter Garino. I won't soon forget him, either. Peter flew planes over the South Pacific. He was part of search missions designed to locate enemy ships.

"From Nazi Germany and Japan, the misguided idea that they were going to control the entire Pacific area, we had to root them out and get rid of that idea," he told me. He had a convincing look in his eye. I believed every word he said.

I could have listened to those men for hours but I had to head back to the TV station. The shoot took a while and I really needed to get back to start editing video and writing my scripts. Television deadlines are pretty strict. I'd said my goodbyes and was turning to leave when Peter's quiet voice caught my ear.

"Excuse me. Can you sit with me for a minute?"

Here's some free advice. When a WWII veteran, who risked his life serving and fighting for your freedom multiple decades before your mother was even born, asks you to sit with him for a cookie and a laugh, you do it. No questions asked. On a tight TV deadline? Suck it up, civilian.

Peter asked me questions about media and the way politics is covered at big networks these days. He told me he loved my station because CBS is where he watched network anchor Charlie Rose. I nodded and smiled. I think he assumed Charlie and I were friends. He longed for the day of the newspaper editorial and fair, honest reporting. I assured him that I agreed with him on the fair, honest part. I told Peter that I marveled at his stories of flight and patriotism. I never wanted to fly but my dad entertained the idea of a career as a pilot at a young age. I relayed my dad's experiences from the sky, about how beautiful the world appeared from such heights. Peter hung on my every word. I could tell he was truly listening. He nibbled his cookie as I spoke. After I finished, he cleared his throat and delivered an incredible line.

"In life, in all of its complexities, we sometimes forget to enjoy the simple pleasures."

How true. This was a man who very likely could've taken a bullet in the chest for this country – for me – and he's sitting on a stool decades later chatting with a stranger about how we should take more time to enjoy the little things in life. If that's not a joyful approach to living, I don't know what is.

We are all in too big of a hurry these days. Our attention spans have shortened since the advent of social media. According to a Microsoft study in 2015, our attention span is hovering around eight seconds. That's strikingly similar to the focusing abilities of goldfish. We are so eager to get to the next thing that we miss out on chances to connect with people the way God intended. We rush moments instead of relish in them. I didn't want to speed through my conversation with Peter. He deserved the respect of a few minutes of my time.

I learned that Peter found joy in educating others on what actually matters. He'd seen a lot in his 90-plus years. Wisdom oozed from his words. Fighting for freedom wasn't always enjoyable. Sharing lessons from his battles was. I learned about Peter's life growing up. I learned about the friends he made and friends he lost. I learned about the hope he has for the future of his nation. I learned a lot from Peter.

The conversation probably only lasted 15 minutes but we covered a lot of topics. I got a good feeling in my chest as I left that veteran art museum. I haven't seen Peter since and may never see him again. If that's the case, it's okay. He gave me a one-liner that is now tacked up on the wall of my desk. I will refer to it for many years to come when I'm running low on joy.

"In life, in all of its complexities, we sometimes forget to enjoy the simple pleasures."

If I made a list, I'd probably run out of ink before I listed all the ways God has blessed me. I know I enjoy holding hands with my wife. I enjoy the early morning bear hugs from my son. I enjoy the giggles from my daughter as we race our bikes in the neighborhood. All simple, joyful pleasures. All things worth remembering.

All things Peter was talking about.

The Bible talks about it, too. It's an attitude. It's a directive. When we trust God, He fills us with "all joy and peace" (Romans 15:13 NIV). The purpose of filling us with that joy is so we can overflow with abundant hope. I'd imagine soldiers in Peter's position, wondering if today would be their last on earth, lived in a bit of a peace-less, joy-less space. His attempt to find joy in the little things probably got him through some tough scenes from war.

I find the more I read from the Bible, the more often I make Kingdom-connections. I didn't know what Romans 15:13 said when I met Peter Garino. I stumbled upon that verse a few days later. As I uncover more of these passages, I'm finding their application is astounding. We all want joy and peace in our lives. We seek them out whenever we can. Peter's advice, to seek joy and peace in life's innocent pleasures, is solid advice. It's Biblical advice. Often, life's innocent pleasures aren't things you can hold. They are gifts from a God, who knows the best things in life are not things. Our simple pleasures outnumber our complex problems.

We can fall into the trap of thinking the Bible is this dusty scroll full of nothing but "thou shalt nots", but it has great uplifting threads. Stop spending so much time trying to impress people you don't know. Stop worrying about what others think. Start worrying about what God thinks. Start seeking and harvesting joy. God wants you to be joyful. Peter helped me realize that some of the most joyful moments in life can be found in the innocent pleasures God gives us each day.

Ecclesiastes 8:15 (NIV)
"So, I recommend having fun, because there is nothing better for people in this world than to eat, drink, and enjoy life. That way they will experience some happiness along with all the hard work God gives them under the sun."

HENRY'S TWO-TON FIRST LOVE

*I*met Henry Witherwax because of his grandson, Scott Earley. Months before I met Henry, Scott was the subject of one of my *On The Road* stories. It was incredible in itself. I drove three hours to meet Scott at an airport to talk about how flying saved his life. He is a paraplegic. He'll be stuck in a wheelchair for the rest of his life thanks to the carelessness of a drunk driver. The life-altering accident happened in 1998. For decades, he sulked. He cried. He quit. He had given up on his dream of becoming a pilot.

"I kind of came to the realization that that dream wasn't going to become a reality because of my paralysis," he told me.

Luckily, not even a wheelchair can keep you anchored to the ground when faith fuels a dream. God's redemption plans are bigger than any earthly diagnosis. Scott's wife, on a whim, convinced him to take a class for paraplegics interesting in flying. It was cool to see the joy on Scott's face as he described the feeling of soaring through the clouds. Years after pronouncing his dreams dead, they were not only revived, they soared!

It was a fun story to put together. I got to use a lot of home video Scott shot himself from inside the cockpit during his six months of training flights. I was happy with how the story worked out. As I tend to do as busy a storyteller, I moved on to the next assignment and didn't give Scott's story much thought after it aired. I'm not malicious. I'm just busy. Months later, Scott emailed me. He told me his grandfather, Henry, wanted to celebrate his 90th birthday in the most peculiar way. He wanted to see elephants. Not just any elephants, either. He wanted to see circus elephants. Scott wanted to know if I could help make it happen.

From 1-10 on the Unusual Scale, this was an 18. Meet-and-greets with giant mammals don't qualify as typical reporter responsibilities. I have contacts all over the country in many different fields, but elephant handlers are not on my speed dial. I felt compelled to try since I liked Scott and enjoyed sharing his story earlier that year. I made some calls and, sure enough, found a farm for retired circus elephants just two hours from our TV station. I arranged for Henry to do what I'm pretty sure almost no other person has ever requested for a 90th birthday bash.

The entire Witherwax crew made the trip up to the Ringling Bros. Barnum and Bailey Center for Elephant Conservation. Henry and his family drove four hours to make this birthday wish a reality. I noticed his joyful grin as soon as he exited the car. He had thin-rimmed glasses and a full head of gray hair. Even with a walking cane in his right hand, there was a little pep in his step.

A few conservation employees met us at the entrance and introduced themselves. They all seemed very excited to meet Henry. We loaded up in a few golf carts and rode out to where the retired elephants spend their days. I remember it was a 100-degree September morning and there was a cocktail of smells in the air that would later require two scrubbings to remove from my skin. It was a glorious day.

Scott told me over the phone that his grandfather loved elephants but he undersold the connection. Henry had a pachyderm passion! As we motored out to see the animals, I heard Henry tell the tour guide why these animals were so special to him. This moment wasn't just fulfilling a birthday wish to see majestic mammals. This was time travel! This was reliving Henry's glory days! This was a trip to see his first loves, the animals that introduced him to his true love.

In the 1960s, Henry worked as an elephant trainer for the circus. That year, the Ringling Bros. show went on the road to Cuba to perform. A young Cuban girl needed to make extra money, so she was hired to ride elephants in the shows. Henry's elephants! She was beautiful and graceful. He was smitten. Side-by-side they worked. He watched her wave to the crowd as he paraded the gentle giants around the ring. This went on for weeks. Their relationship started to grow. Henry didn't know a word of Spanish. She didn't know a word of English. But, love found a way. A year after meeting, Henry and Mercedes were married.

My wife and I met over a two-liter bottle of orange soda at a church

Christmas party. A buddy and I only went to the party so he could introduce me to a different girl. I thought my wife and I had a cool first encounter. Compared to Henry's, our love connection couldn't be any more boring. Henry and Mercedes owe their joy-filled lives to 12,000-pound Cuban performance animals! The Lifetime movie channel prays for storylines like this! No wonder the old guy wanted to spend his 90th birthday visiting the two-ton beasts.

We hopped out of the golf carts near an open field. A trainer brought one of the older elephants out to meet the birthday boy. I slipped a microphone on Henry as he gathered some bread in his hands. I wanted to hear all the intimate banter between man and beast during this sweet reunion moment. The trainer stood nearby to help calm the enormous animal as Henry extended his arms full of treats. The elephant opened its gaping mouth and Henry threw in the bread as if he was tossing a penny down a wishing well. The elephant swallowed nearly an entire loaf of bread in one gulp. I had never stood that close to an elephant before. It was breathtaking. Its eye was bigger than a golf ball! Its trunk alone was easily as tall as Henry. The interaction between the two was remarkable to see. Henry patted the elephant on its trunk and smiled a joyful smile. You could tell by the way they shared that close space that they respected one another. Henry was loving every second.

"Beautiful!" he cried. "It's been many years!" Mercedes smiled as she watched from the golf cart.

Flash forward nine months. I submitted Henry's story for an Emmy award. After consulting with a photographer friend of mine from the station, who himself has won over 30 Emmys, we decided that the piece about Henry's special day was worth sending in for meticulous grading. If it won, I'd be happy. If it didn't, at least I knew that I helped play a small part in making that man's 90th birthday memorable.

When I found out the story was nominated for an Emmy, I emailed Scott to tell him. He called me to tell me the sad news. Turns out, Henry's 90th birthday was his final birthday. I was so heartbroken for Scott. It's the first time anyone that I'd ever interviewed had died. It was a weird feeling.

Henry died just a few days earlier. Scott asked me to tape a short farewell message for his family so he could play it at the memorial service. I was more than happy to do so. In that moment, I didn't really feel like rejoicing. I like to live in life's sunshine moments. Sometimes, it pours. I've found that God gives us joyful moments to help us push through the tough times. I hope hearing that Henry's elephant encounter was eligible for an award somehow provided a few smiles to his funeral.

Henry Witherwax celebrated his birthday with elephants

One of the great things about joy is that it can still exist amidst sorry. You can't really say the same for happiness. We are only happy when things are going well. God gives us the ability to have joy, even during sadness. There can be joy at funerals. There can be joy during death. If your loved one is home in Heaven, there is the possibility of a joyful reunion. Jesus can connect you again.

I'd like to think that Henry is in Heaven riding an elephant with no need for his cane. I can't say for sure. I didn't have any spiritual conversations with him during our afternoon at the elephant conservation. But, I did see the look in his eyes as he relived his youth. It was more than happiness. It was joy! There was personal rejoicing happening between him and Mercedes in the back of that golf cart. They giggled as they experienced a moment they never thought they'd get to experience again. I bet it's the same giggle they shared back in Cuba so many decades ago. To me, it's the kind of moment that only comes from knowing how special God's creation really is. It's the recognition of joy.

If petting a few elephants gave an old man a sense of joy that day, I call it a win. If Henry is looking down from Heaven, he's the winner. I can only imagine what it would be like to hear firsthand the story of how those elephants were made.

John 16:33 (NIV)
"I have told you these things; so that in me you may have peace. In this world you will have trouble. But, take heart! I have overcome the world."

THE STAR OF THE 5ᵀᴴ QUARTER

*I*like to keep the world in perspective whenever possible. Circumstances are almost never as good nor as bad as they seem. We elevate highs and exaggerate lows. Social media has only added to the problem. We live in a second-by-second cycle of information which can trick us into thinking the latest news headline is the only thing happening. It's a brain trap. A plane engine explodes mid-flight. An abusive foster mom goes unpunished. Today's lead stories will make it sound as if the world is ending. It's not. There is so much good out there.

I constantly remind myself to stop and rejoice in the fact that I have a job that I don't dread. I enjoy the drive into the office each morning. So many people hate their gigs. I don't! I joyfully pull into my parking space and thank God for where He has planted me. I'm here on purpose. God planned all of this. He organized this moment in time for my benefit and His glory. The same thing is happening in our life right now.

That perspective allows us to see joy. Not every person sees it. I'd guess that 80 percent of the time viewers see a news vehicle, they suspect something bad has happened. Why else would the news station be there? People who come up to me are typically surprised when I tell them that I do the happy stuff. It sparks great conversation. They tell me they want more of that type of news. They want to hear positive things happening in the community. I agree! We're constantly beaten down by negative thoughts and ideas. It's unavoidable. It's a broken planet. We are stuck in the shadow of evil We are desperately seeking something good to help us break away. It's hard to rejoice when all you see on TV is murder, flashing police lights, and politicians screaming at each other over who messed up the nation more. That's why I rejoice in my position. I get to find stories that remind me of

God's need for rejoicing. Franklin D. Roosevelt once said, "Happiness lies in the joy of achievement and the thrill of creative effort". You won't find joy if you are not seeking it.

Davis Harkey won't be playing basketball in the NBA someday. He won't crack the starting lineup for his high school team either, most likely. But, for his middle school basketball team, he was important enough that his coach bent the rules of both sports and mathematics to get him on the court. The Christ The King Lions disregarded the meaning of the word "quarter". Typically, a basketball game has four. The Lions played five. If you're a math purist, relax. Numerically speaking, there really is no such thing as five quarters. In middle school basketball terms, it makes perfect sense.

I don't remember much about my brother's, birth. I was only three at the time. I've heard my mom talk about how stressful Steven's first few weeks were on this planet. He was born prematurely, just like Davis. Unless you've had a sick child, there is no way to understand the strain it puts on a parent's life. You just can't relate. My mom and Davis' mom, Kim, probably had many of the same thoughts. They probably peppered God with similar questions. Steven's asthma nearly killed him. He was stuck in the hospital for weeks. Davis was born at 28 weeks and faced enormous medical hurdles. He contracted a staph infection in the NICU. He needed surgery to remove it and lost half of a hip joint in the process. Three months after birth, his mother found out her little boy had Down Syndrome. Life was never easy. Even tasks that require little effort for most able-bodied people were agonizingly difficult for Davis. He couldn't go all the places friends could go. His list of available entertainment options was limited. One thing he did gravitate to was basketball. It became his passion.

The sports reporter that still lives inside me searches for opportunities to tell stories like Davis'. I call them hybrids. They are not purely human interest and not purely sports, either. They're a little bit of both with some feel-good elements involved. I remember sitting in a small church gym with about 50 other people watching a bunch of 12-year-old boys dribble the basketball off their feet. This wasn't the highest level of hoops you'll ever see. At that age, winning is a surprising result of the fun. The life lessons the kids learn will last far longer than any box score.

Davis sat on the end of the bench watching his teammates shoot and pass. He wore the bright red team shorts and a pair of black and red Reebok high-tops. He cheered louder than anyone else in the gym. Even if a fellow Lion air-balled a layup, Davis emptied his lungs in support. He was instantly likable and I found myself drawn to his enthusiasm. Standing on the other sideline with my camera, I got a few shots of Davis smiling and shouting from the bench as the final few minutes of the game ticked off the scoreboard.

Kim sat in the stands across from the team bench. She wasn't really paying much attention to the action. She wasn't as invested in the first four quarters of the game as the other parents. She was there for the fifth quarter. It was the main attraction. It was the part of the afternoon that drew the most eyeballs and applause. I asked her why the final frame was so important. She unsuccessfully tried to fight back tears as she described how proud she was of her death-defying son. Our conversation was cut short by the blaring of the final buzzer. Christ the King players high-fived at midcourt. It was time for the fifth quarter.

The Lions gathered in a huddle as their coach charted a game plan. It was always the same play call in the fifth quarter: get the ball to Davis and get out of his way. The Lions broke the huddle with a booming, "1-2-3 TEAM!" The two teams would scrimmage another few minutes and Davis would take every shot for the Lions. Expectations were low but confidence was high. Davis had only sunk one basket the entire season. His shooting percentage was low but he had no fear of failure. Just being on the court was a victory. The parents in the crowd all moved to the edges of their seats as the referee blew his whistle.

Judging from the roar of the crowd each time Davis touched the ball, you'd think Michael Jordan was out there throwing down 360-degree, one-handed slams in the NBA Finals. Davis was the surprising star of the team and his joyful smile was contagious. His teammates encouraged him to shoot each time down the floor. He wasn't the best player. Not by a long shot. But, Davis exuded joy with every dribble. You could hear him laughing as he awkwardly ran down the court. He wasn't graceful but he was grateful. His jump shots routinely peaked a few feet shy of the rim. Kim shouted encouragement from the front row. Rebounds were returned out to Davis and he gleefully kept shooting. The fifth quarter lasted five minutes and the Lions failed to sink a single shot. Nobody cared. Everyone was all smiles as the final horn sounded. The teams gathered around Davis. He got high-fives from everyone in both jerseys.

There was no doubt that Davis knew how to find joy in the small things. He was bursting with joy! He got to play! He appreciated the sound of the ball bouncing off the hardwood. Enthusiasm radiated from him. Davis soaked up every minute of the fifth quarter and when the game ended, whether he'd scored or not, he was happier than when the game first began.

He rejoiced in, as Peter Garino would call it, "life's innocent pleasures".

I congratulated Davis on a great game. There was no way I was leaving that gym without a picture of myself with the Lions' star player. Kim took the photo as Davis and I both posed with five extended fingers, one to represent each quarter in the game. He was a great example of what it looks like to seek out joy in life. Davis Harkey embraced the happy moments God delivered in the fifth quarter.

If you never face your fears, you'll never conquer them. Joy will lose automatically. The Harkey family didn't allow an ugly diagnosis or physical limitation rob them of joyful opportunities. Instead, they considered it pure joy just having the chance to face those trials head-on. Sitting on the sideline was not an option for that unlikely basketball player. There was more joy in the action. It lived in the fifth quarter. It lived inside his heart.

If joy feels distant, get off the bench. If joy seems impossible, lace up your high-tops. If joy seems unlikely, get in the game. Joyful players get rewarded. God is a coach who won't let you fail.

James 1:2-3 (NIV)
"Consider it pure joy, my brothers and sisters, whenever you face trials of many kinds, [3] because you know that the testing of your faith produces perseverance."

THE SNO BALL EFFECT

I have never been a fan of winter. Give me a hot summer day, please. Give me sand over snow. Give me beach over brrr. I want to live where the official dress code includes sunscreen, and Santa Claus needs flip-flops. Eggnog? No thanks. Make mine a lemonade.

Christmas is about 75 degrees where I live, which means finding ways to cool down vital. How vital? My wife once paid $19 for a snow cone. No, I wasn't happy about it, but I do understand why people would pay such an absurd amount of money for ice. Hydration is necessary for survival, and your go-to hydration depends on your style. During a fun *On The Road* story, I learned there is an enormous difference between snow cones and sno balls Don't get them confused, apparently. Them's fighting words among those in the know.

I remember pulling my news vehicle into a snug parking space in front of a beachfront strip mall on a blazing hot day in St. Pete Beach. It was so hot the seagulls were seeking shade. There were tons of folks milling about. They were either eagerly making their way to the beach or even more eagerly searching for shade after visiting the shore. Tucked away in the strip mall was a little sign that read, *Beach Sno Balls*. The glass storefront was inviting and sounded like the perfect place to chill. Inside, a family of six was enjoying a treat while on vacation from Pittsburgh.

I stepped inside and met the owner. Her name was September. Yes, like the month. We chatted about her journey to the west coast of Florida and I thanked her for allowing me to use her shop as a backdrop for my shoot that day. I was scheduled to meet an author visiting from Jacksonville, with a joyful turnaround story to share.

I ordered a raspberry lemonade sno ball and sat down to wait for Abby

Vega to arrive. September tried to educate me on the difference between snow cones and sno balls. I still don't really understand. To me, it's ice in a cup with flavored syrup on top, no matter what you call it. I think the main differentiation has something to do with the shape. It's essentially icy sugar. Whatever I was eating, it was fantastic. I could see why Abby loved them so much.

She arrived a few minutes after I did and we immediately hit it off. She lives in the Ponte Vedra Beach area just outside Jacksonville. It's home to TPC Sawgrass, where the PGA Tour hosts The Players Championship each spring. It's famed 17th-hole is a true island green that draws golfers from around the world. Abby and I chatted about golf for a minute and she invited me up to play sometime. I was putty in her hand at this point. Sno cone? Sno ball? I didn't care.

She ordered an egg custard sno ball with marshmallow topping. It sounded terrible to me, but that daytime dessert transported her back to her childhood. I'd never seen a grown woman savor ice so much. Abby grew up in Baltimore, where sno balls are king. I grew up on the west coast of Florida, where you are just as likely to pour ice on your neck to cool down as you are to eat it. After a few minutes of eating, I flipped on my camera and asked Abby a few questions about her book.

Abby told me she hadn't been very happy. Based on the cheery personality of the woman seated across from me, I would never have guessed it. From the outside, everyone thought she had it made. Her life looked like a Forbes magazine cover. She had everything the world covets and then some. For 35 years, Abby worked at big corporate jobs, pulled in a six-figure salary, and was incredibly successful. She worked in the fancy office, owned the nice house, and had all the notoriety that comes with incredible occupational achievement.

Why would she give that up, I wondered?

"I'll give you one of the secrets to happiness," she said with a spoonful of shaved ice in her hand. "It's not doing something for you. It's doing something for somebody else."

My tongue was too frozen to talk so I just listened. I knew what she was saying was true. It was refreshing to hear it from someone who understood managing a profitable business required. I'm not a businessman. I don't know the first thing about growing a company. I know popular culture tells us that bank accounts carry a lot of weight in life. Commercials lead us to believe that we deserve a shinier and newer everything. Movies portray happy actors who gain the whole world and never face difficulty. Media says to take, take, take, take, take then take some more. We live in a selfish world. Even the device in your pocket has a self-serving name: "i"-Phone.

Abby just plain quit. Enough was enough. No more chasing the unattainable. No more rat race. No more doing a job that didn't make her happy. Sure, she was accumulating tons of stuff, but at what cost? She didn't have much time for her family. She was stressed about work. She wasn't excelling in the areas of life that were most important to her. She wanted to make a change. She wanted to find joy.

I was hanging on her every word. My sno ball was now a puddle of colored water in my cup. The spoon was floating on the surface and making a mess. I didn't care. I wanted to learn from a woman who rejected what the world calls victory and started over in a fascinating way. She smiled as she told me the next bold move in her journey to joy.

Abby bought a snow cone truck.

"One day I sat down and said, 'What are the three things that make me happy?' It was snow cones, children, and music," she said. Abby told a joke about not being able to carry a tune as a vocalist. That made her decision a pretty obvious one. She took another bite of her sno ball. "I went with the snow cones and children."

For one year, Abby hit the road. Every day she would get up and find a way to put a smile on someone else's face. For decades, she had rolled out of bed thinking about ways to put money in her bank account. Now, she only cared about getting tasty iced treats into the hands of children. She journaled throughout the year. She wrote down everything about her journey as the proprietor of a Kona Ice truck. She made stops at birthday parties and corporate events. She sold snow cones at small outdoor markets. Who knew joy could be served in a paper cup? She loved every second of those 12 months.

Joy comes when we least expect it. That's because it's a gift from God, not dependent upon material things. Cars and boats can bring you happiness. They can't bring you joy. That's God's job.

One of the most impactful experiences from Abby's year with the truck came when she answered the request of a desperate parent. It required a day-long trip to Georgia. Typically, Abby would not travel too far from her Jacksonville home to serve snow cones. It just wasn't cost-effective. She wasn't in the snow cone business to get rich, but she also didn't want to waste time or money, either. After hearing the pleas from a desperate parent, Abby made an exception. She and her son drove 130 miles to a drug rehab facility to serve snow cones to a man fighting addiction. He had spent the last few weeks there in a treatment program and depression was setting in. This young man's job was to wash dishes for all the other rehab patients at the facility. It was a tiring job. It was a thankless job, I'm sure. Abby's snow cone truck rumbled into the parking lot on this man's 21st birthday. When the officers at the center told him a snow cone truck was waiting for him outside, the rehab patient didn't believe them. He refused to drop his sponge at for fear that someone was playing a prank on him. He eventually made the walk to the lot where Abby's colorful truck was ready to serve frosty treats. At the request of the man's mother, Abby hugged him and gave him a much-needed snow cone. It was the pick-me-up the struggling addict needed.

She fought back a little tear as she recalled the embrace. That moment reinforced the purpose behind Abby's decision to give up her comfortable corporate lifestyle. More than that, it changed her life. Seeing the gratitude in the man's eyes was worth those 130 miles across state lines. It was worth driving all day for one stop and very little money. The man's family had hoped Abby's snow cones would provide a little confidence boost and some overdue encouragement. It did. Within a few months, the young man was out of the rehab facility and drug-free.

That story plays a prominent role in Abby's book. Her year-long collection of thoughts was published. She called it *Sno-Cone Diaries: A Sweet Route to Happiness*. The pages are filled with inspirational stories from her travels. I thumbed through a copy of her book as she continued to snack on her sno ball, which was now melting, too. *Sno-Cone Diaries* sounded like a tastier version of what I did each day. Her one-on-one interactions with complete strangers gave her the chance to see how putting others first, and yourself second, could lead to everlasting joy. She smiled between bites as she told the story of kids laying down in the road to block her truck and prevent her from leaving parties. That 12-month process of seeking joy was far more rewarding than her previous three decades of seeking possessions.

Abby's journey to happiness is only beginning. She started working on a second book to help women in leadership positions. She hopes to become a motivational speaker and teach others around the country how to chase their dreams and find joy. The decision to give to others makes the journey to joy a lot smoother. Taking only satisfies yourself. Giving has no end. I left that meeting with a blue tongue and renewed perspective on life. If Abby can give up a whole year of her life to enrich others, surely, I can spend my days attempting to share joy with viewers.

King Solomon, the wisest man who ever lived, conducted research to prove exactly what Abby discovered. He wrote about how seeking joy, rather than possessions leads to a fulfilling life:

Ecclesiastes 2:1-11 (ESV)

"I said in my heart, "Come now, I will test you with mirth; therefore enjoy pleasure"; but surely, this also was vanity. I said of laughter— "It is madness!" and of mirth, "What does it accomplish?" I searched in my heart how to gratify my flesh with wine, while guiding my heart with wisdom, and how to lay hold on folly, till I might see what was good for the sons of men to do under heaven all the days of their lives. I made my works great, I built myself houses, and planted myself vineyards. I made myself gardens and orchards, and I planted all kinds of fruit trees in them. I made myself waterpools from which to water the growing trees of the grove. I acquired male and female servants, and had servants born in my house. Yes, I had greater possessions of herds and flocks than all who were in Jerusalem before me. I also gathered for myself silver and gold and the special treasures of kings and of the provinces, I acquired male and female singers, the delights of the sons of men, and musical instruments of all kinds. So I became great and excelled more than all who were before me in Jerusalem. Also my wisdom remained with me. Whatever my eyes desired I did not keep from them. I did not withhold my heart from any pleasure, for my heart rejoiced in all my labor; and this was my reward from all my labor. Then I looked on all the works that my hands had done and on the labor in which I had toiled; and *indeed all was vanity and grasping for the wind. There was no profit under the sun."*

When you read the phrase 'under the sun' in the Bible, it's talking about life here on this earth. So many of us are living for right this very second with no concept of how today's choices impact our eternity. I blame Facebook and Instagram. The news cycle lasts three minutes now. We dwell so much on the instantaneous that we lose sight of the big picture. We absorb in a moment and move on in an instant. We barely digest information. It's all about take, take, take. That's not the path Abby chose. She found a way to give, give, give. It took her 2.5 years and multiple revision to write her book, but the process provided her with the opportunity to plant a joyful spirit into the minds of her readers. She could have called it *Joy in a Cup*. Readers certainly seemed to like it.

"I believe Abby has touched an inner part of us all in such a way, that makes you relate to the struggles we all share throughout the journey of one's life, at one time or another," read one online review of *Sno-Cone Diaries*.

I left that sno ball shop on a steamy afternoon with a new book in my hand and a cool new perspective in my head. I want to be a storyteller who reminds people that there is joy beyond the news headlines. I want to help people find it. Abby Vega provided the blueprint. Doing for others nets far more joy than taking for oneself. As Solomon noted, why waste time trying to chase down stuff God never designed to last? The alternative is so much grander! Abby chose joy. Choosing joy means choosing God's plan.

Ephesians 4:29 (NIV)
"Do not let any unwholesome talk come out of your mouths, but only what is helpful for building others up according to their needs, that it may benefit those who listen."

CLOSING THOUGHTS ON JOY

I once made a meteorologist very mad during a commercial break. We didn't put on boxing gloves or anything but I could tell by this person's tone that I crossed some kind of imaginary line. The atmospheric opinion of the local sports guy wasn't exactly asked for, nor was it welcomed. I simply pointed out that no weather forecast should include a 50 percent chance of rain. Mathematically, it's obvious. It either will or it won't! It's a daily coin flip. A kindergartener could get that right! I thought my observation was pretty astute. This professional weather-guesser did not. In fact, I think I touched a nerve.

After a few minutes of arguing, the commercial break came to a merciful end and my sportscast began. I was just joking around but my innocent little comment sparked a hailstorm of misplaced rage. I wasn't trying to demean this person. They were, and still are, great at their job. I think meteorologist have a good gig. After all, what other profession can you find where you can be wrong a few times per week, still get paid, and nobody complains?

Headlines tend to be overwhelmingly negative. Even weather headlines! Meteorologists coined the phrase "Cone of Uncertainty" to describe the projected paths of hurricanes. That sounds ominous, doesn't it? Does it put your mind at ease when you hear "Cone of Uncertainty"? I watched a Category 5 hurricane splinter Puerto Rico and the Florida Keys. I lived within two hours of the tornados that collectively killed dozens of people in Moore, Oklahoma and Joplin, Missouri. Those are catastrophes and qualify as bad news.

News is easy to forecast. There is a 100 percent chance of the devil throwing haymakers today. There is a good chance he'll land a few, too. Monday? A forty percent chance of a flat tire in the morning will be followed by a ridge of high-tension around 2 o'clock. Wednesday sees an increase in stress levels due to an unexpectedly light wallet. Can't wait for the weekend? There's a 90 percent chance traffic will make you late to your nephew's birthday party. Try to keep your cool. It will all repeat itself next week with the added bonus of an unplanned mother-in-law visit on Thursday.

See what I mean? The devil wants to get you sidetracked. It's all he can do. He knows, if you are putting God first in your life, he doesn't have the power to derail you from reaching your destiny. But, he certainly can distract you along the way. He's just hoping those distractions cause you to detour from the plan God has put in place for your life. Your external forecast can easily lead to internal fear-casts. Headlines are depressing! Channel surfing can leave you in constant states of misery. When it comes to news habits, your headline-intake directly determines your joy-output. You can consume all that terrible news and choose not to supplement it with a steady diet of uplifting content, but plan on feeling sick to your stomach. Don't expect to feel great about the world around you when you consistently absorb adverse headlines. Bombings are going to happen. Politicians are going to tweet stupid things. Shootings are inevitable. That's the reality of living in a shattered world in need of a new seven-day outlook. Digest headlines in doses. Consume them with caution.

Want more joy in life? Download more good and you'll upload more inspiration. Open your mind to more than just the low-hanging fruit of social media and traditional "downer" headlines. The cable news networks are trying to get you to stick around through the commercial break. They know that panels of "experts" throwing verbal jabs at each other will eventually burst your bubble. They introduce provocative topics designed to scare, confuse and engross viewers. Usually, the conversation will ignite an emotional response that keeps your eyes and brain engaged. You become enticed. You stay tuned in for the promise of solutions. More often than not, you're left unsatisfied, fat on filth, and stuffed with negative thoughts you never meant to devour.

Facebook and Instagram do the same thing. They trap you with links, commentary, and images that lead to endless scrolling and create an alternate world in which the consumer must participate to feel included. Social media is nothing but a joy-sucking, life-squelching, headline service. Once you get sucked in, it's hard to escape. How many times have you browsed the internet looking for a topical video on YouTube only to end up wasting 45-minutes on content you never sought in the first place? Similarly, if you start with one salacious news headline, pretty soon, you'll unravel the ball of yarn to the point where you're left with a bunch of clutter to clean up.

Seeking joy in the everyday news cycle is the antidote to a miserable mind. It's easy for our heads to become clouded by the rapid assault on our senses being thrown at us by competing channels. Pursuing the joyful moments will help break up the headlines. It will help realign your thoughts and keep you focused on your priorities. When I start to dwell on the sad stuff, I get frustrated by things that don't deserve my angst. When I put my efforts into seeking joy in the world around me, I'm much more stable. God gives us reasons to smile every day. You may not be as young as you once were. You may not be the best at what you love to do. You may not even be able to control every situation you encounter. But, you can rejoice in the fact that you're here and God has joyful news for you today. Usually, you won't even know when it's coming. Usually, joy comes from an experience you thought would be anything but joyful.

I remember the day my daughter lost her first tooth. It had to come out but she wouldn't let us near that sucker. Her anxiety was too strong. At six years old, here fear was paralyzing. Then, one bite into dinner, it loosened to the point where there was no bribery necessary. She concluded that it was time to take it out. It was so loose a hearty sneeze would have sent this thing flying across the room like mouth shrapnel. I grabbed a napkin and reassured her that it was no big deal. It would be over in a flash. She was still terrified that the pain would be searing and endless. I was finally able to yank out the middle tooth on the bottom row. The removal was so quick that she didn't even realize it had popped out! That six-year-old was the proud new owner of a gap-toothed grin. Her anticipation was worse than the reality. When she saw her tooth in my hand, her expression changed from uncertainty to unbridled joy. It was out! All that build up was wasted worry. The Tooth Fairy was going to visit and our baby girl could not have been happier. Her joy was evident, even after dreading the pain that preceded it. Just like a lot of our grown-up problems, many times the joy is hiding behind the pain. We just have to look past the momentary discomfort to reach the payoff.

Peter Garino saw a lot of loss in his life. Soldiers typically do. He wasn't what I expected him to be. I thought he might be hardened by the terrors of war. Instead, they humbled him. Peter used the devastation from battle to teach civilians like me about what truly matters in life. He could have dwelled on the negative. He could have kept his struggles bottled up inside. Nobody would have blamed him. Instead, he embraced his position in history and chose to highlight the positives. The result was joy.

Davis Harkey didn't care that he wasn't going to play in the NBA someday. He was too busy smiling as he sprinted down the court. His favorite thing to do was to shoot that basketball during the fifth quarter. He missed 99 percent of his shots, but those misses were hardly failures. The fact that he even put on a jersey was a win. The fact that his teammates wanted him in the game was a win, too. The fact that an entire league defied the laws of mathematics to create a fifth quarter allowed a little boy got his chance to joyfully pursue his passion.

I can picture Henry Witherwax up in Heaven right now having a long conversation with God about elephants. Why are they gray? Why such big ears? Why the long trunk? The smile on Henry's face when he touched the trunk of one of those majestic animals is something that is seared into my mind. There was pure joy in his eyes. It was as if he was a young, 20-something again training elephants in the circus. That moment took him back to when he met his wife in Cuba. The two young lovers bonded because of the gentle giants. Seeing them one last time before Henry left this earth provided him and his family a joyful memory to cherish.

Abby Vega knows all about joy. She gave up everything the world considers a benchmark for success to shave ice into paper cups. It doesn't sound as glamorous as her old corner office, making the high-dollar paychecks, but she chose to chase joy over her usual routine. She ditched comfort in favor of the unknown. She chose adventure over stability. She wanted to seek joyful moments and found them in cups full of snow. Her decision to go all-in on a dream ended up touching countless lives. She wrote it all down in her book. There are messages of joy sprinkled on every page.

My wife? She rejoices over homeschooling, now. She calls me at work to excitedly announce that our first-grader spelled all ten of her spelling words correctly. She will eagerly tell me over dinner all about the scholarly adventures that she and our two kids shared that day. She rejoices in the small milestones our little ones achieve. Will my kids learn enough to end up in Harvard? Maybe. Will they learn that, even in the tough times, it pays to find joy in today's shaky forecast? No doubt. As long as I'm homeschool principal, that lesson will be a core requirement to our curriculum. (For extra credit, they can watch my *On The Road* story tonight.)

VERSES ON JOY

Philippians 4:4 (NLT)
"Always be full of joy in the Lord. I say it again--rejoice!"

Psalm 47:1 (NIV)
"Clap your hands, all you nations; shout to God with cries of joy."

James 1:2-3 (NIV)
"Consider it pure joy, my brothers and sisters, whenever you face trials of many kinds, because you know that the testing of your faith produces perseverance."

Nehemiah 8:10 (NIV)
"Nehemiah said, "Go and enjoy choice food and sweet drinks, and send some to those who have nothing prepared. This day is holy to our Lord. Do not grieve, for the joy of the LORD is your strength."

Romans 15:13 (NIV)
"May the God of hope fill you with all joy and peace as you trust in him, so that you may overflow with hope by the power of the Holy Spirit."

THANKFULNESS

*A*re you thankful for newscasts? If you say no, I understand. Plane crashes. Murdered children. Elected liars. Local and network anchors read that stuff every day. I'd urge you to not shoot the messengers. The world is what's messed up. Reporters just present the evidence. The fact that there are so many awful things to talk about makes me appreciate the good stuff even more.

I am thankful for so much in my life. I am thankful for a healthy body, kids who run and play, a wife who loves me, and the chance to drive to work every morning with an eagerness about my job. I have been truly blessed in so many ways. I'm excited about the things God has done, is doing and will do in my life. He is going to bless me in ways I can't even fathom! That's the best thing about God. He never gets tired of throwing us surprises. He has a ton of cheerful tricks up those omnipotent sleeves.

One of my favorite sections of the Bible is in 1 Thessalonians 5. I especially love verses 16-18:

> *"Always be joyful. Never stop praying. Be thankful in all circumstances, for this is God's will for you who belong to Christ Jesus. (NLT)"*

Do you still look for reasons to be thankful, even when the headlines make it easy not to? The Apostle Paul, who wrote those words, was an outspoken ally of Jesus. Yet, that didn't keep him from ending up in a bad position. He and Silas ended up in jail after casting out a demon from a fortune teller. They were being stripped and beaten before being thrown into jail. It wasn't a pretty picture. There wasn't much reason to say 'thank you' to God. Yet, they sang loud praises to Him anyway at midnight. The story ends miraculously, with an earthquake that shakes the prison so violently that all the cell doors swing open. The jailor feared that he'd be executed after his bosses found out all the prisoners escaped. Paul and Silas prevented him from killing himself, and he and his entire family converted to Christianity.

We won't always understand why the headlines look so rotten. But, God is there during our darkest hours. In all situations, He deserves our praise and thanksgiving.

I went to a church Christmas party in 2005 to meet someone and ended up locking eyes with my eventual bride. Six months of constantly asking her out and she eventually caved. We went on a group date to a ballroom dancing class. She hobbled home thanks to my big, clumsy feet, but did so with a smile on her face. I still have the necktie in my closet that I bought just for the occasion and think about that date each time I wear it. I am thankful for Juslin Lewis. God hand-picked her for me before our grandparents were even born. She just didn't know it for a while.

My children are gifts from the Lord. They are sweet and funny. They are caring and creative. My daughter could easily be the first female President of the United States or a shoeless, starving artist who paints murals with her toes. My son? If he makes it to ten years old, we'll call that a victory. He's equal parts cannonball and dynamite. I see E.R. bills in our future.

Even the home that God provided for my family is special. I was brought home from the hospital to that same house 27 years before I ever signed the mortgage paperwork. My grandparents built it in September 1964 after moving to Florida from Ohio. The room my daughter is growing up in today still has my mom's original furniture, just repainted in girlie, flowery paint. My son now sleeps and plays in the room where I played hide-and-seek with cousins after Thanksgiving dinners. Our Christmas tree sits in the same corner where Grandma's used to sit.

I recently started something new with my daughter. I found an old journal with empty, pink pages. I knew she would like it. I got out a brown Sharpie marker and scrawled 'Thankfulness Journal' across the top in my best handwriting. I explained that each night we were going to sit in that same spot and write out three things that she was thankful for that day. The trick is, once she writes something down, she can't write that word again for a whole week. The first night she had me write 1) house, 2) family, and 3) cars.

The exercise is going to teach her a very important lesson. It's going to uncover how much she has to be thankful for and teach her how to find thankfulness on days when it feels like the well is running dry. Sometimes it feels like you can't lift your hands in praise. Sometimes there really is something weighing on your heart. Sometimes life is hard. Yet, no matter the circumstances, there is always something in our lives worth saying thank you for.

Just because you don't *feel* thankful doesn't mean you can't *be* thankful. That's what I want her to learn.

I can't imagine my thankfulness level spiking any higher. I am grateful for the things that God has sent my way. Some of it I saw coming. Much of it I did not. Some of the things that I'd say I'm most thankful for are things that were total surprises from God.

I am thankful that I get to share all my daily news interactions with people. On occasion, I will bump into viewers who they tell me how much they appreciate my uplifting stories. They will share with me how a story really touched them. I have had people cry! It's a weird feeling that's both humbling and odd. Those encounters are always unexpected.

I've been going to the same grocery store religiously every other Saturday for about four years now. I have gotten to know some of the names of the staff there. They are all very welcoming and friendly. They even pretend not to hear my toddler screaming in the cart when he drops his free cookie. About a year ago, the woman who always works weekends and always seems to end up slicing my sandwich meat finally asked me if I worked at her favorite TV station.

"You look like Bobby Lewis from Channel 10."

"That's me," I answered, before explaining my role with On The Road.

Her name was Teresita and she already knew my role. As we chatted, more and more customers started showing up in line. This lady didn't care. She had something she wanted to tell me. As we stood there, separated by bologna, Teresita went on to tell me how she had been so very lonely the last few years since her husband died. They used to travel together all the time. They would visit family and friends in far off places. Now, she sits at home and doesn't do much. I was starting to feel sad for her until she delivered a surprising line.

"Now, I travel with you."

You never know what impact you can have on someone's life. At this point, the people in line for swiss cheese and ham were probably getting a little fed up with my meet-and-greet with Teresita, but I wasn't done. I needed to thank her for watching and tell her how much I appreciated her kind words. She wanted to thank me for giving her something to look forward to each night at 6 p.m.

That conversation with a stranger lasted ten minutes at the deli counter. As she wrapped up my turkey, I remember smiling back with an appreciative grin. I was so glad she mentioned how thankful she was for my stories. In a world full of negative headlines, it was a much-needed reminder that an uplifting report carries a lot of power.

I'm thankful for my niche. I'm also thankful for encounters like the one with Teresita. They remind me that God still has plenty of surprises to share. We need to be ready for them and offer praise and thanksgiving when they arrive.

THE BRICKS THAT BOND

I don't know what your childhood was like but mine was great. My mom made sure of it. She worked many jobs to make sure my two siblings and I were happy. I spent my first five years bouncing around Florida and even had a brief stint in Kentucky. As a child of the late-80s and early-90s, I was all about two things: sports and action figures.

I had every action figure known to man. I was a Darkwing Duck fan, loved Teenage Mutant Ninja Turtles, and TaleSpin characters. On rainy days, when I couldn't go outside, I'd sit on the brown carpet in the guest room of our rural Kentucky home and set up my Ninja Turtle figurines in a diamond formation. I'd call out the play-by-play and act out bottom of the ninth baseball scenes will all my fictional childhood heroes manning the bases. I'm sure I wasn't the quietest kid around. It was hard to pipe down when there was so much action to imagine! Eventually, I graduated from Leonardo and Donatello to a toy that still piques my interest today.

My children are old enough now that we can all gather around the tub of LEGO bricks in our playroom and spend at least six minutes playing. With little kids, attention spans aren't that long, so building a LEGO fortress isn't really in the cards. We're still in the phase of life where my daughter builds a princess castle and my son reduces it to rubble three seconds later with his tiny Lightning McQueen sneakers. Tears ensue and LEGO time is over. Someday, I hope to peaceably build LEGOs with them for 20 uninterrupted minutes.

I totally get why Adam Smyk loves the toys, too. I got an email from a friend of mine telling me about a new store was opening in a shopping mall about 30 minutes from the TV station. It was a LEGO bricks and minifigs store. I admit, I had no idea what a minifig was. Turns out, it's simply an abbreviation for mini figurine. This store had almost every LEGO character, set, and figurine ever made. There was Star Wars LEGO, superhero LEGO, princess LEGO, and movie character LEGO. I mean it was a child's dream!

That is kind of why Adam got the idea to open the shop. I stopped in one day on the way home from church. We arrived at about 11:45 a.m. The mall was open, but the shops didn't officially open doors to customers until noon. For 15 agonizing minutes, my two kids pressed their smudgy little faces up to the glass display window and drooled over Adam's colorful bricks that were just out of reach. There was a table set up right in the front of the store that had minifig pieces in neatly divided sections. There was a bin for just the legs of LEGO characters, a bin for bodies, heads, and accessories. My son was entranced.

A college-aged guy unlocked the floor-to-ceiling doors. The loud thud of the lock signaled to all the other little kids who were gathered near the entrance that it was time to dive headfirst into the brightly colored toys. The young, 20-something guy had a scraggly black beard and long, wavy hair. His smile hinted that he loved his job. I walked up and introduced myself. His name was Daniel, which I would have known had I noticed his LEGO-shaped name tag.

Daniel Smyk, as it turned out, was the son of the owner, Adam Smyk. His dad wasn't around at that moment and I didn't have a lot of time to spend at the store. My kids were nearly buried up to their elbows in LEGO figurines at this point and those tidy, orderly bins were now colorful chaos. It only took five minutes for the kids to totally undo all of Daniel's organization. I left my business card with Daniel and asked him to have his dad call me. I gathered up my kids, brushed away a few tears after denying them Wonder Woman LEGO pieces, and headed for home. A few hours later, Adam called.

I set up a time to come back and tell his story. Adam was a retired Navy man. He spent over 20 years serving the United States of America. He was stationed in Jacksonville, San Diego and, get this, Hawai'i. Yep. He got to serve the nation while living in paradise. He was an electrician and mechanical engineer who helped keep the Navy's fleet up and floating.

When you have a parent who serves in the military, that parent is going to be gone A LOT. Adam served for months at a time and missed important moments in his kids' lives. He was dedicated to Uncle Sam and, sometimes, that meant missing a t-ball game, recital, or birthday party. That is the cost of wearing red, white, and blue on your uniform.

The day I returned to his store with my camera, Adam brought along his two youngest sons. Andrew was six and James was nine. Daniel, whom I met the previous week, was 21, and had been adopted by Adam when he was just a small boy. The four Smyk men were hanging out in the LEGO shop selling toys to cheerful little kids and their kid-at-heart parents. They were loving every second of it.

Good stories cover the essentials well. Who? What? Where? When? Why? The *why* is most important.

Whose idea was it to have a LEGO store? What was the reason behind starting it? Where did you get these LEGO bricks? When did you find out your kids loved this stuff? And, most importantly, why is this important to you?

Adam told me the story of a time when he walked through the airport terminal in full military uniform, with open arms, expecting a giant hug from his youngest son. Instead of a loving embrace, he was greeted by shrill cries from a child who didn't understand why the stranger in uniform was trying to squeeze him.

"When you come back from six months away, the kids don't really trust you," said Adam.

Imagine how that must have made a loving parent feel. Adam was torn between two passions. He had a duty to uphold as a military member. He needed to parent three boys who didn't really know who he was.

The upsetting airport experience led to a plan. Adam thought about what he could do with his kids that would essentially force them to spend time together, get to know each other better, and have fun all at the same time. The answer came to him one night – LEGO! It was the perfect activity. It is like a puzzle, requires you to work together to assemble, and, the best part of all, is time-consuming. Adam knew if he brought the toys home, the boys would sit with him and work on LEGO sets for hours. They could rekindle their relationship and start to build trust in each other.

The plan worked to perfection. Every time Adam returned home from duty, he'd bring new LEGO sets for his sons. It started to become an expectation. Their love for each other grew along with their love for LEGO.

As I began asking more questions, Adam's sons, James and Andrew, feverishly tried to assemble makeshift houses from bricks they found in the used LEGO bins. They meticulously searched for just the right piece to complete their structures. The boys rummaged through the bins with their fingers, which created jingling sounds as bricks careened off the walls of the container. Adam watched them over my shoulder in between my questions. He wasn't being rude. He just wanted to see his sons enjoying the LEGO. After all, he was the one responsible for their love for the colorful bricks.

"Best job I've ever had," said Daniel, who was helping a customer not too far from me. "The fact that I get to make money and spend time with my loved ones, that's probably the best part of it."

When Adam retired from the military, he wanted to spend most of his time building with his kids. They started buying and selling brick sets and opened the resale shop together. Daniel works for his dad and Adam gets to bring James and Andrew with him to the shop on weekends. The family's reconnection reminds Adam to be thankful for every minute he gets with his three boys.

I learned a lot from my chat with Adam. I learned that there is no right formula for being a dad. Being around to help get kids off the school bus and help with their homework is ideal, but that's not reality for many parents. We forget to be thankful for just a few minutes together, sometimes. We should make the most of the chances we get and try not to squander them. I think when my kids arrive at Daniel's age, I'll look back on the crazy moments that we currently share and smile a proud, papa smile. Yes, most of our play sessions end with me assuming the role of LEGO referee, but at least I'm there and get to enjoy the togetherness.

The memory of that airport hug-gone-wrong motivated Adam to be more intentional about the quality time he spent with his kids. Now, he couldn't be more thankful that he did. You can't go back and redo life. You can look in the mirror and be thankful that today is worth celebrating.

"It's been a way to bond my family together," Adam said, just before I turned off my camera. "Kind of like the way LEGOs bond together. That's what it's done for my family and I."

Adam's kids are a gift from God. So is the time they get to share. A few LEGOs is all it took to strengthen their relationship. He is so thankful for what God has done in his life. You could see it in his eyes as he watched his kids play in the store. He was thankful for the lessons he'd learned and the life he'd built. Adam Smyk is a man who understands what it means to be thankful for good times, even in the middle of hard times.

If you're looking for a reason to be thankful, start with the small stuff. You woke up today. You breathed today. Hopefully, you smiled today. Each of those things is a gift. Remember to say a prayer of thanks to the One who provided it.

James 1:17 (ESV)
"Every good gift and every perfect gift is from above, coming down from the Father of lights, with whom there is no variation or shadow due to change."

BEHIND THE WHEEL AGAIN

*I*t isn't exactly a Ferrari, but Willie Reese's 1996 Nissan Maxima is his gleaming chariot. It was probably white at some point in time but today the color-scheme is more of a chipped paint and smudges combo. There is a dent in the driver's side door and the rubber seal on the inside of another door is peeling off. The air conditioning barely works. The gear shift is tattered. The dark blue Yankee Candle air freshener that drooped off the rearview mirror helps, a little.

As I said, it isn't exactly a Ferrari, but it represents an amazing comeback.

I pulled up in the parking lot of the Without Walls International Church with very little information about my story. I knew I was interviewing a man who was recently gifted a car. I knew his name was Willie Reese.

That was about it.

From the moment I saw this man, I knew I was going to like him. He and I were about the same height – a smidgen above 6-foot-2. His Nike Air Force 1s matched his polo shirt and flat-brimmed baseball cap perfectly. In his right hand he held a walking cane and in his left hand, he jingled his new prized set of keys. He had an inviting look on his face. He seemed like a genuinely jolly person. I introduced myself and he shook my hand with a firm grip. There was a gleam in his eye that was inviting.

I found out Willie played professional golf and caddied in the early 1970s. He started rattling off so many names of pro golfers he helped win tournaments that I started to lose count. If you know me, you know that I'm a golf nut. I could have listened to Willie talk about the game for hours. As I was pulling my camera out of the trunk, he assumed a swinging stance and placed his cane between his toes. He took a practice swing and flashed that smile again.

"I haven't played in a few months."

I hadn't played in three days and already had the itch to break away for another 18 holes. Golf is addictive. It's also what led to Willie's addictions and demons.

We squeezed into his car. He turned the key and the engine fired up. I was surprised, based on the look of the outside, that the 1996 model sounded like new. The engine didn't cluck. The tailpipe didn't sputter. I was starting to feel better about letting this 68-year-old stranger escort me around town.

I put a microphone on Willie and attached a tiny camera to the rearview mirror. Both of us were in view of the lens. I secured a small, magnetic camera to the hood of the car and turned on its WIFI feature. It would enable me to get a look at the camera's perspective from the cell phone resting in my lap. On the floorboard of the passenger side, between my feet, I set a larger camera connected to Willie's microphone. I took a second cell phone, plugged in a smaller mic cable, and wired myself for sound.

We were ready to roll.

I'm not sure what Willie thought about all those wires and contraptions but he willingly played along. It looked like we were ready to shoot a scene from an upcoming James Bond film. All we were missing was a set of secret gun holsters in the glove box and exploding cufflinks. The first left turn out of the parking lot was a bit bumpy. Willie hadn't driven a car in 21 years but he sure remembered where the gas pedal was located. During our 15-minute ride, Willie explained why he'd been without a set of wheels since 1996.

The sport he loved so much had led him astray. Golf took him around the country and allowed him to rub elbows with the rich and famous. He found success early on and let it carry him away to a place that ultimately would lead to some very regrettable decisions.

His first sample of cocaine came at age 24. He said it knocked him out. He admitted that the experience forced him to wise up a bit. He didn't touch a drug again for four years. But, at 28, he found himself trapped again in the web of cocaine use. Each time, the dosage increased. Each time, he pushed the limits. He was living for the next high. He was consumed by consuming.

The results were fatal. Not to his life, but his career quickly died. His focus was blurred. His purpose was lost. Three times he found himself in handcuffs. Once, after two family members set him up to sell cocaine to an undercover drug officer in Atlanta. He was as low as he could get without being six feet deep. The third time he was sentenced to jail time, Willie was ordered to begin a six-week drug rehab program.

It saved his life.

Life can get sideways on us in a hurry. Temptation doesn't take a vacation. It's important to stay true to God in the down moments. In the Old Testament, we read a story about an honorable man named Joseph. He was the favorite of his dad's 12 sons. That didn't sit well with the brothers. They sold him into slavery and faked Joseph's death. Later, he was accused of a rape he never committed, was wrongfully jailed and forgotten there. Through it all, God didn't forget him. Joseph ascended to the second-highest position in all of Egypt and kept a nation from drying up during a famine. He even saved his brother's lives when they came to him begging for food. Times were tough for Joseph. God led him through it all.

Despite the grim conversation, Willie kept things lighthearted during our car ride. He had incredible perspective and plenty of reasons to be thankful.

"I never in a million years imagined I'd be driving a car again," he said. He didn't stop talking while checking for openings in the oncoming traffic. "I learned that God puts people in your path for a reason. I've got a lot of wonderful people in my life."

One of those people is the very reason that we were sitting in that Nissan Maxima. About two years prior to our conversation, Willie was panhandling outside a movie theater when Pastor Randy White walked by. He is the leader of Without Walls International Church. He gave Willie a few bucks and invited him to a church service. Willie attended. I didn't ask if he did so reluctantly. Given the stories he'd shared with me to that point, I'm guessing there was at least a little hesitation. We humans don't like roadblocks. We don't like detours. That's because obstacles force action. The devil finds opportunities in our crossroads. He prepares to pounce when times get tough. It's easy to lose sight of our reasons to give thanks when doubts are dancing in our heads. I can only imagine the slimy thoughts Satan peppered Willie's mind with that Sunday morning before he boarded the bus for church.

"*This won't work. They won't accept you. You're not good enough.*"

"Stop kidding yourself. You're a drug addict. You think they want drug addicts in church?!"

You have a choice to make when those evil ideas creep into your brain. You can try to ignore them or you can command that them to leave. If you don't stand up to them, they'll keep coming. A crowded mind isn't a thankful mind.

"You have to catch a bus? It will probably be late. It's been late before. Just sit on the porch today. Don't even bother."

"You're worthless. Everyone will see it the minute you step through the doors of that place."

Faithfully, for two years, Willie shrugged off those persistent attacks. He made it to church and surrounded himself with people who cared about him, possibly for the first time in decades. He made God a priority. He tried to find reasons to be thankful. He let God work for him. Willie rode shotgun.

One month prior to the morning that I first shook Willie's hand, he was standing in that same parking lot. He had made the journey across town for a Sunday service. He had no idea what was about to happen.

"I was surprised," he recalled, with joy in his voice. "Pastor Randy called me up to the pulpit and said somebody donated a car and handed me the key. That was one of my biggest, greatest surprises of my life."

The previous Sunday, Pastor White had challenged his congregation to make a difference in Willie's life. He called for someone to step up and support Willie's journey to becoming a better man continued. One person listened and reacted. Someone donated the 1996 Maxima that Willie and I were sitting in. A church member who ran a mechanic business gave up his time to ensure that the car would run properly.

"After church, I went out, put the key in the ignition and started it up," Willie said.

Drugs had drained his bank accounts. He would not have been able to buy a car on his own! Oh, what a feeling that must have been! Two decades of waiting for freedom had arrived. Freedom from loneliness? Check. Freedom from depression? Check. Freedom from drugs?

Check.

Willie and I pulled back into the church parking lot and he told me that he was just three weeks out from celebrating seven years sober. He was thankful for the things God had provided for him. Willie knew God never stopped caring, even during his storms. Rearview mirrors are helpful. They can help you see what's behind you. But, there is a reason why the windshield is so much larger. Your future is bigger than your past. Just ask Willie.

Remember Joseph's brothers? When they came to Egypt looking for life-saving food, their now-powerful sibling could have easily squashed them like bugs or tossed them in jail forever. Revenge was a very real option. Instead, Joseph showed his brothers the same kind of protection he received from God during his desperate moments. After all he'd been through, he still had enough perspective to realize that it was all part of a master plan.

Genesis 50:20 (NLT)
20 You intended to harm me, but God intended it all for good. He brought me to this position so I could save the lives of many people."

Like Joseph, Willie's setbacks set him up with an incredible opportunity to show thankfulness to God.

"Drugs is a dead-end street. If you want success in your life stay away from drugs."

Life for Willie Reese has included many potholes. His journey was rocky. There were moments when he probably wanted to give up. But God isn't just waiting for us at the finish line. He's there pushing us on towards it. An attitude of gratitude is what got Willie through. He's not at the end of his race yet. There are more years to come.

Thankfully, he now has a proper heading. The best part? He's full steam ahead in a new set of wheels.

"That's no limitation," he said with a smile. "That's added freedom."

1 Chronicles 29:12-13 (NLT)
"Wealth and honor come from you alone, for you rule over everything. Power and might are in your hand, and at your discretion people are made great and given strength.[13] "O our God, we thank you and praise your glorious name!"

◇

GREEN WAS RED

I like flowers, but I have never been much of a flower man. I buy them for my wife quite often, although less often than I should. I get them for my daughter when we go on special daddy-daughter dates each month. Even if it's just the $3 bundle from the nearby grocery store, she doesn't care. She just lights up when I hand her a bouquet. Flowers are great! I have just never really cared about them. On Valentine's Day, I prefer the chocolates.

Well, I had a change of heart in October 2016. I went on a trip to visit my in-law's new home and was reminded of why God made so many beautiful varieties.

My in-laws live in the Costa Rican jungle. Literally. I'm not exaggerating. They don't have a street address and get their water from the rain. They live in a little house between the bustling metropolises of Cachi and Orosi. And by bustling, I mean the roads are lined with cows and coffee plants. They are greeted by chirping parrots in the morning and bid the day farewell with brilliant sunsets overlooking an active volcano. You can feel thunder under your feet and see every star God ever positioned in the sky during the pitch-black nights. It's peaceful, relaxing, and gorgeous.

They have three acres of land on the side of a mountain. The house is positioned in the middle acre between two enormous "farms". The lower farm has tons of food growing, like bananas, coffee, and sugarcane. The upper farm is a floral paradise. There are around 40 different varieties of wild orchids growing intermittently up and down the walking paths. In addition to the orchids, my father-in-law, who helped plant the original landscaping for Walt Disney World in Orlando, has cultivated a natural rainbow. There are exotic plants like birds of paradise, bromeliads, heliconia, and gingers everywhere.

On our 2015 visit, all the newly-planted flowers were just ankle-high. They were tiny buds in the dirt waiting to burst towards the heavens. Twelve months later, I could barely see the house from the driveway. Fueled by years of falling volcanic ash, those little plants got the nitrogen boost they needed to grow taller than me. The colors are breathtaking! The oranges and yellows practically glow. It feels a little bit like walking through fire. It looks like a watercolor painting come to life. It's an amazing natural masterpiece! Up to that point in my life, I had taken flowers for granted.

God connects the dots in funny ways. Shortly after our vacation ended, and we returned home to the United States, I interviewed a man who offered a new perspective on both flowers and thankfulness.

I'm not sure I've met a more grateful guy than Noel Stafford. From the moment that I pulled up in his driveway, I felt welcomed. The flower-loving man strolled up from his backyard to greet me with very dirty hands. The job of a landscaper is never done – especially at his own home. Noel is the type of guy who will probably never have clean fingernails again.

I remember his genuine smile. He took off his bright blue University of Florida Gators ball cap and shook my hand. He introduced me to this wife and daughter before inviting me to come check out his yard. The reason I was there with all my camera gear, was starting to become more unbelievable which each step.

The bright colors were everywhere. Noel had red and yellow hibiscus growing on large bushes near the side door. Fresh annuals provided a pop of pink. The grass was emerald green and stood out against the mulched gardens.

Noel's view on life had always been cheerful. He spent almost his adult life in that home. His daughter, Molly, works with him in the family lawn business. While we chatted, Noel's grandson played with the hose. Noel explained to me how thankful he was for his blessings. His last birthday had been just a few weeks prior.

In that very backyard, in the center of a semi-circle of family members, Noel had fumbled with a small box. His trademark Gators hat was pulled up a little higher than usual. Camera phones recorded him as he unwrapped his gift. A bunch of colorful birthday balloons sat at his feet. Inside the box was a present that was going to change his life forever.

The pair of sunglasses looked like any other pair. He smiled as he slipped them on his face. Then his expression changed. It was hard to tell which emotion was strongest. He wore looks of shock, amazement, excitement, joy, and thanks all at once. For the first time in his entire life, he could see colors properly.

"It's magnified the beauty and it was just breathtaking," he told me, choking back tears. "People who aren't colorblind, my son for example, say, 'Well, dad that's how it is'. I didn't know."

Noel's job as a landscaper is to plant beautiful flowers but he had never truly seen what colorful creations he was crafting. Before the glasses, greens looked reddish and blues looked yellowish. Noel was seeing God's masterpiece for the first time through his new corrective sunglasses. Experiences like that are hard to imagine for people like me who take colors for granted. There was no doubt he was thankful for this newfound sense of sight.

The video of Noel opening his gift of color for his 66th birthday, recorded by his grandson, Carson, was viewed nearly a million times on YouTube. It's a moment that touched countless lives across the world. People with colorblindness reached out to Noel. He became a bit of a local celebrity. His beloved Florida Gators asked him to make the two-hour drive to Gainesville to throw out the first pitch at a home baseball game. Noel said he'd never seen so much beautiful green grass in his life.

Sometimes we don't know what thankfulness is until we realize what we were missing. For 66 years, Noel didn't know what his flowers *really* looked like. He knew he was a bit colorblind, but it didn't bother him. Now, after seeing the true beauty all around him, life would never be the same.

I left Noel's home that day with a new perspective. God gave me two eyes that work just fine. I saw flowers, but I didn't truly recognize their beauty. I saw something that wasn't worth celebrating. Noel saw something special. I saw a pink periwinkle. He saw a pink periwinkle as pink for the first time.

On the drive back to the TV station, I God reminded me to be thankful for yellow daisies. Noel's entire career was based on making someone's yard looking immaculate. He had great success, despite thinking yellow was blue and green was red. The world was inside out for him, yet he saw what I couldn't. When Noel's eyes were finally opened to the way God intended for us to see creation, his appreciation grew even more.

I'm not sure you'll find a nicer man than Noel Stafford. I'm positive you won't meet many as thankful, either. He knew God was working in his life before those special glasses. Now, he can see God's masterpiece even more clearly.

2 Corinthians 9:15 (NASB)
Thanks be to God for his indescribable gift!

ONCE A MERMAID, ALWAYS A MERMAID

The very first movie I ever saw in the theater was Disney's *The Little Mermaid*. The songs engulfed me. The storyline amused me. The characters befriended me. I loved every minute of Walt Disney's under-the-sea epic, until the final minutes of the movie, when the wicked sea witch grew to five-times the size of the prince's ship and started belting hellish cackles. Lighting flashes and loud, booming thunder on the screen didn't help. The giant video that started off so whimsically took a sudden, traumatizing turn. About the only thing I don't remember about the experience was if I cried. It's certainly possible that I purposefully erased that part of the story from memory.

Despite that experience, I still like mermaids. They are easy to like. They can do things that we can't do. I sure would like to know what it's like to breathe underwater without an air tank. They are human fish. They are majestic, incredible and, sadly, fake. There is no such thing as a real mermaid…

Or is there?

Vicky Smith is the coolest old lady with a fresh tattoo that I've ever interviewed. Regardless, she's cool. Disclaimer: I say 'old' as a sign of respect. You're only as old as you feel, right? I met Ms. Smith at Weeki Wachee State Park shortly after her 77th birthday. Her capri pants were just high enough to expose the black ink mermaid on her right ankle. The tattoo was a birthday present to herself seven years prior. We chatted while overlooking a natural spring that has attracted visitors from all 50 states for decades. The icy waters there captivate people. There are slides and beaches and plenty of things to do. But, the big draw is the mermaids. Vicky Smith was one of the first.

You can tell how much someone loves something by their willingness to permanently mark his or her body with that image. If a 70-year-old woman decides to permanently imprint her passion for make-believe underwater sirens on her skin, she must be gaga for mermaids. One of the first things I noticed about Vicky was her infectious laugh. She chuckled as we chatted about her many summers spent at that park. Her storytelling ability was easy to spot. We swapped jokes as we walked down a ramp to the underwater theater that faces the natural spring. In the intimate setting, park guests 'ooh' and 'ahh' as actresses perform dazzling underwater swimming routines to peppy music. With nothing but air hoses for a lifeline, a dozen mermaids entertain crowds during 20-minute shows. I caught a glimpse of Vicky's facial expression during one of the shows. She was lost in yesteryear. The music was familiar. The water looked inviting. The whole experience revived decades-old memories.

After the show, we went back up on the deck above the springs. Tucked under Vicky's arm was a special photo album. I could tell it meant a lot to her. The edges were a little tattered and the gold trim was wearing off. It was obvious that this album had been flipped through many times. The pages were loose and the glue that held the photos in place was losing its stickiness.

"That's me," she said, pointing to a cute young girl in a very conservative one-piece outfit. "All we wore were little pink bathing suits and tutus."

The mermaid tails would be added to the girl's swimming ensembles years later. Vicky grew up a short drive from Weeki Wachee. She knew the spring's history. Even as a young girl, she always knew she wanted to entertain as a mermaid.

"For the girls whose first job was being a mermaid, the rest of your jobs, for the rest of your life, are pretty mundane," she said with a youthful giggle.

Vicky joked that after high school, back then, you either went to the University of Florida, got married, or became a mermaid. At the age of 17, she chose the latter and signed up for her dream job. A fresh high school graduate, she started the process of becoming a performing mermaid for the thousands of visitors to Florida's nature coast each year. She got the job in June and was in the water for her first show exactly one month from the day she was hired.

It was July 7, 1957.

She was a nervous and excited teen. Her childhood dream was finally coming true. Imagine what it must have felt like to slip into the 70-degree water for the first time. It was probably a combination of sensory overload and girly giddiness. She had the anxious energy of performing the routine properly, the excitement of getting to perform in front of park guests, and the joy of finally making it to the underwater stage.

We flipped through a few more photos in her album. She looked so happy in the pictures. Vicky performed thousands of shows during her time as a mermaid. She spun. She twirled. She danced. She brought smiles to the faces of little kids from all over the world.

Vicky shows off her album full of mermaid photos

The great thing about memories is there are always new ones to be made. The reason I made the 90-minute drive to Weeki Wachee to meet Vicky was to reminisce about a historic memory-making experience from July 7, 2017. Six decades to the day after her first performance, at 77 years young, Vicky Smith put on her bathing suit and was embraced by the spring waters once again.

There was a quiver in her voice as she described her emotional swim.

"If I never did it again I wanted to go in that day," she said. "I never, ever dreamed at 17 that I would still be doing the same thing at my age of 77."

There was thankfulness in her words. You could tell the chance to relive her glory days was special to her. I could tell it took her back in time to a place where so many special things happened. Mermaids had always been special to Vicky. Becoming one must have felt so rewarding. So many times, we don't take the opportunity to just sit and be thankful for all the precious things we've experienced. Vicky embraced that opportunity.

We tend to say thank you so often that the words lose their meaning. It's a standard exit from a conversation. The barista hands you a coffee. You casually mumble your thanks as you turn to leave. The cashier hands you some change and you hurriedly spit out a "thank you" as you fumble for your cell phone in your purse. True thanks is heartfelt and sincere. It's eye contact. It's a hug. A "thank you" is more than just being polite. It's more than just another rushed phrase during our day. It's permanent if it's honest.

Vicky is truly thankful for the waters of Weeki Wachee. She's the oldest living, still performing mermaid at the springs. We chatted a bit more after I turned off my camera. Usually, people open up a bit more once their microphone is removed. Still on the dock, the worn, wooden planks creaked a bit as we leaned over the railing to get a better view of performers below. The young women were preparing for the next mermaid show.

Two middle-aged fans who recognized Vicky ran up to snap a mermaid selfie. The shared stories of seeing her perform years ago. It was as if Vicky was their long-lost friend from the deep. One of the park visitors smiled and offered a sincere "thank you" as she left Vicky behind. Vicky smiled back. It's the least she could do for a place that has provided her with so much for which to be thankful.

Psalm 20:4 (ESV)
"May he grant you your heart's desire and fulfill all your plans!"

CLOSING THOUGHTS ON THANKFULNESS

*I*n America, we gather around the table on a special Thursday each November to gorge ourselves on turkey meat and mashed potatoes. We crave gravy, cram yams, and stuff stuffing. Then, just after we unbutton our pants and let out a little (painful) sigh, grandma comes by with a slice of pumpkin pie.

I love Thanksgiving.

There is a tradition in many homes around the nation where family members share what they are most thankful from the previous year. It's nearly obligatory on a holiday based on being thankful. The sad part is that it may be a full calendar year before many folks utter thanks to God again for the many blessings He has supplied. Thankfulness is a lifestyle that never goes out of style. More than anything, God deserves our thanks. Giving a simple shout of praise to the Source of all gifts is a good way to keep them coming. Adonai is another one of God's names. In Hebrew, it means "master, protector, and provider". He is very good at his job.

If there was anyone in the Bible who had a reason to NOT be thankful, it would be Job. The guy was stuck in the middle of a schoolyard bully battle that God allowed. Satan asked God, since he can't do anything without permission, if he could test Job, a man whom God had commended as upright and honorable. God allowed it, as long as Satan didn't physically harm the man. It looks like a peculiar move by God, but He knew this plan would backfire in Satan's face. The devil dashed everything in Job's life. His family was killed. His livestock all died. His home was crushed. Satan hit Job with every bullet, arrow, and mortar he could muster and the man still wouldn't back off his commitment to the Lord. Satan bombed his heart!

Job lost almost everything! But, he still had God. That was enough. He was thankful to still be connected to his Creator.

Job's thankfulness teaches us that our relationship with God is not predicated on anything but the relationship itself. It doesn't come with a catch. He still had faith in God because he knew that faith is not reliant upon what God can do, but rather who God is. Job's praise and thanksgiving were not transactional. It was not based on anything besides the fact that he existed and was part of this amazing universe and awesome life. Maybe you've lost a lot. Maybe your life didn't turn out the way you planned. Maybe Satan's attacks sank your ship. Good news, God is sending a lifeboat. There is no news too damaging and no headline too awful to separate you from God's goodness. Are you seeking God as earnestly as Job? Will you thank Him for the things you have left?

My wife has a cute little habit of searching for heart-shaped things. She finds them everywhere and always saves them. If she can't pick them up and take them home, she whips out her cell phone and snaps a quick photo to remind her of God's love in her life. A heart-shaped rock, leaf, or paper cutout all have meaning. She even found a little heart in her plate of eggs one morning. Sometimes we need a reminder that God loves us. The lead story in the newscasts rarely do that. So many times, the most talked-about news story each day has the potential to blow our minds off course. It's not easy to remain thankful. Keeping our eyes tuned in to God's good news moving throughout the world keeps us aligned with His script. Seeking good and finding it gives us reasons to be thankful.

You don't have to remind Adam Smyk to give thanks. Not after what God has done for him! He knows what he missed during his service in the Navy. He's thankful to have time to bond over LEGO with his kids now.

Willie Reese hadn't clutched a steering wheel since 1996. Two decades elapsed between his driving experiences. The faithful man learned that life is full of roadblocks. He also learned that God offers detours. He wasn't gifted a Ferrari, but he is possibly the most thankful Nissan Maxima owner on the planet.

Do you think Noel Stafford is thankful? The man spent his whole life looking at beautiful flowers just wondering what they REALLY looked like. Imagine the moment when his slipped that pair of corrective sunglasses over his eyes and was gifted a proper view of ever color God made.

For many people, just making it to 77 years old is a reason to be thankful. For Vicky Smith, taking a sentimental dip in the chilly waters of Weeki Wachee six decades after her first mermaid show provided her with an incredible memory. Her thankfulness was as obvious as her smile the day she shared her story with me at the springs.

Maybe you feel like you've lost your reason to say thank you. Maybe you feel like you just don't have much to be thankful about. I challenge you to make a list of all the things in your life that bring a smile to your face. I promise you, the list will be longer than you might expect. God isn't leaving you high and dry. When the headlines of this world tell you that there is nothing good happening, remember that God doesn't worry about news headlines. He's too busy hiding joy in plain sight for you to find.

VERSES ON THANKFULNESS

James 1:17 (ESV)
"Every good gift and every perfect gift is from above, coming down from the Father of lights, with whom there is no variation or shadow due to change."

Philippians 4:6-7 (NIV)
"Do not be anxious about anything, but in every situation, by prayer and petition, with THANKSGIVING, present your requests to God. And the peace of God, which transcends all understanding, will guard your hearts and your minds in Christ Jesus."

2 Corinthians 4:15 (NLT)
"All of this is for your benefit. And as God's grace reaches more and more people, there will be great THANKSGIVING, and God will receive more and more glory."

2 Corinthians 9:11 (NLT)
"Yes, you will be enriched in every way so that you can always be generous. And when we take your gifts to those who need them, they will thank God."

BLESSING

I met a woman named Debbie Entsminger for an interview one morning. She invited me into her home to tell her amazing story. For two decades, she gradually lost her hearing until she became completely deaf. Fortunately, she got cochlear implants placed in her ears and regained the recognition of sound! She has been pastoring college students for almost 20 years.

"I love stories," she told me, "because God writes the best ones."

That's true, we just tend to have more access to the world's defeating stories than God's triumphant ones. We hear the bad stuff so often that we grow numb to it. "If it bleeds, it leads", right? We pick up a TV remote and invite evil in, then get upset when we start feeling depressed. It's a nightly affair. That repetition can breed resentment. It's become woven into the fabric of our routines. You may not sit down at the television set at 5 p.m. sharp anymore to get the news of the day, but I bet you checked your cell phone before picking up this book.

A 2017 study by global tech support company Asurion claims Americans check their cell phones once every 12 minutes. That's a lot of opportunities to absorb headlines that could steer your day into the gutter. Of the 2,000 people Asurion surveyed, a third said they'd rather go without sex for a week than give up those cell phones, which are rapidly becoming the main source of information in our lives. Our news gathering habits may change but our news consumption needs are still very demanding. I remember seeing the local evening news on TV in my house as a kid. My earliest memory of something truly terrible happening was April 20, 1999.

A pair of high school students decided they'd had enough. Enough of the bullying. Enough of the name calling. Just, enough. Eric Harris and Dylan Klebold, both dressed in trench coats on a balmy morning in

Littleton, Colorado, had reached the point of no return as they entered the school campus with loaded rifles. Their unsuspecting classmates were sitting ducks. Homeroom became a war zone at 11:19 a.m. as the duo sent bullets into classroom walls, doors, and students. The mass shooting was the deadliest ever carried out at a school at the time. It was later reported that the shooters targeted Christians. Survivors told stories of victims being asked if they believed in God before being shot. I was 13. Could this happen at my school? I remember standing in my living room watching the national news reports wondering how anything like this could possibly happen. It was terror on the screen. There were body bags on the ground outside a high school. I was going to graduate middle school in a few short months. I remember the chilling feeling those sights and sounds sent down my spine. The entire United States groaned for that little mountain town dealing with so much unexpected grief. The killings sparked national debates on gun control and unnecessary violence in video games. Harris and Klebold murdered 12 peers and a coach. It was as if all 50 states got kicked in the gut at the same time.

Flash forward to now and there are mass shootings every month. People are dying all the time at the hands of crazed shooters. The worst part? It doesn't even register with me anymore. The boyish agony I felt in my parent's living room in 1999 is gone. I'm unfazed by the reports now. They don't hurt the same way anymore. I've become desensitized to the magnitude of evil in our world because of the overwhelming quantity. Maybe it's social media. Maybe it's cell phone cameras. Maybe all this stuff happened four decades ago but we didn't have the capability to post pictures and video of terrible events instantaneously. Or, more likely, the opposite is true. Our ability to share everyday evils from our backyards only heightens our detachment to it altogether.

I was a sophomore in high school when terrorists hijacked jumbo jets and flew them straight into the side of the World Trade Center towers in New York City. The first plane slammed into the North Tower at 8:45 a.m. Moments before impact, the first school bell of the day signaled the transition between class periods. Waves of teenagers flooded the hallways. Most of us were oblivious to the developing tragedy in New York. On the way to my second class, I heard someone say we were under attack. I remember shrugging it off as some silly joke. My mood changed when teachers began quickly pulling kids into classrooms with nervous looks on their faces. I didn't arrive in time to see United Airlines Flight 175 obliterate the side of the South Tower. Some of my classmates did. There were sickened looks on their faces. Was this the end of the world? We sat in silence and watched news coverage. By 10:28 a.m., both towers had collapsed. The world changed on September 11, 2001. My eyes never left the TV screens.

Years later, as an adult, I met a man for an *On The Road* story who has made it his life's mission to collect one million letters from American wars. He showed me a hand-written note from September 13, 2001. It was written by a woman who worked on the third story of the North Tower. I saw the places on the paper where tears had fallen from her eyes. The droplets left dots of blurred ink all over the page. I tried to imagine what it had been like for her to pen that emotional letter just 36 hours after watching two iconic buildings be reduced to gravel.

That fateful moment in New York history is probably the last time I felt a deep connection to a news story that affected the whole world. Events come and events go. Daily, I hear co-workers discuss their story ideas. They talk about their dreadful assignments chasing down crooked politicians and trying to hold criminals accountable. I am swimming in an environment that is tainted with off-putting content. The fact that none of it bothers me is what bothers me the most. The endless cycle of depressing information can start to beat us down if we let it.

In times like these, it is crucial to remember and count all our blessings. They are everywhere. Think you don't have any? God has impacted your life and the lives of those around you in a huge way, even if you don't choose to acknowledge it. Trust me.

Matthew 7:11 (NIV)
"If you, then, though you are evil, know how to give good gifts to your children, how much more will your Father in heaven give good gifts to those who ask him!"

When you think of blessing, what comes to mind? Is it a nice house and fancy car? Is it exotic vacations and designer clothes? Blessing has nothing to do with any of that material stuff. Blessing has nothing to do with bank accounts. That's the secular standard of blessing, and it looks nothing like God's. If your idea of being blessed means you live in a gated community with two cars, a picket fence, and a schnauzer, your expectations for what God wants to do in your life are way too low. Start thinking bigger!

Being blessed means God has His hand on your life. It means He orchestrates goodness to win out in all situations. It means we are encircled by His hedge of protection and shielded from defeating, supernatural attacks. Life is messy! So are the news headlines. God works through messy lives and messier headlines. I know it! Your trust is your ticket to your blessing.

When I got a job offer to return home and work at a TV station in Florida, I got very excited. I called up our realtor in Tulsa and asked him to help us list our home. It shouldn't be a problem, I thought. We lived in a family-friendly neighborhood in one of the best school districts in Oklahoma. Surely our house would sell in a flash if we left it in the capable hands of one of the best realtors in the city.

Oh, but what you don't know can haunt you.

The tiniest of cracks, barely visible to the untrained eye, was discovered by an inspector. We had an unknown foundational issue beneath our master bedroom that presented an enormous roadblock between us and a 'For Sale' sign. Nobody would buy a home with a foundational issue. Not in Oklahoma. Not in our price range.

No way.

Not in a state with mostly clay soil and plenty of tornados and earthquakes.

I joke with people all the time that I wouldn't complain if I was on fire. It's just my personality. I don't get too high or too low. But, this foundation thing? My stress level rose a bit. This was a big deal. How was I going to sell my broken home? I was supposed to leave for Florida in a month. I already had the job there. I was moving, but I didn't know if we'd be able to get rid of a house that, aside from the crack in the side, was just fine.

That's the thing about little cracks. Little ones can lead to giant problems. It doesn't look like much on the outside, but underneath there is a much greater issue. Clay soil can offer a firm foundation when it's dry, but when summer storms come and winter snow melts, that same once-sturdy clay becomes very pliable and starts to slide around. The results are stress-inducing cracks. When your foundation is shaky, everything is off. If it's not fixed, doors won't fully shut, pipes can rupture, and, as we found out, walls can split. Our little crack required five piers. They cost us $500 apiece. Yep, $2,500. A stay-at-home mom and a small-market television salary meant we didn't have an extra $2,500 just lying around to fix foundation issues. Unfortunately, we had less of a choice than we had money. I should have prayed. Instead, I panicked. We can block blessing if we try to handle hardships on our own. I forgot God was there. I forgot that God blessed me with a job opportunity I'd waited on for years. I was too busy worrying to see it.

We packed up and left. I was forced to trust that God would take care of us as we moved. At least forced trust is still trust. All through the hilly roads of Alabama and the swampland of Louisiana, I fretted. Our realtor told us he'd keep an eye on it. That's serious faith! What if my house didn't sell? What if nobody wanted to buy it even after being reassured the problem was fixed? What if I'm stuck with a repaired home 21-hours from my new home? I didn't even know where I was going to live once I arrived in the Sunshine State!

Instead of focusing on the blessing that God had handed to me in the form of a highly-desired job, I could only focus on my present problems. I had a new gig, healthy baby girl, and fresh start in a place I'd always wanted to work. It was an opportunity that only God could have orchestrated. All my previous efforts to secure a job in Florida failed instantly and miserably. It's easy to miss the blessing if you are focused on the burden.

Four long months passed. Word finally came around Christmastime. Our house had sold. I was relieved. I have friends who were saddled with a home they couldn't sell for a decade. All things considered, a few months wasn't that bad. It sure felt like ten years waiting for that phone call. Not only did the old house sell, but the home went to a police officer and his growing family. They paid over the list price and we didn't absorb a huge financial hit from the piers. God blessed us with exactly what we needed when He was ready to provide it. God opened my eyes to the possibilities that come when we give our past, present, and future worries to Him.

I regret that I didn't take advantage of the blessing process throughout that whole ordeal. I was in too much of a hurry. I missed my blessing by getting caught up in my mess. My self-centeredness blocked God from revealing His big-picture plan. He wanted me to have peace about the situation from the moment I pulled the moving van out of the driveway. I didn't. I got a crash course in how to accept God's gifts. Call it, Blessing 101.

One of my favorite reminders about blessing in the Bible comes from Exodus. When Moses led the Israelites out of slavery in Egypt, they were blessed on the way out the door. God hardened the hearts of the Egyptians and they sent their former slaves away with silver, gold, and livestock for their journey. On Monday, there was bondage. On Tuesday, there was treasure! Every need was taken care of by the very people who had been blocking the progress.

James 1:17 ESV
"Every good gift and every perfect gift is from above, coming down from the Father of lights with whom there is no variation or shadow due to change."

If you woke up today and knew where your breakfast was coming from, you're one of the richest people on earth. Over three billion people, around half the world's population, live on less than $2.50 per day. Go check the menu board at the Starbucks drive-thru. You won't get much coffee for $2.50. Yet, we guzzle it down and complain if we don't get our favorite hazelnut creamer. If you own a car, you're in the top 6-9 percent of the wealthiest people in the world, depending on which report you cite. The book of Joshua tells us that "Every good and perfect gift is from above". Did you forget the Source of blessing?

Do you have friends? You're blessed. Do you have a job? You're blessed. Do your kids hug you? You're blessed. Did the piers help sell my house? Yep, I'm blessed.

This chapter will introduce you to people who definitely have God's hand on their lives. Debi Shackowsky started a non-profit with the goal of fulfilling her sister's wish. It grew into an enormous blessing for kids in her neighborhood. Molly DuPont Schaffer saw a need in her community and addressed it. She never thought a wooden box would play such a vital role for a starving population. John Joyce was only trying to do a good job mowing lawns. He was stunned to see how much people cared about him after learning of his struggles. Delwyn Collins was always a giver. When a surprise honor came his way, it marked noteworthy blessing in his life.

God tells the best stories and hands out the best blessings. Good luck trying to manufacture something that can compete with treasure from Heaven. Our most is galaxies short of His least. The temporary "blessings" the world offers will leave us feeling empty. The Bible says, "The grass and flowers wither but the word of the Lord lasts forever" (1 Peter 1:24). Why worry about getting more flowers?

Some of the most impressive people I've met in my quest to tell uplifting TV stories have been the people who decided to trust that God would make the connections click at just the right time. That trust resulted in incredible blessing. I'm just happy I've gotten the chance to share those stories. Simply doing so has been a blessing to me.

THE NUMBER 153

I don't like when people call me a television "reporter". I also don't like doing "interviews". The act of asking someone questions on camera is usually referred to as an "interview", but that sounds too sterilized and rigid to me. Reporters do interviews. They ask all the right questions in the proper order. They relay pertinent facts and vital statistics. Reporters stand out in front of City Hall and regurgitate information from the mayor. They give election polling results. They unscramble complicated funding options for new pro sports stadiums. Reporters are important. They do interviews. Not me. I like to call myself a "storyteller" who conducts "conversations".

When I'm asking someone questions, I consider two things: What is this person telling me and, what does God want me to hear from them? Often, those are very different things. God speaks much differently than we speak. God whispers. When humans converse, we tend to shout. I've got two small children. Trust me, I know what shouting is. I live in shouting.

If you want to find joy, you must listen for God's whispers through the chaos of the day.

I pray for God to show up in the room before all my TV "conversations". If something goes wrong, I want some backup. If something goes well, I want to share in the victory. Sometimes I feel His presence. Sometimes I don't. On a humid August morning in New Port Richey, Florida, I heard His whisper. A few days before school resumed from summer break, I was tuned in to one of Heaven's barely audible lessons.

I stood in a narrow hallway of River Ridge High School with a woman who oozed positivity. When I say oozed, I mean the kind that is borderline annoying. The type of upbeat, giddy-up that most people find off-putting. Not me. I love people like Debi Shackowsky. Her giggle-to-word ratio is sky high! I had only spoken to Debi on the phone once before we met that morning. We didn't really share too much about ourselves during those chats. Shortly after shaking hands, I could tell that we were going to get along like long-lost friends. We babbled on about all kinds of things before I ever turned on my camera. Those pre-shoot conversations are some of the most important detail-gathering moments. That one-on-one "B.M. chat" (which stands for, Before Microphone) allows people to get comfortable with me. That's when Debi told me her story. At 50 years old, Debi's road to our encounter was littered with potholes and flat tires. Disappointments? She'd seen a few. Her headlines were not all positive.

Like I always prefer, rather than doing a formal interview, Debi and I had a great conversation. Debi Shackowsky is a giver. She always has been. Her parents taught her how to value others. She learned how to give away what she could in order to help those in need. It was obvious from looking at the hallway. At 6-foot-2, I was easily a foot taller than Debi. I got a great view of the stuff bags the long purple and white corridor.

"There are 1,500 here," she said, noticing me looking around at all the backpacks. "1,800 more will be here this afternoon."

This is when the whispers started. The word 'blessing' popped into my head. So did 'three' and 'sheep'. It's tricky trying to carry on a conversation and listen to Godly whispers at the same time.

Nine years earlier, Debi had set out on a mission to help the kids in her community get vital back-to-school supplies. In this neighborhood, it was no guarantee that students would return to school with the essentials. This part of town wasn't wealthy at all. Debi didn't want limited finances to limit opportunities in school. She wanted to make a change. When you want to see a change, you have to make a move. Debi moved, big time.

Many people never bother to help solve problems because they feel like their small contribution won't make a difference. They think what they have to offer won't leave a big enough dent to matter. God doesn't work that way. God breaks down barriers one brick at a time. The answers to our biggest challenges tend to come in stages. We may not get every piece of the puzzle today, but what God provides in the moment is enough to start beating back our issues. We all want to knock out problems with a one-time uppercut. But, big solutions can still happen if we are willing to steadily throw jabs. Debi knew that. So, she started small.

In 2008, She scraped together enough cash to purchase 45 backpacks. These weren't fancy $80 bags, but they were perfect for the kid who would otherwise do without. She stuffed each one with a few pencils. She added in some markers and sheets of paper. It wasn't much, but it was more than enough for needy students. That first year, Debi sent nearly four dozen kids to school with more than just supplies on their backs. They showed up for homeroom with a ton of confidence. Somebody cared for them! Somebody helped! Debi left a small dent in the problem. She didn't solve the entire problem, but at least she made a dent.

I couldn't believe my ears or my eyes. The story of her humble beginning seemed so distant based on what I was seeing. We stood in a hallway with hundreds of cardboard boxes overflowing with empty backpacks. Around the corner, in a cleared-out classroom, hundreds of boxes were filled with school supplies and hygiene products waiting to be loaded into backpacks. No wonder Debi had such a giddy personality. She knew what it was like to stand in an empty hallway. Now, I could barely see the checkered tile floor. There were backpacks everywhere! Debi brought me over to a photo album and flipped to the second page. There was a photo of a woman with a giant smile. It was her sister, Marjorie.

"She was amazing," said Debi. "She had a zest for life that many of us adults would love to recapture."

Marjorie died 21 years earlier in a head-on car crash. Debi described her sister as giving and loving. She would do anything for kids. Debi started a non-profit called 'Marjorie's Hope' in her sister's name. It allowed Debi to take in larger donations from the community each year and buy more and more backpacks for kids.

"It was, I think, her hope, wish, and dream to make sure that no child went without, and so it becomes 'Marjorie's Hope' that we continue that," she said. As Debi explained all this, those whispers started again. They were faint, but they were there. They were repetitive and resounding. They were still, yet strong. Quietly and clearly, I heard:

"Feed my sheep".

What in the world did that mean? It was a mysterious message. I didn't know what God was trying to whisper to me. I stood quietly in the hallway and heard it again.

"Feed my sheep".

This command felt familiar. I couldn't pin down where I had heard it before. It's found in a dialogue between Jesus and one of his disciples, Peter. I knew that "*feed my sheep*" meant take care of people who need help. I knew that Jesus said it three times. Debi had no idea my mind was spinning like this.

John 21:1-17 (NIV):

[1] Later, Jesus appeared again to the disciples beside the Sea of Galilee. This is how it happened. [2] Several of the disciples were there—Simon Peter, Thomas (nicknamed the Twin), Nathanael from Cana in Galilee, the sons of Zebedee, and two other disciples.

[3] Simon Peter said, "I'm going fishing."

"We'll come, too," they all said. So, they went out in the boat, but they caught nothing all night.

[4] At dawn Jesus was standing on the beach, but the disciples couldn't see who he was. [5] He called out, "Fellows, have you caught any fish?"

"No," they replied.

[6] Then he said, "Throw out your net on the right-hand side of the boat, and you'll get some!" So, they did, and they couldn't haul in the net because there were so many fish in it. [7] Then the disciple Jesus loved said to Peter, "It's the Lord!" When Simon Peter heard that it was the Lord, he put on his tunic (for he had stripped for work), jumped into the water, and headed to shore. [8] The others stayed with the boat and pulled the loaded net to the shore, for they were only about a hundred yards from shore. [9] When they got there, they found breakfast waiting for them—fish cooking over a charcoal fire, and some bread.

[10] "Bring some of the fish you've just caught," Jesus said. [11] So Simon Peter went aboard and dragged the net to the shore. There were 153 large fish, and yet the net hadn't torn. [12] "Now come and have some breakfast!" Jesus said. None of the disciples dared to ask him, "Who are you?" They knew it was the Lord. [13] Then Jesus served them the bread and

the fish. ¹⁴ *This was the third time Jesus had appeared to his disciples since he had been raised from the dead.*

¹⁵ *After breakfast Jesus asked Simon Peter, "Simon son of John, do you love me more than these?"*

"Yes, Lord," Peter replied, "you know I love you."

"Then feed my lambs," Jesus told him.

¹⁶ *Jesus repeated the question: "Simon son of John, do you love me?"*

"Yes, Lord," Peter said, "you know I love you."

"Then take care of my sheep," Jesus said.

¹⁷ *A third time he asked him, "Simon son of John, do you love me?"*

Peter was hurt that Jesus asked the question a third time. He said, "Lord, you know everything. You know that I love you."

Jesus said, "Then feed my sheep".

After I finished shooting my story with Debi, I headed back to the TV station and dug out my Bible. The numbers in Jesus' chat with Peter caught my attention. I studied 153 and 3.

Numbers that appear in the Bible have specific meanings. If you come across one in the text, it was written there for a purpose. Jesus' disciples hauled up 153 fish. Did the author of the gospel book really sit down and count out 153 fish? Why would such a specific number be referenced? That number, 153, is both literal and symbolic. It is only found in the Bible once. It appears in this story and represents "abundance and overflow". This number shows up in Jesus' penultimate bodily appearance to the disciples before He ascends to Heaven. It signifies how you will be blessed with Jesus is your captain. He won't let you go without meeting your needs. The number three is used 467 times in the Bible. It pictures completeness. It's also the first of four spiritually perfect numbers (7, 10, 12). There are 27 books in the New Testament, or, for all the math whizzes out there, 3 x 3 x 3. It is completeness to the third power. The number is used frequently in the Bible and each time it brings with it a powerful revelation. This is why Jesus told Peter THREE times, '*feed my sheep*'.

If Jesus had commanded Peter just once, it still would have been noteworthy. Everything Jesus said was important to jot down. But, when God's son says something three times, *pay attention*. Saying "feed my sheep" three times drives home the intensity of the directive. Jesus wants us to take care of people and do it with fervor. Standing in the hallway at River Ridge High School, the week before school began, that was the message God was driving home through a well-placed whisper. Abundance. Blessing. Both were there in Debi's mission.

No wonder "*feed my sheep*" was ping-ponging inside my brain. In 2008, she collected 45 backpacks. Nine years later (3 x 3 = 9), she collected over 3,500 backpacks and jammed them with all the school essentials. Yep. 3,500 backpacks! The community heard about Debi's mission and jumped on to the bandwagon with both feet. She now receives donations from area businesses and church groups. She does a fundraiser each year at a local country club where 'Marjorie's Hope' raises a few thousand dollars. Every dime goes back into a fund to buy backpacks each summer.

I called Debi a few months after our story aired to see how she was doing. She was in the middle of a rough season in life. She was about to send another beloved family friend off to Heaven. It was the latest ugly headline in her life. She told me she appreciated my call. I felt compelled to tell her what I learned about the number 153 after our conversation in the school hallway. God may whisper a lesson to you, but that doesn't mean He wants you to keep it to yourself. When I told her what I learned, I could tell her mood changed. Her voice shifted to a more excited pitch.

"You know," she said, "one year we had exactly 153 backpacks."

I was amazed. Turns out it was the third year of her collecting. Abundance. Overflow. Blessing. They were all there in her drive to make her community a better place! The abundance and overflow continue to grow each year. Her efforts to impact lives is thriving. My mind does jumping jacks at the thought of what God was teaching me in that hallway.

"*Then feed my lambs*".

"*Then take care of my sheep*".

"*Then feed my sheep*".

Those whispers shouted blessings into my life.

Debi is living what she preaches. She is making a real impact and her sister's legacy is her jet fuel. Debi is one of the few people that I have had spiritual conversations with while out on a story. I am normally so rushed that I just don't stop and take the time to peek into someone's heart. There may be something he or she needs prayer for in that moment. If I don't ask, I won't know. Going forward, I aim to ask more often. God is begging us to feed His sheep.

Those 3,500 backpacks were distributed on the 21st anniversary of Marjorie's death. There were tears at that giveaway, just like there were in previous years. There will be more tears and more giveaways. There are more sheep to feed. Debi is nowhere near done. Where God has decided to bless you, abundance and overflow always follow. He blesses you so you can become a blessing. Like the disciples in John 21, we're often just fishing on the wrong side of the boat.

Turn your gaze and your heart towards Jesus, and your nets won't be big enough to hold all the blessing.

John 21:11 (NIV)

"So Simon Peter went aboard and hauled the net ashore, full of large fish, 153 of them. And although there were so many, the net was not torn."

FREE FOOD FOR ANYONE

*H*omelessness is a taboo subject. I've met dozens of homeless people in my TV travels. There are a lot of folks out there who just didn't get the right breaks in life and, through no fault of their own, lost everything. Life is cruel, sometimes. There is no way to predict when tragedy will hit. We are all one nail on the highway away from someone etching our tombstone. Some of us are one bad month away from losing our homes. There is no way to know when you'll need a little assistance.

Those who don't understand the struggle can easily view our homelessness issue much like drivers view car wrecks on the freeway. We all creep up to the flashing EMS lights, merge into one lane, crane our necks out the window and let out a loud *"OOHHH!"*. Then we drive away and never look back. That is how we treat homeless folks. Like twisted metal on the interstate. We gawk and escape. We point our attention at the problem just long enough to get an idea of what's going on, then do nothing about it and move on with life.

In July 2015, a family vacationing an hour south of my TV station captured video of a homeless man playing a beautiful song on a piano outside a local restaurant. The city had placed pianos around town to encourage people to embrace the performing arts. Two years later, that video had been viewed over 38 million times on YouTube. Local TV stations reacted like mice on cheese. *"Find this man! Go interview him! Talk to locals! Get him to play the music again!"*

I was shoved out the door to find the guy, too. I drove for over an hour, wondering what I would ask him if we ever did cross paths. This was not an example of negative news. It was actually borderline positive. But, I viewed it as exploitive. All of the sudden we cared about this homeless man? All of the sudden his presence in our newscast was important? Because he entertained us like a monkey at the zoo? Last week, nobody cared about him or his situation.

When I arrived, I found a few of his buddies. They told me all about this man. His name was Donald. He'd been homeless for a while and, indeed, had become an internet sensation. I asked where I could find him and was told that *Inside Edition* had put him up in a hotel. At first, I thought that was a nice gesture. Turns out, it was only so the show could exploit his story and try to extend it by giving him on-camera makeovers. It was shameless self-promotion.

The rest of the homeless community in the area got nothing out of Donald's overnight celebrity. They were just as homeless as they were the week before all the cameras showed up in search of the homeless piano star. They didn't play music. They didn't sing. They were just wrecks on the side of the headline-highway. They were in the way of the reporters trying to hunt down a "story". The walk back to my vehicle was a quiet one. As I neared my car, I saw a homeless man sleeping in an alley gutter just a few feet from a rancid dumpster. If he had been awake, I would have stopped to see if there was anything I could do to help him. Instead, I left him there to nap. I wonder if that was the right thing to do.

Are we out to expose problems or are just exploit them? Are we the rubber-neckers or are we the paramedics? Are we contributors or consumers? Blessing comes to those who work to become a solution. It comes to those who see others for who they are – a child of God.

There is an area near the city where I grew up that is notorious for homelessness. There are lines down the block at the soup kitchen. There are dirty bodies lying along the streets and under tree limbs. They are desperate for some shade and respite from the intense Florida sunshine. The homeless population there has just one public shower available to use and it's only open for two hours per day. You get ten minutes. Then, you're out. Next up. Homeless people are modern-day lepers. In Bible days, people infected with leprosy were forced to live in colonies outside the city gates. They were quarantined. They must stand 50 feet behind healthy people at all times and announce their presence by yelling, "UNCLEAN!" wherever they went. They were viewed as useless and dirty. They were uninvited and uncared for. Nobody wanted to be around them. Sound familiar?

Someone needs to step up and care for the people who seem so ostracized. I'm so thankful I met a group of friends who decided to make a difference. All it took was a little wood, some nails, and an email.

The Little Free Pantry is not a concept that is unique to the little town of Belleair. It is, however, probably one of the last places you'd expect to see one pop up. Belleair is a community with million-dollar homes and breathtaking ocean views. Front yard palm trees seem mandatory. The sun sets over backyard boat docks every night and exotic cars are as common as mailboxes. Celebrities live there. Bankers live there. Maybe that's why the emergence of a Little Free Pantry just a few blocks from the waterfront caught me a little off guard.

I parked my news vehicle in front of a historic church. As I rolled up the windows to my news vehicle, I looked to my left in time to see two women slip out of a streamlined black BMW and pop the trunk. The back of the car swung wide open, revealing what looked like half of a grocery store inside.

"This is a blast," said Cheryl Franzese. "We have all kinds of snack foods."

The Little Free Pantry is as simple of a concept as its name suggests. A small wooden box is displayed on a post in a public place. Food is placed inside by volunteers and is available to anyone who needs a little something to get them through a rough patch. The food might be taken by someone who needs help during the next two days before a paycheck arrives. It may be the sole source of food for a homeless woman who lives near the box. It could just be a place to grab a bottle of water for a jogger who passes by during the afternoon. Whatever the reason, the Little Free Pantry is designed to be a loving, judgement-free opportunity to make a real impact on bellies and souls in a community.

Molly DuPont Schaffer is the one who came up with the idea to add this little wooden blessing to her Belleair community. She wrote an email to a few friends around town asking if they'd like to help her uplift strangers through the Little Free Pantry. It was met with overwhelming support. That's why her friends showed up in their BMW that morning by the church. It was their day to fill the Little Free Pantry.

I watched as the two volunteers hauled over a few heavy paper sacks of groceries. They brought everything from bottles of water to trail mix. It was fast and filling. Better yet, it was fulfilling. I got some video of snacks being loaded into the Little Free Pantry. A laminated sheet of paper tacked to the side of the box caught my attention.

"Leave what you can and take what you need".

Giving back is second nature for Schaffer and her friends. I was happy to learn that they were familiar with the *On The Road* segment I do each night. Meeting people who watch and are uplifted by my stories always makes me feel special. It reminds me that the platform God has given me is important. M story is never first in a newscast. It always comes after the headlines. You won't hear the good news first, but it's there. God is showing up in this chaotic world every day. The headlines make Him easy to miss. I want to chip away at negative news with one uplifting TV story at a time. I love when I get to chat with viewers who understand that goal. Belleair's Little Free Pantry women do. I never know who I'll bump into and how our lives will be changed after our encounter. Getting entangled with positive people is never a bad thing. God puts them in your path on purpose.

This day, I was energized by the chance to share the Little Free Pantry mission. I stood back a few feet from the Little Free Pantry box. My goal is always to capture whatever activities would be taking place if I was not there recording that day. Taking the fly-on-a-wall approach nets the most genuine reactions. It makes the experience feel more natural through the camera lens. The box stood about six feet tall, was made entirely of wood, and looked about the size of a mini-fridge, the kind you'd see in a hotel. Cheryl ripped open boxes of orange peanut butter crackers. She stacked them neatly on the top shelf of the Little Free Pantry.

"It's very rewarding," she said. "I like the anonymous nature of it."

This was only the second week that passersby could take advantage of Molly's free food idea. It had been wildly successful to that point. She gathered 31 volunteers and assigned each of them one day on the calendar. They were responsible for filling the box on that day. Many mornings, the person who showed up to restock the Little Free Pantry found that the contents from the previous day had been totally cleaned out. That was the goal, for sure. Quickly, the homeless community started to gravitate to the available blessing inside that sturdy wooden box.

I hooked a wireless microphone to Molly's shirt. We stood a few feet back from the box as her friends continued to fill it with non-perishable items like water, Vienna sausages, and granola bars. She described what an enormous blessing this project had become in her life. She was elated that the community was benefitting from what seemed like such simple idea. It was needed! There were so many hurting people waiting on something like Molly's Little Free Pantry. It grew to become a bright spot in a dark situation.

Homelessness is no joke and Satan doesn't fight fair with people stuck in that life. He'll use a situation like homelessness to drag you down into depression. When evil starts to take root, discouragement can snowball. Punching back with a God-centered plan is the only way to gain the upper hand against injustices like homelessness. That's exactly what Molly did. She punched back with a box full of blessing. The Little Free Pantry is a daily reminder that people are being blessed by the generosity of strangers. That's worth a news story to me.

The best part of blessing is that it comes with kickbacks. When you do something to bless others, you get the feeling right back. It's like a blessing boomerang. The Little Free Pantry volunteers were getting more out of the box than the recipients, in some cases. Swapping a bag of crackers for the realization that you helped stave off starvation is a trade worth making.

Blessing is funny like that. When you genuinely do something beneficial for strangers, like the Little Free Pantry, the people hand-delivering the blessing get paid back more than they ever could have given. That's being the hands and feet of Jesus.

Proverbs 31:8-9 (NLT)
"Speak up for those who cannot speak for themselves; ensure justice for those being crushed. Yes, speak up for the poor and helpless, and see that they get justice."

GIVE THAT MAN A TRUCK!

*I*became a businessman at the age of 10. There were only two kids on my street old enough to work a lawn mower and the other guy didn't want to cut yards. So, I was basically king of Wildwood Road. I would walk up and down my street cutting the grass for anyone who would pay me. Long before I made those hard-earned $5 bills, my dad put me to work in our yard for no pay. I recall multiple times when he'd (hopefully jokingly) say, "I have kids so I don't have to do any chores", or something to that effect. Paraphrasing lessens the blow, a bit. It seems like parental tyranny, expecting your children to slave away in the hot sun with nothing but the promise of dinner as compensation, but I plan to do the same thing eventually to my kids. It's the circle of life. I can't wait to sit in a lawn chair and bark out orders to my son between sips of lemonade.

John Joyce loves the outdoors more than me. A lot more! I met him on one of those oh-so-hot summer days where you could fry an egg on the hood of your car. Summer in Florida is brutal. John didn't seem to mind the heat. I could tell because he was wearing khaki pants when I pulled into Robert Norton's driveway in my news truck. Robert hired John to mow and edge his lawn. For weeks, like clockwork, John would show up and take care of the property while Robert was at work.

I consider myself a reporter who shoots, not a photographer who reports. I'm forced to do both, so I give both my all. Shooting video for stories can sometimes be the hardest part for me. How many different angles can I possibly shoot of someone mowing grass? I set up my tripod in Robert's driveway to get shots of John pushing his rusty, red mower back and forth. His pace was rapid. Thirty yards from left to right, followed by an about-face, and thirty yards back right to left. Over and over again. John was not a time-waster. For a guy who'd just turned 83, he sure didn't like to sit still. I assumed his tattered Adidas shoes used to be white before all the grass stains. He finished off the front yard in about ten minutes.

John Joyce poses in Robert Norton's yard

John fascinated me. He moved with an almost stealthy finesse for a man his age. He knew every inch of Robert's property and nothing distracted him from his duties. The mower seemed to glide over the blades of grass and turn on its own. While watching him work, I noticed that the midday sun was really starting to beat down. I began to sweat profusely in my polo shirt and shorts. How were John's khakis not soaked? I parked my camera in the little bit of shade I could find and angled the lens towards the side fence. I got a nice, clean clip of the mower's wheels flying in and out of the frame. It was a money shot.

After what seemed like just a few short minutes, John cut the power to the mower. He swapped it out for a trimming tool and began manicuring the property line. He finished almost as quickly as he'd started. Another lawn was complete. On to the next one.

I noticed there was no truck in Robert's driveway. I assumed someone was going to come to pick John up when the job was done. Instead, John briskly packed up his equipment. He laid his electric blower flat on the hood of the mower. He balanced the trimmer on top of that. The mower's handlebars supported the extra weight so that nothing would fall while rolling. Robert and his wife, Nikki, happened to be home this day. John gave them a silent wave before heading down the driveway. The newlyweds waved back to John from the front porch. The 83-year-old was headed home after about an hour of work.

I was there to speak with Robert and Nikki. The couple had an entire garage full of lawn equipment just gathering dust. They certainly could take care of the lawn themselves. They probably would have if John hadn't become such a blessing in their lives.

We sat on the porch and chatted. I found out that John had always been a diligent worker. They hired him months before and he always did a great job on the lawn. Because John mowed during the week when Robert and Nikki were at work, they rarely saw him. All they knew was the grass was always cut and trimmed perfectly. They had no idea what lengths John was taking to ensure it always looked that way.

Robert had no idea that John was without wheels. His 1995 F-150 pickup truck had broken down. John took it to the repair shop but the mechanic broke it even more. John got cheated out of his hard-earned money and didn't have any more to fix his still-broken truck. His ability to drive from lawn job to lawn job was short-circuited. That F-150 was his lifeline to lawn money. He was out of a truck and out of luck.

This is the point where most of us quit. This is the moment where potholes start to look a little too deep. We start telling God how big our problem is instead of telling our problem how big our God is. John had a choice. He could quit or he could find a way. God is ready to break down barriers for you.

Robert knew none of this. So, imagine his surprise one morning when, unexpectedly, John walked up the driveway pushing his lawn mower. Robert was confused. John didn't have a truck to haul his equipment. Yet, there he stood.

"It shocked me because my first thought is, 'If you have no transportation, why are you here?' ", he recalled from the shade of his porch. Nikki nodded from her lawn chair.

"That broke my heart," she chimed in. "Especially when I found out how he was getting here to do what he was doing."

At 83, creaky joints and all, John spent weeks walking 2.5 miles from his front door to Robert's, balancing all his gear on the handlebars of his lawn mower like some game of rolling JENGA. John dodged traffic for an hour to get to the job site. The man who only made a few dollars mowing Robert's lawn was expending incredible energy and effort to make sure the job got done the right way. He had a legitimate excuse! He didn't use it. Robert stood in his driveway trying to process everything he was seeing. He couldn't believe it. John was doing all this for him? It broke Robert's heart to see a man walk so far with his mower.

It amazed me, too. I had just spent the morning watching John strain his body to ensure that lawn looked immaculate, and Robert had no idea the sacrifice it required. The trip from John's house to Robert's took about 15 minutes in a car. I know because I got John's address from Robert and drove over there to see what kind of trek this elderly man was making each week. The Nortons were truly blessed by John's worth ethic and dedication. They felt like they had to do something to help John. They certainly didn't have the money to buy him a new truck. Nikki got the idea to start an online fundraising account. She hoped the generosity of others would eventually provide enough cash to fix up John's old truck.

Before we were even born, I think God implanted a desire in our hearts to help others. We are asked to be Jesus' hands and feet. We are not called to be bystanders to our neighbor's troubles. God needs us to get in the game. We may not be able to do *everything*, but we all have the ability to do *something*. Start swinging your bat. Don't let your inability to hit a homerun today keep you from contributing a single. God can use a single. Doing nothing always results in a strikeout. God can't use you if you're not prepared to swing. Blessing comes from doing, and God blesses doers.

Robert and Nikki wanted to bless John back for all he'd been doing. I told them I'd do my best to spread the word about their fundraising efforts. Deep down, I wasn't sure I'd be much help. I know how hard it can be to convince people to give up their hard-earned dollars. We're all takers by nature. Very few of us are givers. It's easier to snatch a salmon from a grizzly than pry a $10 bill from a stranger. People get really protective of their money. It's understandable. I can't say I'm the type of person who wakes up each morning wondering how I'll be able to give away my cash. I hoped that my *On The Road* TV story would touch enough people, and pull on enough heartstrings, to persuade a few dollars Robert and Nikki's direction. With some luck, maybe they'd tiptoe near the $4,000 goal they'd set up online.

I went back to the station, edited my story, and clicked the 'send' key. I wanted to buy in. I wanted to believe it would generate $4,000, but that seemed like a steep goal. TV stories that ask for donations don't always hit the mark. They're more likely to change the channel. Based on past experiences, I expected this story to end the same way. John's uplifting video aired at 11 p.m. I went to bed thinking I'd done my part and that it was all in God's hands now. That's where the miracles happen. The internet caught fire while I was sleeping. John's story caught people's attention, alright. It popped up on the radar of other local affiliates and re-aired in their markets. The web article I'd written, complete with Robert's high-quality photos of John mowing the lawn, caught the attention of USA Today. The Daily Mail posted it online. The video traveled around the world. The fundraising account starting humming. Within a few hours, it seemed like that hopeful $4,000 goal was within range. I could not believe how deeply John's example of determination and blessing had touched so many people. By week's end, I got Facebook messages from Robert with fantastic news. Forget fixing up John's old piece of junk! He was going to have enough money to buy John a used truck.

I believe God works through channels. It's how He distributes blessing. Blessing doesn't just fall out of the sky. If you're waiting for $100 bills to mysteriously wind up in your sock drawer, good luck. God only sends blessings through available pipelines.

Ephesians 3:20 (NIV) says God is able to do "immeasurably more than we ask or imagine, according to His power that is at work within us". That is exactly what happened to Robert and Nikki. Their plan was nice, but it would have netted chump change compared to God's plan. They were thinking small. God always thinks bigger. Nikki's fundraising site and my TV story were usable channels for God. In just two short weeks, total strangers donated $13,080 into John's new truck fund. God took the Norton's original $4,000 goal, tripled it, and then added some more. That is blessing in action.

Awful news headlines tend to knock my worldview out of line. I hear so much awful news that I get foolishly insecure about the promises of God. I am aware that it is pointless to rely on my own merits instead of God's goodness. Yet, I start to doubt that His goodness will show up after hearing the clutter of the headlines. I love when blessing slaps me in the face like it did with John Joyce. He didn't even know that the Nortons were plotting to improve his life. I did a follow-up story and it was a joy to be there to witness a used car dealer slide freshly-printed ownership paperwork across his desk. John's hand quivered as he signed his autograph. The white whiskers on his mustache spread further the longer his grin sat on his face. I knew this was a blessing from God. There was plenty of depressing news happening that day, too. My heart needed this story.

Robert held back tears. Nikki tried but couldn't. The trio linked arms and walked to the back of the parking lot where a black 2004 Nissan pickup was waiting. The green balloons tied to the side mirror added a nice touch. Friends and family snapped photos and dabbed their eyes with each step. I stood behind the truck with my camera. I had clipped a microphone to Robert's shirt before the three unlikely friends made the slow walk towards the new ride. I put on my earbuds and enjoyed listening to his words.

"I just couldn't bear to see you showing up at my house and pushing that lawnmower and not having a vehicle and I didn't think you were going to have the means to get one. I didn't know how we were going to get you one. I said to Nikki, 'Maybe we can give some of our wedding money'. She suggested we try a (fundraiser). So, this was her idea."

The walk ended at the back bumper. John's grin hadn't faded. His hands trembled a bit as he slipped the key into the driver's side door. The man who walked the five-mile roundtrip to mow Robert's grass would now cruise the streets in style. The truck was 11 years old, but John gripped the steering wheel as if he'd been handed the lease to a new Rolls Royce. I zoomed in tight on his hands as he turned the key. The engine purred.

"I feel like a millionaire!" cried John.

Robert and Nikki held hands as John pulled out of the parking lot. The couple had collected enough money to pay for the truck, gas, insurance, and a few new pieces of lawn equipment. John blessed the Nortons, and God helped the Nortons bless John back. It's amazing how puny our dreams are compared to God's plans. Our grandest plans must seem so small to the Creator of the universe. Thankfully, He continually delivers above and beyond everything we hope for.

God blesses those who work hard without expecting a pat on the back.

Diligently putting forth your best effort is pleasing to our Heavenly Father. John Joyce continues to mow lawns in the hot Florida sun. God continues to look down with fondness on the people who helped make it happen.

Ephesians 3:20 (NLT)
"Now all glory to God, who is able, through his mighty power at work within us, to accomplish infinitely more than we might ask or think."

PAYING BACK SANTA

I chuckle every time I drive past a Powerball billboard. The numbers climb higher and higher and the daydreamer's hopes keep pace. Remember when your parents said you could become anything when you grow up? They meant anything but a lottery winner. It is a much sounder decision to take the $2 you'll waste on a ticket and stash it in a coffee can on the shelf. Over time, it will add up. At 1-in-292 million odds, you probably have a better chance of being struck by lightning while being eaten by a shark than winning Powerball.

I read an article online that conveyed the idiocy of the lotto. A Florida-based study found that 1,900 winners were flat broke within five years of winning. Most people didn't spend all their money in the first two years, but the odds of bankruptcy between years three and five increased for those winners. You'd think all your problems would dissolve the second you match those winning numbers. They actually compound. That's our selfish culture. That's our greedy nature. Why have just two Ferraris when you can have eleven?

I think I've purchased a lottery ticket twice in my life. I bought one when I turned 18 and another when the purse topped $900 million. I figured, why not? I wish I had my $4 back. Even though I know I have no shot at mega millions, my wife and I often chat about what we would do if big money landed in our laps.

I would buy a lot of cars. No, the cars wouldn't be for me. I'd rather buy minivans for single moms who just can't seem to make ends meet. The ones who are working as hard as they can but don't have reliable transportation. Imagine how many minivans I could buy with $50 million! Better yet, imagine how many lives could be changed with $50 million-worth of minivans! That's what having money is for! That is what God envisions for us when he pours down blessing from heaven.

We tend to misuse money. The Bible says money is the "root of all types of evil". Money is neutral. It's neither good nor evil. It's just like any other tool. Planes can be crashed into buildings or used to transport missionaries. Knives can murder or slice wedding cake. Fire can carry out arson or roast s'mores. A tool is only as lethal or as helpful as its manipulator. That means how we use money is important. Money can be a wonderful tool! It makes us more of who we are. If you're a generous person, coming into money won't change that. You'll only become more generous. If you're a stingy person, money won't change that either. God wants us to use money wisely. That's why He gives us chances to put it to work for His kingdom. He knows if we learn to live faithfully with a little, we'll become even more faithful with a lot.

That's why I love people like Delwyn Collins. When I first met him in 2014, his legendary generosity preceded him. I had heard about a man who worked in the basement of Tampa General Hospital washing dishes behind the kitchen. He arrived at work via bicycle at 5 a.m. to get the sinks up and running. Cleaning thousands of dirty dishes each day is a taxing job, I'd imagine. Yet, this man has spent nearly three decades doing the laborious task with a smile on his face and a love for others in his heart.

I rolled up to the hospital on a December morning anxiously awaiting our meeting. I wanted to shake hands with a guy who was so well-known for his abundantly positive attitude. He was totally different from the type of people you usually hear about on the evening news. He didn't fit the typical "news story" character. Newscasts are littered with guys who beat up a cop or men who shot a neighbor during a disagreement. Sprinkle in a woman under arrest for child neglect and you've got a show! You don't often hear about a man who has dedicated his life to spending his own money on Christmas presents for foster kids each December.

The first thing I noticed about Delwyn was his smile. It spread from ear to ear and you could kick a football through the gap between his two front teeth. The man looked a little bit like Santa Claus with his bright red shirt and round belly. He would give Saint Nick a run for his money in the jolly-department, too. He shook my hand with authority and enthusiastically led me to that year's haul of gifts. Unwrapped presents of all shapes and sizes were carefully spread around the 50-foot Christmas tree in the hospital courtyard.

Delwyn proudly gave me a tour of the items. There were basketballs, toy cars, and board games for boys. There were stuffed animals, Easy Bake Ovens, and dolls for girls. It looked like there were gifts for at least 100 children there!

"500," he grinned.

There were at least 50 bicycles with colorful, festive streamers dangling from the handlebars. Those were his favorite gifts to give. I was astounded at what I was seeing. The stories I'd heard from hospital employees about Delwyn were all starting to make sense. He was a real-life Santa without the sleigh.

Delwyn and I sat down on a bench in the courtyard. We gazed out at the presents set to be handed out that afternoon. He explained to me how for the last 25 years, he'd been putting money aside from each of his modest paychecks in order to buy Christmas presents. He knew it could make a difference. Delwyn shopped all year long and had a great relationship with the toy stores in the area. His mission impressed them so much that he was given a few discounts by the big-name retailers. I think everyone wanted to be connected to his dream of making kids happier.

For some reason, he was drawn to helping foster children. Even with help from the state for basic needs, the money for Christmas presents isn't always available for host families. Delwyn recognized that disconnect and made sure the host family trees had presents underneath. Presents for 500 kids per year, for nearly three decades really adds up. He wasn't buying everyone fancy things like iPads, but he was at least providing something. A single guy who lives within his means, Delwyn decided years ago that blessing kids every December was the best use of his money. Appreciative hugs from smiling children was payback enough for a man who never asked for anything in return.

I did my story with Delwyn and wished him well in his quest to make Christmases a little merrier. He really impressed me. There are times when I meet folks for interviews and can tell right away that they are using me to get their message out. That was not the case with Delwyn. He wasn't in this for the fame. He would be blessing families even if nobody ever reported it. Getting his face on TV was not a priority. Being found in a Google search did not appeal to him. Fame? He could do without it. But, God always seems to find a way to shine the limelight on people who are dedicated to blessing others.

Flash forward two years. Before the first game of the hockey season in 2016, the Tampa Bay Lightning called Delwyn. They wanted to invite him to be their special guest on opening night. The hockey arena was just five minutes from the hospital and Delwyn agreed to attend. He was excited to see the local NHL franchise in action. That night, as he arrived for the game appropriately dressed in Lightning blue from head to toe, Delwyn was invited to meet the owner of the team. The Lightning had something for Delwyn.

A hospital co-worker contacted the team and nominated Delwyn for a well-deserved honor. At every home game, the Lightning honored a difference maker with its Community Hero distinction. Along with being recognized during the game in front of the crowd, meeting a player, and being praised for all his or her efforts, the team provided the honoree with a $50,000 grant to be spent on a non-profit effort of their choice.

On opening night 2016, Delwyn was named the first Lightning Community Hero of the season. I was so happy for him! He had $50,000 at his fingertips! After years and years of pulling every spare dime he could afford from his paychecks to give back to kids, the man who was faithful with a few things was finally being entrusted with so much more. His decision to do a lot with a little was being paid back. It allowed him the chance to do even greater things with $50,000 in his pocket. If he wasn't the king of Christmas giving before, he certainly would be now.

Some of the most well-known Bible stories are called parables. They are lessons taught through stories. One that has always interested me is the parable of the talents. These are not talents like singing and dancing, although that is where we derive the modern-day term. Here, a talent refers to a unit of money. In the story, three men are given talents by a wealthy man according to their merits. The wealthy man asks the trio to watch over his talents while he is away. He gave the first man five talents, the second man two talents, and the last man a single talent. When the wealthy man returned, he was pleased with the first two men. The one who had been given five talents put them to work and doubled the money, earning another five talents. The man who had been given two talents put them to work and doubled the money, earning two more talents. But, the man who was entrusted with a single talent did nothing with it. He was scared he may mess up and lose the only talent with which he was entrusted. To avoid the unwanted outcome, the man buried the single talent. The wealthy man was very disappointed in the third man. He took back his single talent and gave it to the man who had amassed ten.

It's a picture of what God wants us to do with the things He has blessed us with on earth. It's what Delwyn is doing. He is the perfect example of a man who is pleasing God with his actions. He did not start out with very much. He doesn't make a surgeon's salary. He is not a highly-compensated pediatrician. He was the guy tasked with washing their dishes. He is probably a lot like the man entrusted with one talent. The difference is, Delwyn put what he had to work. He used what he was given and was blessed with the opportunity to do more.

For the last two Christmases, since winning the money from the hockey team, Delwyn hasn't changed a bit. He's still eagerly scouring Toys-R-Us aisles in January and Walmart shelves in April. He's still on the hunt for the perfect Christmas gifts. He's still searching for summertime bargains. Only, now he has more resources than he's ever had. He can make a bigger impact than ever before. He'll dip into his $50,000 each year and foster kids will be the real winners. He has blessed so many of them in the last 28 years and will continue to do so for as long as he can. Delwyn was faithful with the little things. Now, he'll be faithful with the bigger blessings God sent his way. He knew Delwyn could handle it. He proved it from Day 1.

On its own, that would have been a wonderful *On The* Road story. But, the blessing didn't end there.

Three years after I first met Delwyn, I was chatting on the phone with one of his hospital colleagues. She simply adores this man. So do I. When his name came up in our conversation, she mentioned how happy she was that the staff had been able to do something nice for his birthday. I was a little caught off guard. I knew Delwyn well enough to know he's not the type of person to accept handouts. It makes him a little uncomfortable. It's not in his nature. He is a giver, not a getter. On many occasions, he's mentioned that he wants for nothing and chooses to give away most of what he earns. So, imagine my surprise when the ultimate giver wound up on the receiving end of another blessing.

Hurricane Irma ripped through the state of Florida on September 10, 2017. The Keys were demolished. The west coast was battered and broken. The storm had weakened to a Category-1 hurricane by the time it skirted just to the east of Tampa General. The eye of the storm narrowly missed buzzing the top of the hospital. In natural disaster terms, it was a win. The next day was Delwyn's 59th birthday. The hurricane was the latest smear in his year. A major heart attack nearly claimed his life a few months prior. Had he not called 9-1-1 on his own when he began feeling short of breath, doctors at his very own hospital said he may not have survived.

Another blessing.

Unable to celebrate his birthday, one that almost never happened, hospital workers were forced to wait a few days to give Delwyn a surprise gift. A few dozen of his closest friends at TGH took up a collection to buy Delwyn something he'd always wanted – tickets to Walt Disney World. A few days following Irma, when the life inside the walls of the hospital returned to normal, staff secretly gathered in an upstairs meeting room and lit the candles on his cake. The Mickey Mouse frosting was ready and waiting.

"SURPRISE!" they all shouted as he entered the room. The Happy Birthday chorus followed, along with photos of Delwyn in a Disney t-shirt. He hugged everyone in the room and posed for another shot with his cake. A few weeks prior, he'd casually mentioned to a co-worker that he hadn't been to Disney in 30 years. It was the same co-worker who had nominated him for the 2016 Community Hero award. She knew it was something that would make the perfect thank you surprise. After all he'd done for his community, it was something they felt was important to do. The group raised $3,500 for Delwyn to go to Orlando for a week, stay in the nicest hotels, and visit all the theme parks. It was a fitting way to give back to a man who never asked for anything.

A few weeks later, Delwyn and I sat in a secluded hospital room surrounded by that year's foster presents. Delwyn was planning a wrapping party for the upcoming weekend. It was his favorite thing about Christmas.

"It was shocking," Delwyn told me, describing his Disney surprise. "It caught me off guard."

He reiterated how he really didn't like surprises but was looking forward to his trip to Disney. A gift is a gift, after all. He planned to take a friend with him to experience the fun. They scheduled their visit to the parks for January. December is a pretty hectic month for Delwyn. He didn't want to take any time away from his Christmas mission. I sat back in my chair, toy cars to my left and princess dolls to my right, and smiled. It was so great to see something special happening to someone so deserving.

Delwyn Collins has provided Christmas for foster kids for nearly 30 years

Delwyn had been faithful in a few things and now God was paying him back in a big way.

Matthew 25:21 (NIV)
"Well done good and faithful servant. You have been faithful in a few things. I will put you in charge of many things. Come and enjoy your master's reward."

CLOSING THOUGHTS ON BLESSING

*W*e are all surrounded by idiotic takers. They are everywhere. Because of the digital, technical, social world we live in, EVERYONE has a megaphone at his or her fingertips. It's all about selfish gains and a look-at-me lifestyle. Hollywood is full of those people. So are middle schools, dentist offices, and supermarkets. You can find a self-promoting braggart on any corner of this globe. We live on a planet with 7.5 billion other people who are mostly seeking affirmation over information. We all want to *be* right, not *get it* right. In this self-indulgent existence, we forget that everything we have is on loan from God. That house you live in? God's. That car you're driving? God's. That wife you married? Yep, a blessing from God. We improperly and frivolously claim ownership of our blessings.

The first man was made from dust. God breathed life into Adam's lungs and human history began. Centuries later, God is still breathing life. You were born naked after a nine-month construction project inside your mother. One day, you'll end up naked in the ground. Some of us will be cremated back into that original dusty form and be sprinkled along the grass. In between, we go, go, go, trying to make a buck and show off how "blessed" we are by all the junk we accumulate. Our earthly "blessings", like watches, clothes, boats and every other vain pursuit, are ultimately worthless. We go into debt over things that enslave us. We live to impress people we don't know. Earthly treasures rot and a beautiful, Botox-ed corpse is still a corpse. It's a shame, what really consumes our time and attention.

The whole point of life is not to gain, gain, gain, but rather to give, give, give. It's about being a blessing, not getting a blessing. It's about loving unconditionally. It's about becoming a source of help for those who are barely holding on to what little hope they have. Jesus was asked what the greatest commandment was and He didn't hesitate to answer:

Mark 12:30-31 (ESV)

"And you shall love the Lord your God with all your heart and with all your soul and with all your mind and with all your strength.' The second is this: 'You shall love your neighbor as yourself.' There is no other commandment greater than these."

It's that easy. Do those two things and you'll be blessed. That fact alone is a reason for you to put this book down on the table and do a little jig. Who cares if the people in the booth next to you at Starbucks think you're odd? You have the blueprint for a blessed life right there in Mark 12! But, there's more. Your life's story doesn't end there. The best part of *being* blessed by God is the awesome responsibility He offers us to become a blessing to others.

Debi Shackowsky is a big-time blesser. In a backyard blessing match, I'd pick her first for my team. She put what little she had into action. The Lord took it and multiplied it. Talk about an investment! She had enough money to provide 45 kids with backpacks in the first year of her mission. By year nine, she had 3,500! I'm no math whiz but I do own a calculator. That's a 7,677% increase in less than a decade! Debi's sister's legacy is blossoming thanks to her willingness to be a blessing to others.

The Little Free Pantry screams blessing. The folks who fill it have made a conscious decision to get in their cars, drive to the grocery store, fill a cart, and swipe their debit card at least once every month for people they will most likely never meet. They are spending up to $100 a pop to ensure that their little wooden box is stocked with enough food to get Belleair's homeless and less fortunate population fed. That food means someone won't go to bed with a howling stomach – again. How many nights did a family of four have to scrape together whatever they could find before the Little Free Pantry came along? It's an enormous blessing! It's a lifesaver! It's exactly what Mark 12:30-31 is talking about!

John Joyce is a shining example of what it's like to receive a great blessing. He didn't do anything to earn it. Yeah, you could say that the generosity of others only came his way because he's a genuine, hard-working man, but that isn't why he's driving around a new truck today. God stirred the hearts of people who heard John's story and planted a desire to bless him. Countless community members chipped in. Robert and Nikki Norton's original plan paled in comparison to God's overflow of blessing. You cannot and will not out-give God. It's impossible. When you are blessed, and choose to become a blessing to others, the divinely designed circle is completed.

Delwyn Collins has probably purchased more Christmas presents for children in his town than any other individual. He's a real-life Santa Claus with a joyful heart. It hasn't always been easy. Health issues threatened to eliminate the gift giving. But, when you have a plan backed by God's blessing, nothing can stop you. The $50,000 grant Delwyn was awarded will help him continue to impact the lives of those in need. He doesn't have to worry about having enough Christmas cash anymore.

I've made the decision to use *my* career for *God's* cause. I believe my career will be blessed because of that decision. The choice to put God first, and live "second", is one that sets you up for blessing. You want to live a blessed life? Don't wake up with an attitude of taking. Wake up with an attitude of giving. Be a contributor more than a consumer. That's exactly what Debi Shackowsky did. The women who run the Little Free Pantry are living for others. That's what Robert and Nikki Norton did for their friend, John Joyce. Delwyn Collins' unselfishness is an enormous blessing to his community.

I chuckle at people who denigrate the Bible yet unknowingly recite common phrases from it every day. Ever heard someone say, "turn the other cheek", or "treat others the way you want to be treated"? Yep. Word for word, taken right out of the text. The "love your neighbor as yourself" classroom rule that lives on the wall of every kindergarten teacher's room is biblical, too.

The best part is, when we follow those rules, blessing will find us. And, when you receive blessing, you get the amazing opportunity to be a blessing right back.

VERSES ON BLESSING

Psalm 34:14 (NLT)
"Turn from evil and do good; seek peace and pursue it."

Ephesians 1:3 (NLT)
"All praise to God, the Father of our Lord Jesus Christ, who has blessed us with every spiritual blessing in the heavenly realms because we are united with Christ."

Genesis 12:2-3 (NIV)
"I will make you into a great nation, and I will bless you; I will make your name great, and you will be a blessing. I will bless those who bless you, and whoever curses you I will curse; and all peoples on earth will be blessed through you."

Hebrews 13:5 (MSG)
"Don't be obsessed with getting more material things. Be relaxed with what you have. Since God assured us, "I'll never let you down, never walk off and leave you," we can boldly quote, God is there, ready to help; I'm fearless no matter what. Who or what can get to me?"

LOVE

*T*he news media slobbers over opportunities to tell us how God-centered love doesn't work. It isn't sexy enough, I guess. In our culture, politically-correct love outranks Biblically-correct love every day. That's a huge problem for me. Want examples? Check the headlines.

How many times have you heard the phrase "domestic dispute" during a newscast? Or a story about a bakery owner who refuses to bake a cake for a gay wedding? Headlines about rape, abuse, and pornography are as common as they are disgraceful. Culture, including the news media, does a terrible job of highlighting what true love looks like. We're all too busy seeking a blueprint for relational happiness in movies and television dramas. Why trust Jesus when you can tweet a Kardashian?

Love is a four-letter word. So is lust. Too often, we improperly interchange them.

The world lies about love. It lies a lot. It tells us the way to a man's heart starts in his bed. It tells women they must wear as little clothing as possible in order to be considered attractive. The world is a 24-hour sex-crazed machine that pushes the boundaries of what's proper and permissible. The world's definition of love is constantly changing and rooted in fiction.

Love is supposed to be patient. Instead, our self-centered relationships often end as soon as they begin. Speed dating is a thing. We have invented dating apps where you swipe one direction if you find the image on your screen attractive, or swipe the other way if it's not. I recently read about a new trend where millennials are establishing temporary marriages. Sounds like an oxymoron to me.

Love is supposed to be kind, yet I can barely go a week without hearing a story on the news about human trafficking. Lost souls laugh at monogamous relationships because they don't mesh with the world's point of view. If love was kind, babies wouldn't be born addicted to illicit drugs. We're told we can love anyone or anything we want. Truth is, we don't even know how to love ourselves.

Love is supposed to protect, yet anchors read stories of children taken away from abusive parents nightly. Love is supposed to endure all things, but divorce rates hover around 50 percent in the United States. Love is not supposed to be easily angered, yet panicked phone calls reporting domestic violence are common sounds on 9-1-1 scanners.

I was asked to emcee a Meals On Wheels annual fundraising breakfast at a brand new, no-penny-spared, gorgeous Jewish Center that was funded by the owners of the Tampa Bay Buccaneers. Hundreds of people had gathered. It was standing-room-only in the back. I recognized many of the faces in the crowd from my *On The Road* segment. There was the headmaster of a local charter school for underprivileged kids, the aforementioned owners of the city's most popular sports franchise, and even a mayor or two. In my hand I gripped an index card containing a barely legible scribbling of **1 John 3:16 (NLT)**:

"We know what real love is because Jesus gave up his life for us. So we also ought to give up our lives for our brothers and sisters."

It's a great verse. It's powerful. It explains that love is a decision, not just a feeling. Love is an action. It's a choice. I was a little nervous. I don't know why. For some reason, I was a little hesitant to drop that lesson on the crowd of the newly-minted Jewish recreation center. I should have been ready to speak with confidence.

But, I was tentative.

I'm sure the fine folks at Meals On Wheels mentioned their biggest benefit of the year was going to be held at the Jewish Center. I'm sure I even wrote it down. But, while preparing my remarks, it never donned on me that the Jewish view on Jesus was much different than the Christian's.

A buddy from my church also happened to be there that morning. He must have seen me mumbling to myself on the stage. He came over and said hello. I explained my predicament. He told me to go for it anyway. I stood at the podium and delivered my message of what love truly is based on Jesus' teaching in the Bible. I'd envisioned a room full of people shooting awkward glances to each other. This was not a religious event. I hadn't disclosed my plans to quasi-preach that morning with the Meals On Wheels folks.

Just a few sentences into my speech, I could tell that things were going to be just fine. I was really worried over nothing. That's what happens to me sometimes. I get the opportunity to share my faith and clam up for some reason. I don't want to. I think I have good stuff to share. I think I'm a lot like the majority of people out there. Most people don't want to ruffle feathers. That's fine, unless we're smoothing over a situation that Jesus calls us to stir up. When it comes to talking about love, we need to set the record straight.

Explaining misunderstood topics like love becomes easier for me to do when I fix my gaze upon the one who designed love from the beginning. God gave us love to show us more of what He is like. Love is God's idea. It's a gift! God created it, so God gets to define it. When we love like Christ, we love in a way that pleases God. Whenever I do a TV story that involves love, that's my aim. I seek out stories that highlight people who understand what unconditional love is all about.

Love was on display at the downtown Tampa courthouse the day I witnessed a family adopt little Andrew. He was born with Down Syndrome and will be confined to a wheelchair the rest of his life. He'll need 24-hour care every day. None of that deterred a family from showing love like they never had before.

Love was on display on Valentine's Day 2017, when I met a man who, just a few months earlier, thought his love story was on its final chapter. He'd spent all of 2016 fighting cancer, wondering if he'd ever get to buy his wife Valentine's chocolates again. Doctors told him he was destined for a coffin, but God gave him new life. He beat cancer and rejoined his beloved barbershop quartet. I tagged along the morning of February 14, just one day after his wedding anniversary, to hear him sing love songs around the city. His wife was there smiling and fighting back tears every step of the way.

I smile when I read the first three verses of **1 Corinthians 13 (MSG):**

> *"¹If I speak with human eloquence and angelic ecstasy but don't love, I'm nothing but the creaking of a rusty gate. ²If*

I speak God's Word with power, revealing all his mysteries and making everything plain as day, and if I have faith that says to a mountain, "Jump," and it jumps, but I don't love, I'm nothing. ³⁻⁷ If I give everything I own to the poor and even go to the stake to be burned as a martyr, but I don't love, I've gotten nowhere. So, no matter what I say, what I believe, and what I do, I'm <u>bankrupt</u> without love."

Bankrupt. Nobody wants to run out of money. Do you ever worry about running out of love? We'd have nothing left without love. The headlines get it wrong. I'm so glad my *On the Road* travels have provided me with plenty of loving storylines to share.

In this chapter, you'll meet four people who understand what it means to love like God loves. Julie Clarke would do anything for her daughter, Amelie, and spends a little extra time each day making sure her school lunch includes a handmade love note from mom. Ken Deka wishes he could hug his buddies again. He plays a special song for them each night as he bids the day farewell. The Stantons prove true love knows no age. The newlyweds are spending their remaining days sharing life's adventures in each other's arms. Brent Kraus' heart is broken but he's mending it as best he can. He's dedicated the rest of his life to showing love for his brother, who was lost too soon.

God's love is undefeated. You can be sure of that. You may feel broken. You may feel lost. Cancer may be winning. The devil's footsteps may be getting louder. Good news! God's love is a crutch that can handle your weight. It's there pushing you towards the finish line.

Love is a choice, and the perfect example of how to love properly comes from Jesus' life. He's the one who designed it eons ago.

DEAR AMELIE,

I'm sure you've heard the catchy, politically-correct slogan, *Love Wins*, right? It's misused in popular culture but the premise behind the words rings true in a Biblical sense. Love wins because God successfully executed a master plan to send His perfect son to buy us back from the clutches of death.

One of the many examples of love that I have seen during my *On The Road* segment was born out of a tragedy. I met Julie Clarke during a shoot for a story about keeping the art of letter writing alive. A group of women gathered weekly at a ritzy paper shop to write letters to kids who were stuck in the hospital. Those tiny patients could use a smile and personalized cards were just what the doctor ordered. It was very sweet, actually.

I showed up with my camera. Julie, a part-time employee at the shop, was working that day. There were colorful sheets of paper scattered on a table next to boxes of ink pens and scissors. Women of varied ages giggled and swapped stories as they created handmade wonders. Each card included a heartfelt message and lots of glitter. The crafting went on for an hour. Julie and I got to chatting after most of the other women left. I like to have conversations with people on camera and off camera to get a feel for what they are truly like. Some people put on an act for the camera and show their true colors when the interview ends. It's a way to fool viewers. Julie was not that way at all. I could instantly tell she was genuine. We discovered we had daughters about the same age. Hers was in kindergarten at a nearby school. Mine was in preschool on the other side of town. As we chatted, she grabbed a few sheets of blank paper and started doodling the most stunning stars I'd ever seen anyone draw freehand.

"Those are beautiful," I remember saying.

She smiled and explained that they would be part of tomorrow's lunch note for her daughter, Amelie. It was Julie's favorite thing to make. Those notes helped Amelie learn to read letters and form words (with the help of her teacher). They reminded Julie's sweet little girl that she was loved, even when mommy wasn't around. I was impressed. These were not folded sticky notes on a PB&J. These were works of art! Kindergarten Bobby would have loved something like this in my lunchbox.

The notes are a parallel of what God does for us. He sends beautifully crafted reminders that He cares for us. He sends a sunrise and sunset each day. He sends the sound of birds chirping. He sends the beauty of an evening rain shower and paints mountainsides with colorful leaves each fall.

I was so impressed at the love notes that I asked Julie if she would mind me doing an *On The Road* story about her colorful connection with Amelie. She agreed. Later that week, I found myself in a sticky lunchroom full of rambunctious five-year-olds fighting over who would get to stare into the camera lens and paw at the microphone first. Amelie read her lunch note to me between bites of apple. The cute little story aired on the Friday night news. I thought it turned out great.

Julie and Amelie's world crumbled two days later.

On Sunday, working in the front yard, Julie's husband was stung by wasps. He didn't know he was allergic and died within five minutes of being stung. The family that smiled together Friday night while watching Amelie read lunch notes on TV was now sobbing. I can't imagine it. I was heartbroken for Julie and Amelie.

But, even during tragedy, love wins. It always does.

Amelie missed a week of school but got a huge surprise when she returned. Her kindergarten classmates had each written Amelie a love note for her lunchbox. There was no way they were all going to fit in there! That is the type of love, that never-quit kind, that God wants us to experience. Julie's notes didn't stop. They had a different tone now that a single parent was penning them, but they still oozed with love.

It's the kind of love that Jesus displayed when His friend Lazarus died. It crushed Jesus. We know it was emotional because the Bible describes Lazarus as "the one Jesus loved". Jesus wept when he heard the news. I'd imagine it wasn't a dab-your-eye kind of weeping, either. It was probably the uncontrollable kind where you shake and use your sleeve as tissue. A Kleenex just wouldn't do in this situation. His friend was dead!

We know the rest of the story. Jesus performs a mighty miracle! He raises Lazarus from the grave and everyone is astonished at Jesus' power. But, it was out of love that Jesus performed such a death-defying wonder. His love for Lazarus, just like the love He showed for all people in His three years of ministry on Earth, overcame tragedy.

Love won.

Giant sequoia trees are remarkable. If you cut one down and lay it on a football field, it would almost stretch from end zone to end zone. The biggest sequoia on record is nicknamed General Sherman. It's 275 feet tall, 102 feet around and weighs roughly 2.7 million pounds! Those are mighty measurables! Yet, as big and burly as General Sherman is, it would topple over easily in a stiff breeze if it weren't for its noteworthy roots. They do not penetrate deep into the ground like other tree species. Rather, they creep around near the surface and mingle with the roots of neighboring trees. Sometimes, those nearby roots will fuse together. It creates incredible stability and makes them stronger. If it weren't for these interlocking roots, a mild storm could topple the top-heavy trees with no problem. With a community of intertwined roots anchoring the trees to the ground, even the fiercest storm has no chance to bring down a sequoia.

Amelie and Julie needed help to get through their difficult loss. They needed each other. They needed a loving community. They needed loving roots. They found support in friends and lunch notes from classmates.

A loving bond between hurting humans can help us withstand the storms of life. On her own, the tragic news of a lost husband could have crushed Julie. Bad news is always tougher to handle alone. If we uplift each other by linking in love, we will be able to ride out the bad news that comes our way. There will be a lot of bad news in life. Will you try to survive it alone?

Romans 12:9-10 (NIV)

"Love must be sincere. Hate what is evil; cling to what is good. Be devoted to one another in love. Honor one another above yourselves."

A NIGHTLY SUNSET SONG

There are a few different types of love described in the New Testament. Four original Greek words translate to 'love' and are all used to describe it in very different forms. *Agape* is the most commonly used term and it refers to an unconditional love, like that shown by God to His created people. *Eros* means sexual love or attraction between spouses. *Storge* refers to natural bonding among family members but is not mentioned much in the text. *Phileo* means brotherly love for a friend. All are important. This story is about phileo love. It's about a man who won't let people forget what his buddies did for complete strangers.

I have great respect for the men and women who have volunteered to bravely serve our nation with the understanding that it could cost them their lives. Hundreds of thousands of United States military members have died fighting wars to protect the American citizens. Men and women of every color, shape, and creed have bled to keep us safe. I have met countless veterans during my time as a feature reporter and shake each and every one of their hands with as much respect as possible. My tone changes around them. I am thankful to the one percent who serve for the 99 percent who don't. I hurt for those who didn't get a handshake.

I met a man on the beach one night that understood better than me what it's like to lose a friend in combat. I've lost friends but never at the hands of enemy fighters. Ken Deka lost many friends during battles in Vietnam.

The departments of Defense and Veterans Affairs keeps tabs on everyone who has worn a military uniform. Unfortunately, many become casualty statistics. Over the course of a century or so, the United States has buried hundreds of thousands of soldiers.

American death tolls by war:
World War I: 116,516
World War II: 405,399
Korean War: 54,246
Vietnam War: 90,220

Those aren't the only wars where Americans have lost their lives. There has been plenty of death. There have been plenty of tears shed. There have been too many funerals planned. Freedom isn't free.

I originally learned about Ken from an emailer who visited our area each year for a few weeks. We call them snowbirds, a class of traveler who trades the cold northern winters for warm, humid ones in Florida. I can't blame them. Santa Claus wears flip-flops and sips piña coladas here. This emailer told me I should join her at Indian Rocks Beach to hear the most stirring rendition of 'Taps' she'd ever heard.

I knew what 'Taps' was but wasn't really that versed in the meaning behind it. It's a song played by a bugler, typically at dawn or dusk, during flag ceremonies or military funerals. It's the ultimate tone of respect. It's a 24-note symbolic "thank you" to loved ones who have passed on. It's the song that inspired Ken to buy a bugle in the first place. He served in the Army and has mixed memories of 'Taps'. It would greet him in the morning during training and was played when a fellow soldier perished in battle. He experienced tinges of guilt over getting to see his loved ones after returning home from war. He entered the service with a handful of buddies. Many died.

He loved his fellow soldiers like brothers. It's the reason why he learned to play the bugle. He shows up every night, to the same spot, to send the sun off with a song. He plays those 24 musical notes every 24 hours to honor his fallen comrades.

I feel fortunate to live where people vacation. Sunsets in Florida are beautiful. The sound of the waves gently kissing the sand provides romantic ambience. People come from nearby restaurants and homes to bid the day farewell as the sky slowly turns from light to night. Some bring beach chairs and wine. Others pull out their cameras. No two sunsets are the same and are all worth capturing. Amelie and Julie needed help to get through their difficult loss. They needed each other. They needed a loving community. They needed loving roots. Oranges and purples blend together on the edges of the clouds and highlight those picturesque moments. Ken shows up to set the scene about 30 minutes prior to the last glimpse of daylight.

He always brings a lawn chair and is normally wearing a straw hat. He carries two small flags in his black bugle case. One is the familiar red, white, and blue of Old Glory. The other is a black POW-MIA flag, representing the prisoners of war and those missing in action. He carefully and strategically places them upright in the sand a few feet in front of his lawn chair. He sits down for a few moments to process the duty ahead and thinks about the reason he's there. Everyone respects his space.

After a few minutes of reflection, Ken rises to greet everyone. There is practically a line formed down the beach. He's a bit of a local celebrity who always has a smile on his face and nothing on his feet. Ken knows the sunset forecast better than any weatherman I've ever met. He knows exactly what time the sun will dip behind the sea and if the clouds will hold off long enough to give beachgoers a show.

While Ken was greeting everyone, I was planning my shots. I had to be strategic about how I got video of Ken playing 'Taps'. The song is less than a minute long, meaning there isn't much time to capture his rendition of the iconic tune. I placed a camera on a stand just in front of his eyes. I placed another small camera in the sand pointed up towards his face. I then took a third camera and shot video of the faces of the men and women waiting to hear his notes. I wanted to get all angles covered. I was as prepared as possible.

Ken removed his bugle from the case and slowly moved into position. The men who died at his side during war decades ago were no doubt on his mind as he stared at the last glimpses of the sun that day. He glanced down at his watch. It was 7:55 p.m. Almost time. One minute to go.

The crowd sat silently as he lifted his instrument to his lips. All eyes were on the bugler. The caw of seagulls and splashing of waves set the mood. Ken closed his eyes and took a deep breath. Hands were placed across hearts as the music began. He emptied his lungs and the music filled the sky. A family on vacation stood nearby. This was the third time this week they'd stopped to hear Ken play. The notes escaped the bugle and rode on the breeze out over the waters. It was a powerful moment. Onlookers shed a tear. It lasted less than a minute. Seemingly as quickly as it began, Ken finished his song and returned the bugle to his side. Applause erupted for the man who serenaded the sea. He nodded in appreciation.

"It's one of those songs that makes you want to smile and cry at the same time and a lot of people do," he said softly.

Ken loved those men who bravely wore the uniform alongside him. They all loved their country. The Bible teaches that the greatest thing a man can do is lay down his life for a friend. Jesus did it for you and me. Ken's buddies did, too. The soldier's sacrifice fostered freedom in our nation. The world understands that the United States is to be respected and feared because of the actions of men and women like them. Love is much more than a feeling or an emotion. Love is a decision. Love is a choice.

John 15:11-13 (NIV)

[11] I have told you this so that my joy may be in you and that your joy may be complete. [12] My command is this: Love each other as I have loved you. [13] Greater love has no one than this: to lay down one's life for one's friends."

I lost a friend to a car accident in college. It hurts. I can't imagine how much Ken misses his Army brothers. I'm not much of a crier, but hearing those notes from his bugle was a special thing. After his showing, Ken turned and trudged through the sand to his chair. Little kids waved to him. He waved back. He packed away his bugle and flags in the sturdy black case. As he gathered his things, a woman walked up and gave him a little hug.

I didn't see them, but I bet angels were there patting Ken on the back as he retired for the day. Why wouldn't they? He'd once again paid tribute to men and women who laid down their lives for strangers in an act of perfect love. Their selfless decision to serve mirrored the actions of Jesus. A few dozen people walked away from that shoreline feeling thankful for the man who played 'Taps'. If I polled them, I'm guessing they'd also have an increased measure of love and gratitude for the soldiers who never got to hear it.

The headlines tonight will focus on war. A man who knows all too well what war can do, chooses to play music full of love.

Proverbs 17:17 (NIV)

"A friend loves at all times; a brother is born out of adversity."

LOVEBIRDS SOAR

*M*y wife and I were sitting in church one Sunday morning and the pastor got up on the stage to relay the weekly announcements. There were a few odds and ends to discuss and, truth be told, a lot of it went in one ear and out the other. My eyes were probably wandering around the room. I'm a sermon man. There is nothing wrong with the worship music and the mingling with neighbors, but I dig in for the sermons. It's the meat and potatoes portion of the experience and I am a meat and potatoes kind of guy. So, it's highly likely I was daydreaming a bit right up until the moment where my wife's elbow found a soft spot between my ribs.

"Let's do it," she said with an excited look in her eye. Still surprised, and a bit sore, I nodded and smiled.

That's how I became a marriage mentor.

I grew to enjoy it, but I can't say I was totally on board from the start. On the one hand, I think it's a great thing when experienced couples lend advice to people diving headfirst into the potentially tricky waters of holy matrimony. Why not offer a life vest or two? That's just being helpful, right? On the other hand, I felt a bit underqualified. My wife and I had only been married a little over eight years when we signed up to be mentors and didn't have a long list of pitfalls to speak of. My wife and I aren't fighters. I can't really think of a time when we've had a major disagreement. I never have and never will raise my voice at her. I've never slept on the couch. From what I hear, those things happen a lot in marriages. Not mine. We get along great! What was I going to say to a couple who isn't even married yet and already fights every day? Could I really help anyone? Worse yet, what if I offered bad advice and derailed a relationship? That's a lot of pressure.

We did it anyway. We felt like it was time to put our marriage to work instead of just sitting idly by watching relationships fail. The key to a strong family is a rock-solid foundation and that starts before the "I dos". There were preparative classes, meetings, workbooks, and all the typical stuff associated with mentoring. It was a bit overwhelming at the start. I felt like I had been assigned grown-up homework. I had to learn all the right topics to discuss with folks nearing their wedding day and try to keep them on track. All they were probably thinking about was the honeymoon. All I wanted to do was make my wife happy (which, by the way, is Lesson No. 1 for a happy marriage). After a few sessions with couples, I realized that, per usual, my wife had come up with a good idea. We learned more about ourselves by talking with other couples than we would have ever learned at home on our own. We debated more topics. We worked together on more projects. We asked each other questions that we would never have entertained had it not been for the mentoring curriculum. We grew closer as a result.

The thing about the mentoring that continues to be the most surprising for me is the session that covers communication. I thought my wife and I were good communicators. I suppose we are. I just had no idea WHY we were so good at it. I just assumed it was because I was a wordsmith who always knew the right thing to say in a sticky situation. Nope. That's not it at all. Apparently, only seven percent of the communication we do comes from words. Just seven. That's it. According to a study by Dr. Albert Mehrabian, the rest of our communication comes from body language (55%), facial expressions, posture, gestures, and tone of voice (38%). Learning to communicate in a loving manner is a lifelong journey through a garden studded with both briars and blooms.

Marriage is a great thing and should be treated with respect. It's not a flippant agreement made haphazardly or on a whim. It's an enduring choice to honor God with your union. If you've been married five minutes or five decades, the structure is all the same. Marriage was designed by God for a man and a woman to work together to honor and bring Him praise. I learned throughout the mentoring process that you never stop learning how to love. Marriage at every stage is something that constantly builds upon itself. If it's done correctly, the most successful marriages are the ones where each spouse enters the committed relationship expecting to get nothing and striving to give everything. Marriage is adventurous if you do it right!

That's how Fran Stanton ended up in the WWII biplane. My wife elbowed me in the ribs and I wound up in a cool, air-conditioned meeting room at the church. Fran's husband petitioned her to get out of her comfort zone and she ended up a few thousand feet in the air over a busy highway. Like I said, marriage is adventurous if you do it right!

I am not much of an airplane buff but my dad sure is. From the moment I saw the sleek 1941 Boeing Stearman sitting on the runway, I knew if I showed up to the next family dinner without a few dozen photos of that aircraft I'd be eating alone in the garage. This thing was gorgeous! Even decades after being built, it was still a show-stopper. It was hard to believe that the plane sitting in front of me had trained some of America's top pilots before battles in WWII. It had sleek body lines and the paint was a vibrant blue. It looked like something straight out of a Snoopy 'Red Baron' cartoon.

I arrived at the airport before Fran and her husband, Dick. I unpacked all my camera gear and walked to the hangar to meet the pilot, Keith. He was a jolly guy with white hair and a genuine grin. He had been flying for many years. Keith led me over to see his plane. My dad would have been so jealous. We chatted for a few minutes about what made his aircraft unique. I attached a camera to its tail in order to get an action shot once it left the ground. I was already picturing clouds rushing by the lens as the plane soared high above me. This Stearman had all its original gages and instruments and topped out at 100 miles per hour. The 75-year-old bird was primed and ready to make a dream come true for two adventurous seniors. The orange windsock above our heads flapped lazily in the wind, which had picked up a bit while I waited for the guests of honor to arrive. The sun was bright and the sky was nearly cloudless. This had all the elements of a great *On The Road* story.

No sooner than I had gotten my camera fastened to the wing, Fran and Dick walked up the path that led from the parking lot to the runway. I smiled when I saw them. They looked exactly as I pictured. He walked with a cane and wore over-sized sunglasses. She walked with a pep in her step and her outfit matched perfectly. Both beamed with excitement from the front of a pack. Some half-dozen retirement home residents made the 40-minute trip to the airport that day to seek a thrill in the skies. I walked over and introduced myself to the happy couple. They were warm and welcoming. Fran was 87 and smelled like roses. Dick was 96 and had a firm handshake. The newlyweds couldn't wait to hit the skies in a real biplane.

"He's always getting me into these things," Fran told me with a girlish giggle. She didn't look a day over 80.

She and Dick met in their retirement community two years prior. The lovebirds hit it off and married shortly after. No need for a long engagement, I guess, when triple digits are in view. The couple vowed to do something wild and crazy together each year to help them stay young. They took a hot air balloon ride the first year of their marriage. Now, in round two, they wanted to go a bit faster.

Neither had military experience but both were amazed by the WWII training plane. Dick slowly walked around the tips of the wings with a youthful look on his face. There was excitement in his smile. If he reached his arms out as far as they'd stretch his wingspan would barely exceed the length of the front propeller. The plane was only about 20 feet long, but he sure looked small standing beside it on the runway.

Both were given the chance to feel the rush of cool wind in their white hair that day. Fran volunteered to go up in the plane first, even though she admitted that the whole thing was Dick's idea. She told me she was nervous enough for the both of them, but I would never have guessed it. She hid her fear pretty well. She loved her husband and was going to do this for him. It was a joint activity. They'd made a promise to each other to do something brave together. Whatever nerves she had were not strong enough to make her chicken out. A team of assistants from the retirement home helped Fran climb a short ladder and into the tiny cockpit. Fran pulled a vintage flight helmet over her curls, drawing the straps through the buckle until it was nice and snug under her chin. These planes could accommodate two passengers. That configuration allowed military men the best opportunity for training back in the early 1940s. Fran wasn't going to be firing any weapons or executing top secret missions on this flight. She was just along for a care-free cruise. She took her spot in the cockpit.

I got shots of the wheels, wings, and cockpit, my brain kicked in. Fran's flight was not about Fran. It was about Dick. I looked over to the shaded porch to see Dick beaming with pride. His bride was about to conquer a fear and sprint down a runway at 100 miles per hour before lifting off the ground and towards the heavens. This was his idea! I left the small group of people at the plane's side and walked over to Dick. I wanted to watch this flight with him. He was going to be my focus during Fran's short eight-minute flight.

That old machine was ready to provide some new fun. The engine roared and the propeller sputtered before beginning to spin rapidly. The sound got to be so loud that I could barely hear Dick's good luck cries. Fran, dressed in her butterfly t-shirt, lovingly waved to her husband as the plane taxied to the end of the runway a quarter mile away. Once the plane was far enough away that the engine could no longer be heard, I asked Dick what this was like for him to see his wife take to the skies. His answer surprised me.

"Every day is special but this is extra special," he said. I asked if he was proud of his wife. "Oh, you bet."

Dick and Fran Stanton flew in a 1941 biplane

The reflection of the plane could be seen in his black sunglasses as Fran left the safety of land below. As she steadily climbed higher and higher, Dick's grin grew wider and wider. He told me about how he'd always loved planes and was born before the Stearman was ever built. For 96 years he'd wondered what it would be like to ride in a biplane. After learning how much this opportunity meant to him, it impressed me that he still let his wife take the first flight. Only 9,783 of these biplanes were built in the United States during the 1930s and 1940s. They were used as a military training aircraft. Dick knew all about them. He'd just never touched one before.

For nearly a century, he watched from the ground, wondering what it was like up there among the clouds. When his wife returned to earth and handed him her helmet, he playfully asked her, "Should I do it?"

A wind-blown Fran answered, "Sure, go for it!"

This was amazing to me. The Stantons had logged 183 total years on this earth and were acting like teenagers infected with puppy love. It was refreshing and inviting. It was loving and enlightening. Fran and Dick had each seen world wars, financial recessions, and political unrest through the decades. They'd learned that the most important thing to hold on to in life was love. Love is stronger than all the other junk that invades our calendars, Facebook feeds, and newscasts. Love is what keeps us grounded.

In Dick and Fran's case, it's also what lifted them off the ground. As Dick took off, I asked Fran which spouse was braver.

"My husband, definitely," she said with a chuckle.

Ecclesiastes 4:9-10 (NLT)

"Two people are better off than one, for they can help each other succeed. [10] If one person falls, the other can reach out and help. But someone who falls alone is in real trouble."

ELLA BING

The most effective way to accurately track your priorities is to look at your calendar. Whatever demands most of your time holds the most weight in your life. Time is our most valuable resource. When I was a kid, I spent almost all my time playing baseball. I spent time on it because it mattered to me.

That's just a sport, though. When it comes to relationships, time is even more valuable. When you love someone, you prioritize them. Getting married totally upended my schedule. I used to do things for myself. Now, I have a partner in life that I want to be around as much as possible. I want to be home in time to kiss my kids goodnight. I love my family, so I put time into making my relationship with each of my family members meaningful.

Love and time are linked. They always have been and always will be. I once heard a preacher say the average person spends three minutes per day in prayer. Just three minutes! How can you expect to have a deep, meaningful relationship with the Creator when you only spend three minutes a day chatting with Him? Try having a successful connection with your spouse on just three minutes per day. That won't fly. Your marriage will sputter and die. Love is about connection. Love is about putting in the time. What consumes your calendar captures your heart. Want more love? Spend more time.

The problems come when you still have love, but have run out of time. That is the story of Brent Kraus.

I liked Brent the moment I met him. We are roughly the same age and both have daughters around the same age. We grew up within two hours of each other and both seem to have an affinity for pizza and neckwear. Both of us are thin crust dudes. I'm more the traditional, long necktie kind of guy while he's strictly a bow tie man. There are a lot of similarities between us but the one glaring difference is what brought us together. I have no idea what it feels like to lose a brother to suicide.

As I drove to meet him for the first time, I couldn't stop thinking about how tough that must be. The drive was a long one, so I had plenty of time to think about the immeasurable pain Brent must have felt the day he got the call that his brotherly bond was over. He'd never see Matthew Kraus again. I can't imagine it. My brother is three years younger than me and we were always around each other when we were little. We shared a room from the time he was born until the time I graduated college. I commuted back and forth for much of the four years I attended school and would sleep in my old top bunk on weekends. My mom famously tells the story of the day she walked into our room to find me in the middle of duct taping a dividing stripe across the orange carpeting in our bedroom. I'd clearly marked my territory from his. I grew weary of his drum set. I didn't always like the noise. But, looking back, I wouldn't change a thing. All this was in my head as I sped towards the Kraus home.

How many times have you flipped on the news and heard these headlines?

"Local man found dead in his home after self-inflicted gunshot wound."

"Woman takes her own life after fight with boyfriend."

"Gunman opens fire on a recreation center then takes his own life after shootout with police."

It's too common. It's too painful. Those headlines make us want to turn away in either disgust or disappointment. Suicide is a topic that comes up frequently in the news but is usually left untouched after the script is read. It's an uncomfortable subject. But, for the families left behind, it's unbearable. I have no idea what it would be like not to have one of my siblings around anymore. For those who have lost a loved one, it's a reality I wish they didn't have to know.

Matthew Kraus was four years younger than Brent. On September 1, 2010, he took his own life. He was a culinary student living in Manhattan. Just two short months earlier, his dad had made the 1,100-mile trip to New York to see Matthew. There were no signs that he was unhappy. There was no indication that he was contemplating ending his life. Brent was blindsided. The news that his little brother was gone landed like a sucker punch.

Evil lurked. Darkness lingered. Love was severed. Time was up. Brotherhood was broken. Suicide had shattered the loving family dynamic that the Krauses had built over 25 years. Love looked like it was losing.

I don't care much for the popular phrase, "Everything happens for a reason". It's used to dissect disappointment. People use it to explain away the unexplainable. Sometimes, the reason for bad things happening is simple: The devil is a crook, out to steal joy and populate the headlines. Suicide isn't God's plan. It's one of the devil's deceptions. But, God can still spin tragedy into triumph. Even when it looks like nothing good can come from something as sad like Matthew's death, God can send a new plan.

That's exactly what happened with the Ella Bing bow tie company.

My wife says I have a problem. I have an entire closet dedicated to my professional attire. I own dozens of ties. Maybe 100. I have organized them on a display rack that hangs over the back of my closet door. It's shameful, really. No man needs all that dress wear. Matthew was just like me. He was an avid bow tie collector. I can associate with the man's fashion sense. It's classy. It's professional. It looks downright spiffy and I think wearing a tie distinguishes a man. It shows that you care about your appearance and want to be taken seriously. Ask anyone who knew Matthew and they'll tell you it was his defining feature. It was one of many things his family loved about him.

Brent is a fashion guy, too. He could have spent the rest of his days crying over Matthew's September 2010 decision. Of course, there were tear-filled nights. Many of them. The two brothers were close.

When I finally finished the two-hour drive from our TV station to his parent's house, I felt very welcomed. Brent showed me a few pictures of him goofing off with Matthew. There was love in their eyes. There was so much laughter in the photos. If I didn't already know that Matthew had committed suicide, I would have never guessed the jubilant person in the frames would be capable of it. He looked so happy. He looked so content.

The photos were tacked up on a corkboard in Lisa Kraus' sewing room. Brent's mom is a keen and capable seamstress. Her spare time was devoted to crafting things for her fashion-forward boys. She was always stitching them something trendy and eye-catching. Lisa had grown especially close to Matthew in the years before he died. She worked long hours to handmake his neckwear on her sewing machine. I looked around her room as the sewing machine hummed an efficient rhythm. It looked a little bit like an upscale boutique. There was neckwear everywhere. The very first bow tie she ever made for Matthew sat on the desk under his picture. The simple blue and yellow tie still held a very special place in the family, even five years after Matthew's passing.

She grinned as I asked her about her hobby. Talking about losing her son was therapeutic. It was healthy to get her feelings out. Enough time had passed that she was able to relive the loving moments without dwelling on the painful ones. My camera zoomed in on her fingers as she worked her fabric cutter over a bright, jazzy pattern. There was a pile of bow ties on the corner of her table. She'd completed them earlier in the week. There were patterned styles and more formal designs as well. Being the connoisseur that I am, I could not help but window shop. I saw a lot of stuff I liked. Lisa was talented and made a really nice bow tie.

A small pile of ties on the corner of the sewing table caught my attention. They were all different shades of brown and looked different from the rest. I moved my tripod around the table to get a closer look and was surprised to see something I never knew existed.

"Wooden," said Brent.

I wandered out to the garage where his father, David, flipped the power switch to his table saw. The machine whirred as he adjusted his protective glasses. I stood back at a safe distance as he carefully lined up a bow tie template. David traced the border onto a fresh piece of cedar. I had never seen anything like this before. I only *wear* neckties. I don't have any ability to make them. David carved a bow tie out of the wooden plank and set it on the workbench to be sanded later. It joined a pile of about a dozen others. It was like Santa's workshop in there!

The family named its bow tie company Ella Bing. I love their flamingo logo. The skinny bird with the long neck and bow tie was tropical and trendy. What was going on in the Kraus' home was astounding to me. Dad carved. Mom sewed. Son sold. It was a family assembly line with a deep-rooted passion. Their purpose was anchored in the love for their son and brother. Matthew would have been more excited than any other Kraus about the budding bow tie business.

Suicide headlines are common. I hear them weekly at the TV station. No doubt you've heard them, too. I have always considered suicide the most selfish decision a person can make. I remember tweeting such feelings after famous NFL player Junior Seau committed suicide in 2012. I was eviscerated online by fans of the football star. They called me every name you could think of from behind the safety of a keyboard. My words irritated them. My stance outraged them. None of those vile retorts changed my opinion. A person who takes his or her own life leaves behind a long line of heartbroken people who will never get answers. They will never get another hug or phone call. Suicide puts everybody else's feelings behind your own. It's quitting on life and quitting on family. God wasn't done with you yet. You cut off His chance to use you in a mighty way.

Suicide is the tenth-leading cause of death in the United States. Each year over 44,000 people die of suicide. Matthew was one of them in 2010. The Ella Bing website summarizes its mission this way:

"The roots of the company Ella Bing were started out of necessity, to heal and to bring our family back together."

Love is a powerful thing. If it is real, love has the ability to last longer than the relationship that produced it. David and Lisa still love their son. Brent still loves his brother. Even though Matthew is gone, the love his family has for him remains. The Kraus family put in the time required to build that loving relationship. Those emotions are as real today as the days leading up to Matthew's suicide. Giving in to sadness would short-circuit the possibility of growth. Allowing depressing thoughts to become common thoughts concedes victory to darkness. Matthew could have just been another sour headline on the news. Instead, with God's help, the family is turning his death into a positive storyline. Carving, sewing, and selling Matthew's favorite neckwear has given his family an amazing platform to promote love like never before.

Ella Bing's cheapest bow tie runs about $100. Some cost nearly $400. It seems steep, but there is a purpose behind the price. Every bow tie the Kraus family sells will be used to help others struggling the way Matthew struggled during his final days. Ten percent of every sale is donated to the Crisis Center of Tampa Bay. It's a hotline facility for people who are contemplating suicide. It's a place devoted to preventing the agony of separation for family members. In the first five years of selling bow ties and hosting charity fundraisers, Ella Bing donated over $50,000 to suicide prevention and awareness. That's unselfish! That's communal! That's Godly love on a mighty mission. Not only that, it's now Matthew's legacy. His death could have extinguished all joy in the Kraus home. Instead, the family turned a difficult situation into an uplifting opportunity. Ella Bing is saving families from feeling the same horrors the Krauses felt after losing Matthew. It's such a simple idea to craft bow ties for strangers. Simple, but monumental! Every dime they generate for the Crisis Center could lead to mended self-esteem. Love will survive. Love will thrive. Love will win. God doesn't want families torn apart. God wants love to cement families together.

I left the Kraus' home that day with a renewed feeling. My *On The Road* stories don't feature a lot of death. They are designed to avoid it. We see death in almost every other segment of the news every day. My segment is supposed to be a break from all of that. It's supposed to be encouraging. It's about moving past difficulty. I think this story, one of the few that featured the sad reality of suicide, was more about love than death.

I own two Ella Bing bow ties. Brent gave me one to wear to the Emmy awards in 2016. On a night where the best-of-the-best television stories are honored, I was happy to end the night posing with a trophy, while wearing a piece of neckwear with a pretty special story itself. Every time I wear one of my Ella Bing bow ties, people ask me where I got it. It gives me the chance to share Brent's story. Not just Brent's, but Matthew's story.

The Ella Bing bow ties are colorful and creative. More than that, they are special. They remind a family of a love that was severed. But, they also serve as a reminder that, if you put your heart into something, and time too, love can never be totally disconnected.

1 John 4:11 (NIV)
"Dear friends, since God so loved us, we also ought to love one another."

CLOSING THOUGHTS ON LOVE

I was a cool 11-year-old. I was the tallest kid in my class. I wore a size-9 shoe and read every R.L. Stine *Goosebumps* book cover to cover the same week it hit store shelves. I'm sure my best friend and I personally funded the purchase of Stine's Cadillac in 1995. I had a sweeping, whooshing haircut that I'm sure drove all the gals batty.

I remember getting into some love-related trouble when I was in fifth grade. There was a girl in my class who clouded my judgment. All men fall prey to puppy-love problems at some point. I was smitten. We were in the same class at Ponce de Leon Elementary school and sat in the same row. Sitting as close as we did, I could smell her fruity shampoo. She had short blonde hair and a cute little smile. As is the custom with most 11-year-olds, we *never* spoke to each other. Rather, I scribbled love notes on lined notebook paper and passed them across the classroom.

Do you want to be my girlfriend? Check Yes or No.

Life was simpler then. No taxes. No deadlines. Just boyish-enthusiasm. I knew I was going to get a *yes* check someday. I was confident. But, things started to go south around the time of the annual school book fair. My mom gave me money for a few books. I decided to buy a small birthstone ring featuring a ruby red gemstone, instead. It was perched in a not-quite 24-carat gold setting. To a boy on a lunch money budget, it was stunning. I took it home and proudly presented it to my mom.

Like any soothing mother, mine gushed over the gift. I was proud of my decision and that feeling lasted at least two hours. Later in the evening, I thought about how that ring could work in my favor as school-yard leverage. Up to this point, I was not getting anywhere with my dream girl. Maybe she was intimidated by my height and good grades. I wanted a 'Yes' check from this girl so badly! She had it all! She always ran fast during kickball and could throw a football further than I could. When you're pre-pubescent, those traits are practically Miss America pageant-level talents. Who could concentrate on long division math work when recess was right around the corner?

So, I made a very poor choice. I snuck into my mom's bedroom and found her jewelry box. I swiped the ring that I purchased with her money earlier that day. She wouldn't mind, right? What's the big deal if I took back the jewelry that I'd originally given to her and re-gifted it to a much younger blonde?

My plan crash landed faster than a wet paper airplane. I snuck the ring to school in my pocket and presented it to my little crush. She gleefully accepted the ring and, at that point, I think, we were going steady. That's how elementary relationships work. Give a gal a $3.15 ring and she's yours forever. Or, at least until that night when your mother finds out that her new red ruby ring had mysteriously vanished from her jewelry box. Being the loving mother that she is, she'd gone to put the ring on her finger to show me how much she appreciated my kind gesture. Instead, I got a lesson on stealing and considering other's feelings.

The next day I had to go back to the younger woman and take back the ring that I'd originally given to my mommy. Talk about embarrassing! It's not the best way to seal the deal on a new romance. Try it with your wife today. Take something out of her jewelry box and give it to some cute chick at the office. I'm sure she'll understand. As a much older man now, I can see how my mother would have been a bit upset over my decision. I never got a *yes* check from that girl. Oh, what could have been.

Love is the most powerful emotion in the world. It has the potential to bond, to build, and to inspire. The problem is we can't seem to get it right. That's because love has been watered down. We don't even know what true love is anymore. We use the word to describe our feelings about clothing, food, and places. God didn't introduce love to our languages so we could use it to define our emotional connection to a Starbucks latte. We flagrantly throw around that word like it's loosely defined. It's not an interchangeable adjective.

So often, what we call love, God calls temporary. God's definition of love is eternal.

I didn't love my fifth-grade classmate. I was infatuated with her ability to throw a slant pass. Infatuation is brief and can make us do and say stupid things. If we're not too careful, our hearts will trick our minds into feeling something that isn't really there. To learn to love, we must follow God's blueprint.

True love is about showing kindness, mercy, and compassion when it's not deserved. It's about putting someone else's needs above our own and deciding to live as a perpetual second fiddle. It's about establishing clear and open lines of communication that minimize anger and consequence, no matter the topic. Love is about seeking God's definition for how to treat people. It's not relying on our own feelings to make decisions.

Love is a choice more than a feeling. The feeling we call love is the world's best imitation of God's eternal expression. True love is the example Christ set for us all by choosing to exit the comfort of Heaven, to descend to this dusty, undesirable planet, and be born in a pig trough. Love was allowing six-inch nails to be driven into His hands and feet for our sake. Love was hanging for hours on a wooden cross. Love was choosing to get up and walk out of a tomb three days later. Love is a decision. It's one that we must make afresh each day.

Love never loses, either. My *On The Road* experiences remind me of that. There are so many negative headlines about love competing for space in our brains. If we're not careful, they'll take root. If you're feeling like true love is unattainable, remember that God loves us more than we could ever love another human being. The Creator will always love the created more than the created could love the created. Not even our love for the Father can compare. Yet, God gave us the ability to love because He knew it was one of the most important choices we could make.

Love is thriving for Julie Clarke. She lost the love of her life. Her world changed dramatically after her husband passed away but she didn't allow that tragedy to negatively impact the bond she had with her daughter. The family tradition of writing personalized lunch notes for Amelie's lunch box kept a little girl's heart feeling loved. It was a midday reminder that someone would be waiting for her as soon as she got home, to snuggle her and beg to hear about her day.

Ken Deka left behind a lot of friends on the battlefield. He chooses to show his love and appreciation for their service and sacrifice at the close of each day. Every time that bugle touches his lips, and he unleashes a thankful blow from his lungs, a loving melody wafts over the waves and up towards heaven. It's apparent how much they meant to him. Love can be heard in those musical notes. It's a moving melody.

Love can take you places you never expected to go and the Stantons found that out firsthand. The newlyweds left the comfort of solid ground by pledging to take their love to new heights. At 96 and 87 years old, respectively, Dick and Fran are still challenging themselves to seek new adventures. A flight in a WWII biplane certainly qualifies as adventure. Their decision to support each other's thrill-seeking spirit shows how much they care for each other. How many other seniors do you know who sign up to feel clouds on their faces? Soaring together was a loving reward for putting each other first.

The greatest expression of love is laying down your life for another person but, perhaps, the second greatest expression of love is living your life to honor someone you lost. Brent Kraus and his family suffered a huge loss when Matthew took his own life. Yet, God created love to be so strong that it even breaks the bonds of death. The Kraus family may never know how many people they've saved from suicide on this side of Heaven. Someday, maybe they'll learn the number. Until then, their decision to donate money from the sale of their wooden bow ties to a suicide prevention center is a poetic picture of true love.

Love is more than mushy Valentine's Day cards or Ryan Gosling scenes from *The Notebook*. It's an outward declaration of an internal understanding that we are here to connect with others. God designed love this way. He wants us to know it to the fullest. His way of love is not archaic, impractical, or old-fashioned. When we allow God to plug in to our hearts, the results will open us up to loving connections like we've never experienced.

VERSES ON LOVE

John 15:13 (NLT)
"There is no greater love than to lay down one's life for one's friends".

1 Corinthians 13:4-8 (NIV)
"Love is patient, love is kind. It does not envy, it does not boast, it is not proud. It does not dishonor others, it is not self-seeking, it is not easily angered, it keeps no record of wrongs. Love does not delight in evil but rejoices with the truth. It always protects, always trusts, always hopes, always perseveres. Love never fails."

1 Corinthians 13:13 (NLT)
"Three things will last forever—faith, hope, and love—and the greatest of these is love."

1 John 4:7-8 (NIV)
"Dear friends, let us love one another, for love comes from God. Everyone who loves has been born of God and knows God. Whoever does not love does not know God, because God is love."

1 John 3:18-19 (TLB)

"Little children, let us stop just saying we love people; let us really love them, and show it by our actions. [19] Then we will know for sure, by our actions, that we are on God's side, and our consciences will be clear, even when we stand before the Lord."

GIVING

*H*ave you ever watched a news story that made you want to throw up? I constantly hear from people in my community who reiterate what I already know – upsetting local and national news content turns them off. We are flooded with a never-ending flood of doom and gloom. Stories of rape, lies, stealing, and depression live on every news channel. Even my colleagues get tired of talking about it! Viewers tell me they are tired of hearing about abused children, families who have been cheated, and politicians who don't do what they swore to do. The world has a sin problem. The media interviews it, then regurgitates it back up through its microphones. There is an obligation to cover certain ugly events. I get that. The world will never be free from sinful headlines. But, a steady diet of junk news leaves you fat and feeling dejected.

I'm not easily angered, but there are some stories that really get me steaming. Sexual abuse that warps a child's life? Disgusting. Hit-and-run crashes that leave worlds shattered? Unnecessary. The all-too-frequent reports of innocent people get cheated? I hate all that stuff. I met a man a few years ago whom I grew to really like. He is kind and decent and puts others first. Imagine how upset I was when I found out his bike was stolen? It was his only reliable mode of transportation to and from work and somebody swiped it! Who would do that? Thankfully, some co-workers helped him get a new bicycle. I get so tired of waking up to a news alert on my cell phone saying a wrong-way driver slammed head-on into a school bus full of students.

The devil must wear track shoes because he is sprinting all over the planet. We live in a combative world. It's a daily fight. There is an invisible war going on all around us. The results of these battles sometimes end up on the front page of the newspaper or the scrolling ticker on the cable news channel.

"Politician kills himself after allegations of child abuse"

"Tsunami levels third-world town and leaves few survivors"

"Officer suspended after shooting compliant civilian"

Satan wants us to believe that the only thing happening on the planet are headlines like those. We know that's not true, but negative news makes that hard to believe sometimes. The devil is a cheater and I hate cheaters. The most effective strategy to beat back the devil is to whack him with a God-sized microphone. He's a taker. I want to highlight stories about givers. When you give, you gain.

There was a string of murders in central Florida during the fall months of 2017. It left a community terrified. The killer was a monster. He was a cheater, not a giver. He cheated people out of their futures. He cheated them out of chances to do God's good work. One of the murdered men was a volunteer at a homeless shelter. That community servant was robbed of the opportunity to continue being a blessing in his neighborhood. That killer will either die in jail or get the death penalty. When he was caught and arrested, it was all people in the city were talking about.

That morning, I was on a mission to help remind people that killers don't win. I was on a mission to make my day count for God and kick the devil off his perch. I spent the day at two different places trying my best to shine brightly for God. I went to a local community complex for people with intellectual disabilities. I went to see those special people hand-paint brilliant pieces of art that would be transformed into festive Christmas cards. The sale of the original artwork would be split between the artists and training center. The money from sales would help fund their art program and offer the artists a boost in life. I was so impressed that I bought ten Christmas cards.

My second stop brought another smile to my face. I got to profile a non-profit which had truly morphed into a grassroots giant. Seven years earlier, a few buddies decided to buy and deliver a couple bicycles to needy kids on Christmas. Now, 1,000 volunteers packed a downtown arena to build 800 bikes in one day. Talk about giving back! Santa's little helpers were going to provide an enormous number of smiles for kids dealing with cancer diagnoses, financial setbacks, and more. What a blessing it was to see both of those groups of people in action!

However, I noticed that in both locations, as happy as everyone was to be spreading cheer and excitement, the topic of conversations eventually leaked over to the catching of a killer. Even inside two upbeat atmospheres, a cloud of confusion and hurt hung in the air. The fresh capture of a man who had done such horrible things was cemented on everyone's mind. It was a dominating negative news event. It was a like a giant mudslide in the middle of two joyous picnics. When I find myself in those situations, I pray I can plug into the transformative power of God's goodness.

Headlines can hurt. I don't spend much time-consuming them, but I'm not naïve to the current events in our lives. I hear the cries of upset, hurting people. To me, it was necessary to take the time to remind people that a sin-filled killer was not going to win. Telling two stories about groups of people willingly giving to others was important. God's good work was being done right there in the same town where a killer had done so much evil.

God build us to be selfless, but from our first breaths, we have rejected that. We need to get back to our original design. The greatest thing we can do in this world is give. Putting someone else's feelings and needs ahead of ourselves is the highest compliment we can pay them. Giving has consequences, and they are all the kind we *want* to have. Learning to become a cheerful giver is God's intention for us all.

One of the biggest thrills I've had in my life was the day I bought a woman some gas. I was probably about 25 years old and my wife and I were on a quest to help a stranger. Our church wanted to be an example of godliness in the community around Christmas time. The pastors there decided the best way to do that was to just love on people through the simple act of giving. Each church member who wished to be part of the experience was given a $25 gift card to a local gas station. It may not have been enough to even fill up an entire tank, but I was so excited to surprise an unsuspecting person with a bit of holiday cheer.

I remember it was a cold, dreary day. It was one of those wish-you'd-stayed-in-bed mornings. The sky was gray and the looks on people's faces matched. I pulled into the QuikTrip gas station a few blocks from my house and shut off the engine. I scoured the parking lot looking for the right person. I didn't care who God put in our path that day. I just wanted Him to put a face in my line of sight and give my heart a nudge. This was a busy gas station at the corner of a well-traveled intersection. There were people everywhere. At a pump to my left, a lady got out of her old rusty car and closed the door with a thud. She was the one. I could feel it. She pumped a few dollars of gas and started for the convenience store door. I slowly got out of my car and followed her inside.

There were two people in front of her in the checkout line. Everybody was bundled up in heavy coats. It was frigid outside and every time a new customer triggered the automatic door, an icy gust of wind deepened the snarl on everyone's face. The first person in line finished buying her items. Then the next. Finally, it was my lady's turn. She'd picked up a newspaper from the stand by the front door. As she laid her paper down on the counter, I stepped to the front of the line.

"Excuse me," I said. "Can I buy that for you?"

You would have thought I asked her to strip down and do the hula. Her eyebrows raised nearly to her hairline. This was unexpected! A few people by the adjacent register heard my humble offering and looked at me bewilderedly. Normally, strangers don't offer to buy things for other strangers. We are natural takers. This was an act of giving! The woman, still a bit stunned, asked me to repeat myself. She must have thought she was hearing things. I told her I wanted to buy her paper and gas. Then the most amazing thing happened.

She started crying.

She was overcome with emotion right there in the line at the QuikTrip. She hugged me and I started to get a little misty-eyed too. I'm not a crier, but she was wet-faced enough for the both of us. She asked me if she could get a coffee, too. I smiled and told her she could buy whatever she wanted. I handed her the gift card and told her it was a gift from our church. I told her God loved her. I told her we'd love to see her for a service on Christmas if she didn't already have somewhere to attend. She was blown away by the gesture. The rest of the folks in line at the store were probably checking out my pockets. Maybe I was hiding a few more gift cards, right? Nope. Just the one. And, this one gift card had hit the mark. Maybe she was down to her last few bucks. I'll never know. I was so glad that God provided the right person at the right time in that gas station parking lot. It was only $25, but it meant so much more. I couldn't stop smiling.

I never asked the woman her name. I wish I had. I have no idea if she ever came to church for Christmas. Even if she didn't, that's okay. Church had come to her that day in the form of a free gift. She got a tank of gas, a newspaper, and some coffee. I got the satisfaction of seeing what a little bit of giving can do. It can provide a much-needed jolt for a weary soul in search of something positive. That's the type of thing I wish made every newscast.

Giving to others is a major theme in the Bible. The world's most frequently quoted verse displays how important giving is to God:

John 3:16 (NIV)
"For God so loved the world that he GAVE his one and only son, that whoever believes in him shall not perish but have eternal life."

God gave up His most precious possession. He gave up Jesus. I have two children. I will not give them up for anything. I just can't picture a scenario where I would let my mind go there. It's impossible to fathom that God so willingly gave what He gave for all the crooks, criminals, and evil-doers in the world. Even the murderers. And not just them, me.

I've met so many givers during my *On The Road* segment. I have met givers of all ages. They give time, effort, energy, and money to make the lives of others exponentially better. I met a pair of elementary buddies who collect thousands of books. They give them away to inner city schools where students don't own a single book. I met a young lady who started a campaign to get backpacks filled with non-perishable food so classmates without enough to eat wouldn't go hungry after school. I met a teenager who takes handicapped children fishing on her boat for free. Many of those kids have never been out on the open water before. I met a middle school student who felt compelled to buy shoes for local low-income elementary kids. She collected over $7,000, bought 150 pairs of shoes, and handed them out right before summer vacation.

You'll read about four special givers in this chapter. Lee Hardy has personally put an Easter smile on over 7,000 kid's faces. For over a decade, she's filled and given away free Easter baskets each spring. Scott Hand drives for hours each month in search of jagged collectibles. He finds shark teeth on Florida beaches and ships them back home to New Hampshire for his nephew's third-grade students. Becky Gama learned how tough life can be when you have no roof over your head. She started a clothing drive at her hospital for patients in need. A pair of UPS drivers I met have spent their careers making deliveries. The most important one saved a best friend's life.

There are givers on every corner of this world. They are the ones wearing the biggest smiles. They are usually the ones you don't hear about on the news, either. There are two types of people in the world. You are either a consumer or a contributor. The things consumers collect only gather dust. The payoff for contributors can't be held or measured. Giving far surpasses getting. If we all took a little more time to give, we would have far fewer gloomy mornings and far more joy-filled interactions.

THE "EASTER BASKET LADY"

When you think of someone who is generous, most people think of someone wealthier than themselves. It's a common misconception. Your bank account has nothing to do with your generosity level. Your heart dictates your giving nature. You can be a stingy rich guy or a generous poor guy. Both are possible and both are common. I've encountered both in my *On The Road* stories.

Count Lee Hardy as one of the most generous people I've ever met. We crossed paths just before Easter in 2015. Lee is a glass-half-full kind of woman but was dealing with heartache that spring. Death had stolen away her daughter far too soon. For a religious woman, her heart was especially pained during a time of the year that typically brings lifted spirits. Nobody wants to lose a loved one, especially around a holiday. I would never have known she was hurting when she greeted me at the front door with a smile as bright as the Florida sun.

I had to turn sideways to get all my camera junk in the doorway. Her living space was super cramped! I made the trip to meet Lee and talk about how much her passion for giving was impacting her community. I never expected to see so many baskets and toys in one place. Her house was crawling with Easter baskets! I could only see the pink carpeting along the edges of the room. For the next hour, Lee explained to me that her purpose in life was to provide some joy for little kids in her neighborhoods. It wasn't an overly affluent area. Some would even call it run down. Even in her situation, she found the ability to give.

All year long, Lee saves every penny she can from her income. Every penny has a purpose and every dime can do damage. She frequents the dollar stores and thrift shops around town. The employees there all know her by name. She asks church friends for cash donations and even collects the toys from their fast food kid's meals. Throughout the year, she eyes mailing flyers for toy sales to stretch her nickels as far as they can go. She rents a storage unit just to house her haul. After 12 months of collecting, the result is a mountain of blessings for strangers in need.

I'm not easily impressed, but this was something I had to take some photos of. There were pink baskets with fluffy bunnies and blue baskets with toy cars. She had princess-themed baskets and sports-theme baskets. There were coloring books and hard candies. There were racecars and stickers. Each one was hand-packed by Lee. Some nights, the grandmother would stay up until 3 a.m. stuffing newspaper in the bottoms of baskets, neatly placing toys inside, and wrapping the handles with bows. She played praise and worship music to keep her going. Eventually, she'd fall asleep on the couch surrounded by colorful packages and that fake Easter grass around her feet. Each year, the workload seemed insurmountable. Each year, the task seemed like it would never end. Each year, she somehow got it done.

Lee Hardy has given away over 7,000 Easter baskets

The year I met Lee, she had shopped wisely enough that she was able to fill nearly 800 Easter baskets. Her neighbors appropriately nicknamed her, "The Easter Basket Lady". It's a title she gladly accepted. I kept asking her why this was important to her. She just kept saying that it was what she felt called to do. She gave the 800 baskets away for free at a local park on Good Friday to parents who would otherwise not be able to buy one for their kids. Anyone who showed up got a basket from Lee. The appreciative looks on the kid's faces was enough payment for her. The Monday after Easter, she'd start collecting all over again.

The story we did that day was not complicated. I showed up, asked a few questions, and left. But, the connection that happened in Lee's home was a special one. We still talk on the phone a few times every year. She always calls to see if I'd like to come back out and interview her again before each Good Friday. Regrettably, I can't always make it. I do keep up with her progress. Her goal is to put together 1,000 baskets in one year. It's a huge number to hit. I hope she makes it. She's a giving soul with a heart for others.

It's one thing to want to be a giver. It's another thing to prove yourself as one. 2015 marked a decade of packaging Easter baskets for Lee. I could hear the joy in her voice as she described the feeling she gets from handing out those baskets. The Bible says God loves a cheerful giver (2 Corinthians 9:7). Being a Bible reader, Lee knew that. Her fingers proved the verse true. I left her home after meeting her for the first time with an increased appreciation for the power of giving. Her dedication to the less-fortunate in her community was astounding. Such generosity! Such willingness! Such unselfishness!

I wish I could tell you that Lee reached her 1,000-basket goal in 2016. Sadly, her total dipped. It dipped again in 2017 and 2018. Housing issues forced her to leave her larger home behind and move into a much-smaller apartment across town. The reduction in space made the task of putting together baskets a lot more difficult. Her location changed and her resources declined, but Lee's spirit remained unwavering. She still has the storage unit. She is still on a first-name basis with the clerks at all the dollar stores within ten miles of her home. She still has a heart for children and pledges to make a difference in their lives.

Life has thrown a lot of curveballs at Lee Hardy but she keeps on swinging! Her goal of 1,000 baskets may never happen. If not, there is no reason to feel down about it. The number isn't important. The willingness to give is what matters to God. The desire to help others is a trait He finds commendable. Lee gives from what she has and does it generously. She does it willingly. She does it faithfully.

My *On The Road* segment is all about highlighting people like Lee. It's about shining a light on the good in our world, not the darkness. I want to have a giving spirit like Lee Hardy. When my time here is done, I want to leave the world a better place. She has set an incredible example.

Proverbs 14:21 (ESV)
"Whoever despises his neighbor is a sinner, but blessed is he who is generous to the poor."

SHARK TOOTH HUNTER

*S*harks are amazing. They are, in my opinion, God's coolest underwater creatures. They are torpedo-shaped, armored, toothy killing machines at the top of the ocean's food chain. They are stealthy and sleek. They are dangerous and dazzling. They are incredible animals with so many mind-blowing characteristics. God was showing off when He made the ocean's top predators.

I'm an unashamed shark geek. This nerd session will continue now with a few quick shark facts:

There are over 500 known shark species in the world. They are basically made of the same material as your earlobe. The smallest shark, the pygmy shark, is just 17 centimeters long and the largest, the whale shark, is longer than a city bus. Sharks can be found in all seven oceans of the world and some live at depths beyond 6,000 feet. Sharks can detect a single drop of blood in an area of water the size of an Olympic swimming pool. Oh, and they eat basically anything. Scientists once dissected a tiger shark and found a full suit of armor in its belly. A suit of armor!

The best place to find stories are the places where you'd never expect them to appear. A co-worker of mine went to breakfast at a Bob Evans restaurant. He overheard the manager telling a waitress about how much he loved the lamp on his nightstand. Small talk led to a story idea. Scott Hand owned a glass lamp with hundreds of shark teeth inside. He made monthly trips to Venice Beach to go kayaking with a friend. They went in search of shark teeth! I called and asked Scott if I could tag along on his next trip. Thankfully, he agreed.

The teeth are the most fascinating part of the shark. The animals have a conveyor belt of chompers in there! Sharks will go through 3,000 teeth in their lifetimes. They have rows and rows of razor-sharp teeth ready to make quick work of fish flesh. They swallow their prey whole, so getting a good grip on their grub is important.

Venice Beach is known as the shark tooth capital of the world. Nobody really knows why that stretch of beach turns up the most shark teeth on the planet. Venice is located on Florida's west coast and attracts tourists from all over the country. I've taken my kids there! It's fun to dig around for fossilized incisors.

I prepped my camera as Scott unloaded two kayaks from his SUV. He walked them down to an area behind some mangrove trees where a small opening provided access to the Gulf of Mexico. I could hear the waves crashing against the exposed tree roots as I got a shot of Scott trudging through the sand with his second kayak hoisted on his shoulder. The salty sea air promised adventure. We loaded up and made our way across the water to a small inlet where the weaker waves didn't disturb the sand too much. Scott piled out of his kayak and started pacing the shoreline. His eyes never left his toes. The water was only a few inches deep and allowed him to see the sandy bottom clearly. He looked and looked and looked. After a few minutes of searching the sand, he found one. Scott snatched up a small, black triangular shape that looked a lot like a stumpy rock. He rolled it over in his hand. It was a fossilized shark tooth, aged after years of being tossed by the sea. He slipped it in his pocket and stared back down to his toes.

"I'm not the type of person who's going to sit on the beach and catch a tan. I get bored with it," he said. "There are some days I've come out and found ten teeth and other days I've found 900."

I was having fun documenting the search. We hopped back in the kayaks and paddled to another one of Scott's favorite hunting spots. We tied our boats off to the mangrove roots. I grabbed my camera out from the dry well. Scott grabbed his special tool.

"This is a Florida snow shovel," he joked.

Scott lived in New Hampshire for many years. There, you'd be wise to own a *real* snow shovel. His "Florida snow shovel" is essentially a sand strainer with a wire basket attached to the end of a long metal pole. It was perfect for scooping up clumps of wet sand, shells, and shark teeth. Scott waded out into the gulf and plunged his shovel into the sand. He returned to the shore with a soggy clump of earth. He emptied his shovel onto the beach and started inspecting the pile for shark teeth. Buried at the bottom was a gem he'd driven hours to find. Scott held up a tiny tooth that fit on the end of his finger. A smile spread across his face. One more tooth for his collection!

Scott and I harvested shark teeth from the ocean all day. Some were easily recognizable to my untrained eye while others just looked like rounded-off rocks. Scott gave me lessons in the differences between species' teeth. Some are serrated. Others are sleek and pointy. A few are curved back towards the shark's mouth to help guide prey down their throats. It was all very interesting. You can learn a lot about the animal just by examining its tooth. I learned a lot more about Scott after he told me how those tiny teeth were making a huge difference in the lives of kids "back home".

Scott's nephew, Stephen Molloy, was a teacher in New Hampshire. The two were chatting on the phone one day about all the fun new adventures Scott was having down in Florida. The topic of collecting shark teeth came up. Stephen was intrigued by the idea of *real* shark teeth washing up on the shore for anyone to find. It sparked an idea for Scott. At its fullest, Scott's glass lamp contained 10,000 shark teeth. Now, most of them sit in his nephew's elementary school classroom, 1,400 miles away, in the tiny New Hampshire town of Manchester.

Scott packed up thousands of shark teeth in cardboard boxes to ship up north. His nephew needed some motivation for his third-grade students during an ocean-themed unit that semester. The shark teeth were given out as prizes to students who studied hard in school and showed real enthusiasm for the ocean. Scott started getting thank you letters in the mail from kids he'd never met. The letters included photos of themselves holding his shark teeth. One showed a little boy proudly displaying a massive tooth in his outstretched arms. The jagged tooth nearly filled the entire palm of his hand.

"Just to see their face like, 'Wow, I want to find some!', it's awesome," said Scott.

He could have kept those tiny treasures but knew they had a powerful purpose. Scott used to gather teeth for himself. Now, he gathers to give. Those photos are the driving force behind Scott's monthly escapes to Venice Beach. The sun and relaxation are nice, too. Now that there is a mission fueling his hobby, he's never worked so hard to find penny-sized pieces of disposable shark bone. It was encouraging to me to see someone do such a selfless thing with his time. The third chapter of Hebrews demands that we encourage others. Verse 13 says "encourage each other daily". That's exactly what Scott is doing. He's encouraging by giving.

My wife used to teach in classrooms where the kids didn't see a lot of encouragement at home. There were days when the only positive interaction those students received was during the six hours in her care. Scott's shark teeth put smiles on faces of children he'll likely never meet. His impact can't be measured. Giving up a little bit of his time each month could lead to a lifelong passion for a New Hampshire third-grader. Maybe one of them will grow up and become a marine biologist someday. Maybe Scott's giving is sparking a career. Maybe his hobby is really his calling.

Galatians 6:9-10 (NLT)

"[9] So let's not get tired of doing what is good. At just the right time we will reap a harvest of blessing if we don't give up. [10] Therefore, whenever we have the opportunity, we should do good to everyone—especially to those in the family of faith."

WHAT'S IN THAT CLOSET?

*W*hen you think of a hospital, what descriptive word comes to mind first? Sickness? Needles? Doctors? All are perfectly understandable descriptors. When I think of hospitals, I think of the word *white*. Yep, like the color. Somewhere, somehow, someone must have sent out a memo to all the hospitals in the world demanding that everything be painted the same, boring hue. I think it's a stylistic requirement for every hospital to be painted white! There is no other shade that will do! It's neutral, but it's also a snooze for your eyes. White is generic. White is plain. White is just about as average as it gets. Heck, the hospital even smells a little white to me, if that's even possible.

I've spent plenty of time in hospitals for work. I highlighted a group of florists on the day they delivered their 50,000th free bouquet to sick patients. I shared the story of a nurse who delivered two generations of babies from one family. I've met children who have beaten cancer. I even met a young woman who, rather than requesting birthday presents each year, asked her party guests and family members to give cash donations to the Shriner's facility where she received care. Add in her charity fundraising donation dollars and sometime around her 18th birthday, that amazing kid surpassed $1 million in donations. The hospital put a plaque on its Wall of Fame in her honor.

Hospitals are interesting places. They are interesting (white) places with plenty of great stories, if you know where to look.

The day I met Becky Gama was memorable. The veteran nurse has spent her life helping people – no matter who they are. We walked down the long (white) corridor together at the hospital. Becky was wearing a microphone. We chatted a bit about her 11 years working in those halls. It was a special place to her. I'd pointed my camera towards a curved mirror on the roof. I used the angle to get a creative camera shot of us rounding the corner towards Becky's favorite spot in the building.

Our walk ended at a bustling intersection where two elevators, a breezeway, and the entrance to surgery rooms joined. Becky pulled a set of keys out of her nurse scrubs pocket and walked towards a closet door. It was tucked away near the elevator doors. It was almost unnoticeable. Becky slipped the key in the knob and opened the closet. She smiled as the doors swung open. I could see shelves and boxes filled with colorful clothing for men, women, and children of nearly every size and shape. There were even shoes on the floor. It really was impressive. Becky beamed with pride.

"Some people think I'm crazy," she joked. "It is pretty full."

Full was an understatement. More like jammed to the gills. Sweaters, pajamas and more sat ready for the picking. For five years, she had been accepting donations and putting aside a few bucks from her own paychecks to stock that closet. Her devotion to the closet came from a single encounter with a patient. That encounter changed her life.

"I've found that everyone has a story if you just listen," she said.

While working on the second floor, Becky realized the person she was treating was a little different than most of her patients. She got to talking with a scraggly man who eventually confided in her that he was homeless. He was grateful to be in her care. The hospital was his sanctuary that night and she was his lifeline. Becky and I stood in the crowded hallway in front of the open closet doors. She poured her heart out. I could tell she had built a connection with this patient. She explained that this gentleman refused her offers to help with basic needs. He didn't want to be a burden. He only asked her for a cup of coffee, but Becky felt like she could do more.

During that night's shift, Becky asked co-workers if they had any clothes they would be willing to donate to her patient. News of her request traveled to every floor of the hospital and by the next day, the donations came pouring in. When it was time for her patient to be discharged, Becky presented him with a few shirts and a sweater. She certainly was going above and beyond her typical nurse duties. That's what givers do. Givers willingly go above and beyond normal expectations. They seek and surpass expectations.

The experience sparked an idea for Becky. She and her daughter emptied their bank accounts and went to Target. They went to all the sale racks and cleaned out the clearance isles. They stocked up on shirts, shorts, and any other essential items she could afford. She filled up boxes with all her clothing items. She had so many things to give away to homeless patients that the hospital didn't know where to stash it all. The temporary space in the storage area wasn't sufficient and the boxes Becky used to pack all her clothing were overflowing onto the floor.

The idea to move the items to the closet provided a chance for growth. The closet started getting so full, it needed a proper name. "Becky's Closet" stuck. Nobody who passes by those double doors knows what sits behind them except for the people who work in the hospital. Becky has tried to run her pseudo-thrift store as quietly as possible to respect the situation of her homeless patients. It's been an abundant success and staff from almost every department on every floor contributes to "Becky's Closet" when they can.

"We have sleepwear, underwear, pretty much anything you could need," she said as she sifted through a crowded shelf. "We want to be able to send them out with at least one set of clothing that they're going to have.

I could not believe this woman's giving spirit. I think we all know what a blessing Goodwill or Salvation Army can be for people who need a little something. Essentially, Becky built her own Goodwill store inside her work environment after seeing the need in her community. Her giving spirit shined through and started to infiltrate the mannerisms of her hospital peers. Her generosity spilled over into everyone else. In just a few short years, "Becky's Closet" has helped countless people exit the hospital in better clothing than what they entered with a few days earlier!

Giving can become contagious. It's kind of odd to wish for something contagious to spread at a hospital, but as I pulled out of the parking lot that day I hoped Becky's attitude for helping others would spread like the plague. I wanted everyone to be infected! The actions of one woman were impacting an entire community. Never had a closet been so inviting.

Proverbs 22:9 (NIV)
"The generous will themselves be blessed, for they share their food with the poor."

◊

WHAT CAN BROWN DO FOR YOU?

The Jacob K. Javits Center is a mammoth, 1.8 million-square-foot structure that takes up six New York City blocks alongside the Hudson River. It's one of the largest convention centers in the world and is home to hundreds of exhibits each year from car shows to business events. In March 2012, the annual New York Times Travel Show was held at Javits. Countries from all over the world set up elaborate displays pitching their homelands as stunning, worthwhile destinations for your next getaway. Each nation chose a slogan to entice visitors to come see their mysterious land.

As I read about this event, this slogan mystified me:

"There's a Little Bit of Israel In All Of Us; Come Find the Israel in You"

Um, what does that mean? I don't get it. Is it God-related? I assume it's a reference to the beginning of faith. It's a little confusing. Slogans should be clear and concise. Israel's current travel slogan is, "Land of Creation". I like that better. According to Forbes, that 2012 travel campaign cost $10 million for the country to piece together. Who knows if that *"There's a Little Bit of Israel In All Of Us; Come Find the Israel In You"* line generated an influx of travelers. It got me wondering about slogans, though.

Some slogans are heard so frequently that we can immediately match them with their company:

McDonald's: *"I'm lovin it"*

M&Ms: *"Melts in your mouth, not in your hand"*

Nike: *"Just Do It"*

These were a little more peculiar:

Häagen-Dazs: *"Pleasure is the path to joy"*

The Red Cross: *"The greatest tragedy is indifference"*

Calvin Klein: *"Between love and madness lies obsession"*

Those are clever, if nothing else. One of the most recognizable slogans of my lifetime is now out of rotation. The United Parcel Service has been around 110 years and has only used six taglines since August 28, 1907. UPS now brands itself with the company phrase, "We Love Logistics". I guess when you have over 430,000 employees, getting the logistics right is pretty important. However, I preferred the slogan that was used from 2002 to 2010:

"What Can Brown Do For You?"

UPS went all-in on the change and debuted it during the broadcast of the opening ceremonies for the Olympic Winter Games in 2002. The company spent $45 million to re-brand itself based around those recognizable brown delivery trucks. Because of that, we can tell which company is dropping off packages just by looking at the vehicle in the driveway. No wonder the company chose to weave its iconic color into its now-retired, iconic slogan. It was a perfect fit.

In 2015, I got to see that old slogan come back to life in a way I never expected.

Friends, especially best friends, are often described as being 'true blue'. The better descriptor for Joe Clement and Noel Keesling's relationship is probably, 'true brown'. The duo has worked side-by-side for UPS for over 25 years. Nowadays, that's impressive. I don't know too many people who have stuck it out in the same profession with the same company for that long and still get joy out of heading to work each morning.

Noel met Joe when he joined UPS as a pre-loader in 1989. They spent long hours stacking, packing, and labeling boxes to be shipped all over the country. It was tough work. It was sweaty work. The diligent duo put on those brown pairs of shorts and matching shirts each morning and got the job done. Both men are blue-collar workers with a heart for hard work. In those early days, they would talk sports for hours while loading trucks. They'd even grab a beer after work and watch ball games.

When they graduated to new posts behind the steering wheels of delivery trucks, they didn't see as much of each other. Joe and Noel would show up at the loading center to collect their packages for the day before heading out on separate routes. The days of chatting side-by-side were over. They worked in the same county most days but hardly ever saw each other anymore. As they got older, they got married and added kids to their respective families. Life got even busier. They saw each other even less. Their friendship was still there but the opportunities to enjoy it had dwindled. It's amazing what finally reconnected them.

I chuckled a bit when I first met these guys at the local UPS office. They could not have looked much different. Noel is a buff former Marine. The buttons on his shirt practically scream for help trying to stay fastened over all the muscles. Joe looks a lot like me. He is a tall, lean guy whose shirt could probably use a safety pin to keep it fitting snuggly. The only shared characteristics between the two men were those brown uniforms and their graying mustaches. After all those loyal years, they had developed a trust with each other. They shared many of life's triumphs and problems, too.

In December 2012, Noel discovered he had a big problem. This one couldn't be fixed with packing tape.

"Renal kidney failure. Complete kidney failure," he told me, seated on the bumper of a delivery truck. "I was kind of like, 'What? Really? Are you kidding me?'"

Pain followed. There were days when the once-fit man felt like he'd never be well again. He used to run triathlons. During treatments, sitting up in bed was a struggle. Noel endured a month in the hospital. His kidney dialysis lasted 8½ hours, seven days a week, for two years. It left his body weakened and stunned. None of it repaired his damaged body. He was stuck in complete kidney failure with only one option. Noel needed a transplant and stay alive.

I've never had an organ replaced but it sounds quite scary. The tough part for folks in Noel's position is the constant uncertainty of the process. Transplants can be hard to come by. It takes a perfect match. It takes a person with a transferable, working organ who is willing to give it up to save the life of, in many cases, a stranger. It takes a giving person to even become a donor. Approximately 3,000 new patients in the United States are added to the kidney transplant wait list every day. That's one person every 14 minutes. Noel was made well aware of the sad statistics and knew he didn't want to become one. He was also aware that he was running out of options. For over two years, from the time of his diagnosis in late 2012 to the beginning of 2015, nearly everyone in Noel's family was tested. No one was a match. In 2014 alone, 4,761 people died while awaiting a kidney and 3,668 more patients became too sick to receive one. Becoming a statistic was becoming more likely for Noel. Every morning he woke up nauseous, he was reminded of what would happen if he didn't get a transplant soon. It was a constant barrage of tension. Negativity lurked in his life. He just needed one person to give the perfect kidney. To try and keep his mind off his failing health, to help him persevere through the pain, Noel continued to put on his brown uniform and go to work. He suffered through grueling daily routines of treatment, work, sleep, repeat. He wondered if it would ever pay off.

Imagine the thoughts that went through his head. Imagine the 'what if?' game he constantly lost. Imagine the hopelessness he must have felt each day during those 8 ½ hour treatments. Persevering through that takes major courage. More than courage, it takes hope. It takes faith! When every family member's blood that was tested came back as incompatible, it must have felt like he was one jab closer to his knockout blow. He was getting pounded with rejection. He was getting slammed with dismissals. Imagine the uncertainty he lived with each day.

Imagine, too, the joy he felt one morning when his longtime friend shared incredible news. Joe casually walked by Noel in the UPS hallway and told him he'd found him a kidney.

"He went and got tested and it shocked me," said Noel. "I got tears in my eyes and I'm not easy to do that."

Joe had grown tired of hoping for a solution for his friend. He was sick of looking at Noel's shriveling frame. He wanted to make a difference, so he went and got his blood tested. Doctors told Joe his kidney could be transplanted to Noel. What an amazing feeling it must have been to learn that they were a match! What an even better feeling to get to tell your buddy the good news! Sour headlines dominate our lives. This was a sweet success! Joe was potentially able to save Noel's life. He found it in his heart to give what he had to help someone in need. This wasn't giving someone a few bucks or loaning a neighbor a tent for a camping trip. Joe was going to willingly let someone cut open his side and yank out an organ! God put that kidney there for a reason. The reason was to save Noel Keesling.

Joe had a great example to follow for his life-changing decision. He told me he was inspired to go get checked out by the doctor because of his wife, Jodie. A few years prior to Noel's diagnosis, one of Jodie's friends went into kidney failure, too. She made the decision to donate her kidney to save her best friend's life. Now, both Clements would have just a pair of kidneys between them.

"I asked the doctor what the odds were of that and he said, 'One in a million,'" she told me. "I said, 'No, really. What are the odds?', and he said, 'One in a million'. It becomes a bond that no one can understand."

Joe has made thousands of deliveries in his lifetime. His biggest came on April Fool's Day 2015. No joke. The transplant surgery was successful that day. Joe's kidney now lives in Noel's body. The two recovered together in the hospital room by, how else, watching old episodes of the *'Friends'* sitcom. What an appropriate way to celebrate providing a second chance on life with a best buddy.

"We're blood brothers now," joked Joe.

Noel returned to work five weeks after surgery. He and Joe ride bikes together and are closer now than even in those early preloading days. I'd like to think God had a hand in putting Joe and Noel on the same packing line back in 1989. I would like to think that they were in each other's wedding parties for a reason. I'd like to think that God knew brown would look good on them. To give of oneself is the ultimate loving trait. To do it the way Joe did, it doesn't get much more special. For 25 years, working side-by-side, the duo had formed a bond as strong as brothers. Even though life changes pulled them in opposite directions for a while, the two men were always connected by a solid friendship. That selfless connection turned out to be a life-saving one.

"*What Can Brown Do For You?*" is a great slogan. In the case of the two UPS delivery men I met for my *On The Road* segment, the answer is, save a life.

Philippians 2:3-4 (NIV)

"Do nothing out of selfish ambition or vain conceit. Rather, in humility value others above yourselves, not looking to your own interests but each of you to the interests of the others."

CLOSING THOUGHTS ON GIVING

Mark was not one of Jesus' 12 disciples, but he accompanied Paul on his first missionary journey. Mark was an observer and a man who didn't waste words. His gospel book is the shortest of the four and is full of facts. The gospel of Mark includes an interesting story only seen one other place in scripture. He records Jesus' lesson about a widow's sacrificial gift. It is an incredible example of giving. Squeezing it into his short book tells me that this is a lesson worth paying attention to.

> ### Mark 12:41-44 (NIV)
> *"⁴¹ Jesus sat down opposite the place where the offerings were put and watched the crowd putting their money into the temple treasury. Many rich people threw in large amounts. ⁴² But a poor widow came and put in two very small copper coins, worth only a few cents. ⁴³ Calling his disciples to him, Jesus said, "Truly I tell you, this poor widow has put more into the treasury than all the others. ⁴⁴ They all gave out of their wealth; but she, out of her poverty, put in everything—all she had to live on."*

I can imagine what life was like for this woman. In this time period, women did not work and relied on their husbands to provide for them. We don't know if she had any sons to help her. It's very likely that these copper coins were the only thing she owned in the world. She gave them freely and hopefully. I'm not suggesting you should sell your house and give all the money to the local church. I do think this story portrays a beautiful message to those of us trying to live like Jesus. This widow gave with proper motivation in her heart. She knew her gift, even as tiny as it was compared to the other rich men in the room, had the power to change lives. We are called to give according to our abilities and not worry about comparing contributions. That means give what you can and give with a willing spirit.

I didn't have a lot of money back in my college days. What I had was time. My roommate and I decided to give up some of our free time to coach a middle school basketball team. The league played its games at the church where we attended services. I thought it would be fun! We were not very good. I blame my assistant coach. What mattered more than victories were the relationships we built in those few hours each week. I remember talking to players who didn't have much else to look forward to outside of basketball. We hung out with them and shot free throws. We made them feel important. All it required was for us to give what we had – time.

You may not be in a position to give a few extra dollars to non-profits each month. You may not be able to give up a weeknight to mentor a kid. You may not be able to go on a missions trip for two weeks. But, we all have something we can offer. God implanted a talent in you. Some of us are great teachers. Some are great communicators. Some are great listeners. Are you willing to give by using your talent this week? It will bless someone. I promise you.

God is the ultimate giver. He gave us His son as the roadmap to Heaven. God poured talents and abilities into each of us and expects us to use them for Him! Start small and gradually give more when you're able. It can be hard to find motivation. The news headlines tend to be all about takers. Lead stories don't typically feature giving. The easiest way to find good news is to look for the people doing the most giving.

Lee Hardy will be a giver until the day she dies. She has a heart for others and has made it her mission to provide Easter baskets for kids in her neighborhood. Think of all the money she's poured into her community over the last 13 years. She's given a lot, but it's not the amount that matters. It's the heart behind the baskets. She's someone who wants to make a difference. She truly is.

Scott Hand loved collecting shark teeth but found out he loved his hobby even more once he started to give those teeth away. He's lost count of how many teeth he's shipped up to New Hampshire, but each one led to a smile. The purpose of giving is to please others. Scott learned that giving provides a great feeling, too. He'll keep hunting and kids will keep smiling.

Becky Gama's life was forever changed by her decision to help a stranger. She pleaded with coworkers for clothing donations and was able to give a homeless man a new outfit he desperately needed. The giving didn't stop there. She now has an entire closet stuffed with clean clothes to give to any hospital patient who needs them. Her giving inspired an entire hospital to begin looking for ways to donate.

UPS drivers Joe Clement and Noel Keesling never thought that their friendship would reach this level. When Noel needed a life-saving organ donation, Joe volunteered to give up one of his kidneys to save his best buddy. The bond between them is unbreakable and built on giving. For over 25 years, they've had each other's back. Now, Noel has Joe's kidney, too.

It's easier to see God working in this world when we adopt an attitude of giving. Consumers get the headlines. Contributors get God's blessing. If you want to be more giving, start hanging out with more givers! Behavior is contagious, and giving routinely pleases our Heavenly Father. God doesn't care much for bad news. He is a God of good news! I am thankful that He has led me to stories of a few wonderful people who know exactly what benefits come from giving.

VERSES ON GIVING

2 Corinthians 9:11 (NLT)

"Yes, you will be enriched in every way so that you can always be generous. And when we take your gifts to those who need them, they will thank God."

Philippians 4:9 (NIV)

"Whatever you have learned or received or heard from me, or seen in me—put it into practice. And the God of peace will be with you."

Mark 12:41-44 (NIV)

"And (Jesus) sat down opposite the treasury, and began observing how the people were putting money into the treasury; and many rich people were putting in large sums. A poor widow came and put in two small copper coins, which amount to a cent. Calling His disciples to Him, He said to them, "Truly I say to you, this poor widow put in more than all the contributors to the treasury; for they all put in out of their surplus, but she, out of her poverty, put in all she owned, all she had to live on.""

PERSEVERANCE

*E*vil is everywhere. I don't think I'm breaking any news with that statement. You were subjected to evil today the moment you opened your eyes and registered a pulse. There is no escaping evil. We are bombarded with terrible images, thoughts, and actions every day of every week. I don't have to convince you. The headlines can do that:

> *October 1, 2017: "Las Vegas Shooting: 59 Killed and*
> *More Than 500 Hurt Near Mandalay Bay"*

The deadliest mass shooting in United States history sends people shrieking into the night during a country music concert. The gunman fired shots from a nearby hotel window. He took his own life.

> *October 5, 2017: "Harvey Weinstein accused of*
> *sexual harassment in New York"*

The well-known Hollywood movie man is accused of inappropriate behavior with countless actresses over a period of decades. Dozens of women surface with similar stories after the initial report. A Pandora's box of sexual misconduct is opened across multiple American business sectors as a result.

> *October 30, 2017: "8 killed as truck plows into*
> *pedestrians in downtown NYC"*

A man driving a U-HAUL truck rams innocent people walking on a busy sidewalk. He didn't show much remorse from his hospital bed. The attack went according to plan.

November 5, 2017: "At least 26 dead in church shooting"

Barely a month removed from the Vegas nightmare, a tiny town in rural Texas lost almost 10 percent of its population when a man barged into a Sunday morning service and began shooting. He later died from a gunshot wound while trying to escape the scene.

November 11, 2017: "7.3 Magnitude Earthquake Jolts Area Around Iran-Iraq Border"

Over 450 people died in one of the strongest earthquakes on record. Thousands more were injured. This came just two months after a quake killed over 200 people in Central Mexico.

This is just a 42-day sample size of terrible news headlines. If I expanded the headline search out to a full year, this book would be a lot thicker. Those are national and global headlines. Imagine what kind of horrors were reported *locally* during those six weeks!

Hearing horrible news leaves us looking for a place of comfort. That fork in the road is where most people leave God behind. When terrible things happen, people ask questions like, 'Where was God?' and 'How could a loving God allow this?'. We forget that God is there in the chaos. God doesn't turn His eyes away from us on messy days. He stretches out his mighty, comforting hands further to help console us. Unfortunately, not everyone reaches back. Bad news is going to continue to grab a majority of the press. Will you panic or persevere?

I'm so thankful I get to find and tell bright stories in a dark world. My job gives me the opportunity to break up those negative feelings that weigh us down following horrendous news. It may not seem like it, but I promise you good news happened today. It may not be the first thing you hear about, but God did something awesome today. He provided a rainbow for a single mom at her weakest moment. He made a connection for the dad struggling to keep his business running. He sent a friend to a widow's side on the anniversary of her husband's death. God is working, even if you don't see it. These were the *On The Road* stories from the same dates as those earlier headlines:

October 1, 2017: "Firefighter's Run Honors Co-worker's Fallen Brother"

John Robinson, a local firefighter and Marine veteran, ran the Tunnel 2 Towers 5K in New York City to honor the brother of his firehouse captain, who died in the 9/11 terrorist attacks. He ran in his full uniform, just like the first responders did the morning the USA was attacked.

October 5, 2017: "Swimmer Competes With Lost Coach in Her Heart"

Isabel Minnis became the first swimmer in the history of her high school to advance to the county championship meet. Her motivation to reach that goal, and to eventually earn a college scholarship, was born out of the tragedy of her coach's death five years earlier.

October 30, 2017: "Lemons and Cycling Could Help Save Toddler's Life"

A local nurse pledged to ride his bicycle across the Sunshine State in three days to raise awareness for a rare disorder affecting a dying child he read about online. He stopped at four hospitals and asked employees there to bite a lemon and post sour-faced photos to social media so ill kids could see them and smile.

November 5, 2017: "BBQ Restaurant Hires All-Kid Staff"

A Kansas City BBQ champion-turned Florida restauranteur decided to hire all high school kids. The opportunity offers the teenagers a chance to decide if a career in the culinary world would suit them. He gets to mentor students and keep them out of trouble.

November 11, 2017: "Moffitt Honors WWII, 2-Time Cancer Survivor"

The day before Veteran's Day, a world-renown cancer hospital threw a party for a man who survived the Japanese air attack on Pearl Harbor in

1941. He would later beat cancer twice! At 96 years old, George Kondas is a military hero.

I am in no way saying that my positive human interest stories are more important than the catastrophic events between October 1 and November 11, 2017. But, I do think they are important. They are important reminders of how God is working in our world on the days we think He's absent. People were shot in Las Vegas the same day a firefighter honored his friend by running in New York. Don't get so lost in the headlines that you miss God's blessed appearances. He's a God of good news! Life is about perspective and perseverance. The feel-good stories help us keep perspective on the reality of news and persevere past the sad stuff that gets so much of the attention. If we allow our minds to absorb only the darkest headlines, our hearts will become hardened to the truth – that there is a lot of good out there waiting to be uncovered. Light is stronger than the darkness and good stories can drown out bad ones, even on the same day.

I firmly believe what is written in the first chapter of James. He comes out of the gates hard! He was the half-brother of Jesus. He saw firsthand that life wasn't going to be a cakewalk. He knew that, occasionally, there would be a headline or two that would make you want to cry, scream, and give up at the same time. He also knew that good can come from those headlines.

James 1:2-4 (NIV)
"² Dear brothers and sisters, WHEN troubles of any kind come your way, consider it an opportunity for great joy. ³ For you know that WHEN your faith is tested, your endurance has a chance to grow. ⁴ So let it grow, for WHEN your endurance is fully developed, you will be perfect and complete, needing nothing."

The key word is "when". Notice James didn't write "if" troubles come our way. Ugly headlines are inevitable. He would know! He wrote his book to new Christians who scattered after Jesus' death because of intense persecution. If you claimed to follow Jesus, you signed your death certificate. You think our news is bad? Followers of Jesus were beheaded, stoned, and burned alive. Faith in Jesus required incredible perseverance. It still does.

Life got hard the moment Adam and Eve took a bite of forbidden fruit. It remained hard when God's people were enslaved for hundreds of years in Egypt and when King Herod murdered thousands of children, hoping to slay the chosen 'King of the Jews'. It was clear that life was hard when that newborn king grew up and accepted nails in His hands and feet to save us. But, there is good news. Opportunities to grow our faith come through standing strong in adversity. The *reason* something happened doesn't matter. Our *response* is what matters.

I met a woman whose son died a few months into his life. I sat at her dining room table as she showed me a framed photo of her boy. His little smile left no indication of the disease that was attacking his body. She had to bury that child. Instead of letting that horrendous life-altering event cripple her, she decided to volunteer to bake and decorate cakes for critically-ill children who are stuck in the hospital on their birthday – for free. How is that for a Godly response! That's powerful perseverance! Most of the time, the people I interview never see the sad news coming. What catches my attention is how they persevere through their trial. Perseverance can be hard, but it's not impossible. Awful news doesn't have to paralyze us. It doesn't have to be anything more than a pebble on the highway to happiness God has paved for you. I want to share triumphant recovery stories!

2 Chronicles 20:17 (NASB)
"You need not fight in this battle; station yourselves, stand and see the salvation of the LORD on your behalf, O Judah and Jerusalem.' Do not fear or be dismayed; tomorrow go out to face them, for the LORD is with you."

God didn't say our lives would be filled with unicorns and glitter. He guaranteed us there would be tough times in life. James wrote about it. WHEN you have troubles. WHEN your faith is tested. Sad news is going to happen, but God promised to walk with us through those days and never leave our side. If necessary, He'll scoop us up and get us to the finish line himself. You aren't walking through tough times alone. In fact, sharing your story with others can really make a difference. That's why I enjoy sharing perseverance stories. They are everywhere! I see God in those victories. When we face trials and setbacks in life, God is there, giving us the grace, strength, and drive required to get out of the pit. God is just like a loving parent urging a toddler to walk. It will be wobbly. There will be moments of concern. But, He will be right there to catch us as we fall.

Jackson Carter was diagnosed with a rare former of cancer at nine years old. He needed 22 rounds of chemotherapy to beat the disease. The following summer, with his hair all grown back, the fourth-grader decided to host a lemonade stand. When word got out that the little cancer conqueror was selling lemonade and intended to donate the money to the Pediatric Cancer Foundation, minivans started flooding Jackson's neighborhood. The line extended down the block! In all, young Jackson donated over $2,500 to cancer research in one summer! Now that's good news that bloomed out of perseverance.

After doing an *On The Road* story with Jackson, his mom asked me if I would like to emcee a fundraising gala for a local hospital where her son received treatment. I was honored to do it. I got to share Jackson's story of perseverance and resiliency. I asked those in attendance to find it in their hearts to support a hospital and a child that had beaten the odds. That night, enough money was raised to buy a new ambulance for the hospital.

What a comeback story! God is good! And, He doesn't want you to get sidetracked. You're meant to persevere. There is a devil who wants you to crumble under the pressure of your situation, but God is there in the weak moments. God was there for the woman who lost her son. God was there for Jackson's chemo treatments. He's here with you now.

Psalm 112:7 (NLT)
"They do not fear bad news; they confidently trust the Lord to care for them."

You'll read about people in this chapter who understand how hard life can be when the devil starts throwing curveballs. You'll also read about how they won a great victory over their situations by persevering through them. Holly and Brian Festa went to great lengths to build a family. For the longest time, it looked like it would never happen. The Orban family always had Bill around for Christmas. It just wasn't the same without him. Remembering his lessons and pushing through the pain helped make the season merrier for their community. Al Vaughan thought his once-mighty body may not be strong enough to conquer cancer. He had enough muscle. What he needed was a miracle. God provided. Eric Piburn has so much joy in his heart. Unfortunately, he needs a new one. He perseveres every day, waiting to see if an answer to prayer will come. In the meantime, he's glued to his favorite TV show and I got to help him meet his heroes.

The devil cannot destroy you. He can only distract you. If you stay focused on God's plan for your life, the devil doesn't have a fighting chance to derail you. When you persevere, it gives God his chance to author your comeback story.

A FIGHT FOR FAMILY

*T*here is no delicate way to ask people how they are feeling on the worst day of their lives. If you have even a sliver of a soul, those interviews are excruciating. I can recall the first one I did as a fresh-out-of-college reporter living in Louisiana. A family near our TV station lost everything in a house fire. I remember driving around town with my manager and seeing smoke rising over the trees. We got there just in time to whip out the camera and record the firefighters dousing the flames. Luckily, nobody was there. As I expected, I was asked to go back to the charred shell of a house the next morning to capture the family's emotions as they returned home to find that a fire had consumed their possessions.

I have always viewed that sort of opportunistic reporting as unnecessary and wicked. What do you expect them to say? They just lost EVERYTHING. It's probably not a good day for them. They just became homeless. Sticking a microphone in their faces is cruel. That's a human being on the other side of the lens with raw emotions and real pain. The whole idea of interviewing people in that moment is idiotic to me. But, it provides a headline for the top of the newscast:

"A local family is devastated tonight after a fire consumed their home"

I didn't want to do an interview that would end with tears on TV. As a new reporter, I had no choice. I remember driving up to the house and smelling the smoky wallpaper from a block away. It stung my nostrils. Everything the fire left behind was black and crunchy. I can still visualize where I was standing. I was a few feet off the curb between the mailbox and the leftovers from the porch. I held out a microphone as a woman tearfully told me exactly what I thought she would say. She was devastated. I tried to end the interview quickly. It was the proper thing to do. I got a weird feeling leaving that place knowing I was going to broadcast that family's misery to the whole city.

In the summer of 2014, I did something I would never wish upon any journalist. I met a family at the beach to discuss the heartache of losing their child. I'd been forced to ask tough questions before, but this was a different kind of tough. It's one thing to ask questions about burned up furniture. That can be replaced. It's totally different to ask about an irreplaceable life. I was a new parent at the time. I could not possibly put myself in Holly and Brian Festa's position. It was gut-wrenching to hear their story. As the waves crashed against the shoreline behind her, Holly wiped away tears. Recalling those final moments with her precious baby girl must have been agonizing.

Sawyer Festa died after just four days on earth. A lung defect took her home to Heaven.

Reports of families losing children are hard to swallow for me. That kind of news makes me want to scream and punch and kick and cry and shut off my brain to the pain. Since I'm personally removed from the reality of the lost child, eventually, I can. But, the shattered parents can't. Holly and Brian will live the rest of their lives wondering what Sawyer's laugh would have sounded like. They will wonder if she would have been a loving sister. They will wonder what she would look like in a prom dress, blowing out birthday candles, or swimming at the same beach where we were standing.

It doesn't exactly sound like an encouraging *On The Road*-type story, does it? It wasn't, until I learned about the incredible messages the Festas received from strangers. Those messages help them persevere.

I was put in touch with Holly's sister, Heidi. She, also being a new parent, was distraught over the loss of her little niece. Our introduction via email directed me to a website that Heidi built titled SawyersCrossing.com. I clicked on the link and marveled at the photos. Heidi left this personal message for site visitors:

> *"Sawyer was my niece. She was born on May 29, 2014 with pulmonary hypoplasia (i.e. severely underdeveloped lungs). She lived for only four days, but those four days mattered. She mattered.*

She arrived a few weeks shy of her due date. My sister and brother-in-law were as prepared for her entrance as any new parents could be.

She was beautiful. She had dark hair, her mother's nose and her father's ears. She fought as hard as she could for as long as she could. She was born to two of the sweetest people you'll ever meet. They loved their daughter deeply, though she was only with them briefly.

When my sister was pregnant I would fantasize about chasing Sawyer up and down the beach. I'd picture her running to keep up with her three-year-old cousin, my son Henry.

The day after she died, I took Henry to Pass-a-Grille Beach in St. Petersburg, Florida. We swam in the warm gulf, collected shells and watched a school of stingrays glide along the shore. I soaked up every solitary second of this solitary moment knowing full well that our lives are fleeting, whether we're here for days or decades.

Henry and I stayed well past sunset. As the sun dipped behind the horizon, we wrote Sawyer's name in the sand. We stood there until the water lapped it away."

Her words jumped off the screen at me. My mind wandered to the scene of her sandy day. I know exactly where she was standing. It's a well-known patch of beach that caresses the doorway of a prominent seafood restaurant on Florida's west coast. People come from all over the state to dine there and enjoy breathtaking sunsets. Only, on that day, Heidi didn't come to gaze at God's beautiful sun-kissed sky. She came to mourn. She came to honor her niece the only way she knew how.

S-A-W-Y-E-R

She probably scratched those letters into the sand through tear-filled eyes. Unthinkable tragedy had found her sister. The six simple letters in the sand must have felt so insignificant at the time. Heidi had no idea what an uplifting spark she had just ignited. The waves would eventually wash Sawyer's name away, but the impact of that special child's name was only beginning. Heidi went home and posted a picture of Sawyer's name in the sand on the internet.

I scrolled through the website some more and began smiling wider with each click of the mouse. Its photo gallery featured Heidi's original picture along with dozens of others that strangers snapped and sent to her from across the globe. People saw Heidi's shot and were moved. It was a photo of Sawyer's name, birth date, and death date, along with a heart in the sand. Touched by the scene, strangers recreated it in their own environments. Sawyer's name was written in the sand of Gordons Bay, South Africa and on a notecard in Brooklyn, New York. It was formed with seashells in Rhode Island and folded into origami in Tokyo. One family even used their bodies to create S-A-W-Y-E-R for a photo in Black Rock City, Nevada. All these pictures flooded Heidi's email and she decided to share them with her sister. She then shared them with the world on the Sawyer's Crossing website. Sawyer was gone, but support for the family had shown up from multiple continents. It was the encouragement the Festas needed. It was the springboard to perseverance.

Turbulence is inevitable in life. When trying to persevere, it helps to have a co-pilot. A shoulder to cry on can serve as a solid crutch. Brian and Holly were slowly absorbing the blow. Nothing was going to bring back their precious daughter, but knowing that people around the world were sharing their heartache meant a lot. Through long odds, the Festas persevered through the loss of a child.

They had no idea they would have to do it again.

Just 18 months after Sawyer's death, Adelyse Sawyer Festa was born. She greeted the world on October 6, 2015 at 8 pounds and 20.5 inches. She had her sister's memory written into her birth certificate in the form of her middle name. She had a cute little smile and warm, inviting eyes. Holly carefully counted all the toes and was reassured by doctors that this child did not have the same debilitating lung defect that caused Sawyer's body to fail her so quickly.

Holly and Brian are both school teachers. Holly returned to work on a Monday and answered every joyful question from co-workers about little "Addie". The same happened for Brian at his school. Their daughter was their pride. She was their special gift. She was Holly and Brian's second chance to be parents. All day on Monday, the giddy couple gushed about their precious child. Tuesday, January 5, 2016, started the same way but took a terrible turn. A daycare worker called and told Brian that Addie had stopped breathing. Panic set in. Fear followed. Addie never woke up from her nap. She died from Sudden Infant Death Syndrome. It was the second time Holly and Brian held a dead child.

Two years after we met on the beach to talk about losing Sawyer, the Festas willingly opened their home to me to talk about losing Addie. They wanted me there, but it was still a tough space to enter. There is a noticeable thickness in the air when something like this happens. It's like a rain cloud in the room. There is no way for me to relate to their pain, but it's my job to ask the questions that will properly convey their story. It's a difficult topic to approach. I had questions to ask, but all I really wanted to do was hug these poor people. I felt so bad for them. I sat in their living room and mourned with them. I had no idea what to say. I'm not a crier, but there was good reason to sob. Holly opened her heart to me as she clutched Brian's hand. Photos of their two daughters hung over their shoulders on the living room wall.

"When I got the call, it was the daycare provider hysterically screaming, 'She's not breathing!', and it was probably the worst day of my life," Holly said through tears. An experienced journalist understands when to cut in with another question and when to, professionally speaking, shut up. I hate stale air. I don't like silence. I naturally want to fill it. But, in this case, I had to bite my tongue and let her get out whatever it was that she needed to get out without interrupting her thoughts.

After a few sniffles, and a long pause, she continued.

"It was a complete shock. It's like the worst nightmare. It's the one thing I feared most. You hear about it but you think, 'It couldn't be me. How could it happen? We've already had one pass. How could it happen twice that we've lost a child?' I almost thought it was a joke. I thought it was a sick joke. It was only after, I don't know, two weeks, three weeks that it went on, that I realized it wasn't a sick joke. That it really happened. Two very rare things happened to us. There's no explanation for it."

It's like my mouth didn't work anymore. She stared at me with a pained look in her watery eyes. She was reliving the moment she received that phone call for my camera. I try to prepare for conversations like hers but there really isn't a way to prepare for an emotional response like this. It was like someone woke me up at 3 a.m. and slapped me in the face. I had no idea what to do. The human side of me wanted to embrace this woman. The storyteller-side of me wanted to capitalize on the moment by asking a follow-up question. I was torn. I had a job to do but also had a broken family sitting just a few feet in front of me. Brian and Holly showed me the two bedside memorials that hang on the wall in their room. Pictures of their girls hung next to stuffed animals and angels. Collectively, Sawyer and Addie were alive for less than 100 days. I was incredibly impressed with how Holly and Brian handled themselves during my few hours with them that evening. I expected them to be an emotional wreck. Maybe they were on the inside and just hid it from me well. I have a feeling these tragedies have taught them to be brave out of necessity. They were forced to face their sadness head-on. Even when indescribable pain was pushing back, they had to move forward. The had to persevere. They had to trust God that everything would be okay.

Perseverance isn't easy. Anyone who tells you it is is probably lying. It's especially tough when there is no explanation for the tragic events that required perseverance. Brian and Holly's dreams of a big family, with festive, happy holidays, wasn't coming true. Instead, it seemed like they were stuck at the intersection of heartbreak and disaster. After years of hoping for a child, their first baby only survived four days. Then, after they were given a second child to love and cherish, she died before her first birthday.

Picking yourself up after tragedy isn't about forgetting what happened. It's about showing the world you can survive waves of evil and thrive in their wake.

Thankfully, that wasn't the last chapter penned about the Festas. After months and months of working overtime, selling anything they could find, and even hosting painting parties, Brian and Holly finally saved enough money for an adoption. I went to one of their painting events. Holly, an art buff, taught a group of women how to paint a festive martini glass on canvas.

"It's for a good cause, right?" one woman told me as Holly demonstrated the next brush stroke. Brian quietly counted $20 bills in the corner. Each one got them a little closer to their goal. They didn't reach it alone, either. The Festas got hundreds of dollars in donations, too. They were finally going to have the family they wanted. In April 2017, a baby boy was born. The Festas were a family of three, again.

I was so happy for them. Adoption is something that my wife and I have discussed as a possibility for ourselves someday. The Bible says taking care of orphans and widows is "true religion". I'm a big believer in helping those who can't help themselves. All children need of a loving home. Brian and Holly had more than enough love to share. I was so pumped they adopted a son! I texted Holly to congratulate her and she surprised me with bigger news. She was pregnant! They welcomed little Tatum Festa to the world on September 27, 2017. She is a healthy and happy answer to prayer. So is her adopted big brother.

When life gets hard, you can either fly or you can try. You can fly away from your problems and attempt to ignore them. You can shut yourself off emotionally and try to forget your pain. Or, you can try to do your best to press on through sorrows. God holds your hand when it's trembling. He guides your steps when your confidence is shaky. He wants you to get through this. It might mean asking for others to help. It won't be easy to be vulnerable, but persevering is about embracing and surpassing. It's about accepting and conquering. It's about having faith to endure trials. It's about looking your obstructions in the eye and remembering that there is a God in Heaven who understands your hurt and wants to carry you through it. I promise He has great things waiting for you on the other side.

Romans 12:12 (NLT)
"Rejoice in our confident hope. Be patient in trouble, and keep on praying."

100,000 POINSETTIAS

The toughest part of my job is just finding a good story. I get phone calls and emails all the time asking me to share a story about a quirky business that "everyone has to hear about". Typically, it is not worth going. If the hardest part of my job is finding good stories, the second hardest part is explaining to people why I don't think the rest of the viewing public will care about their idea as much as they do. I'm in the *unique* business. I want to find one-of-a-kind stories. Re-hashing something we've already seen doesn't appeal to me. Another Christmas parade? Why should I care? Little league all-star? Snooze. For me to care, it's got to stand out.

In 2016, I got an email telling me I needed to visit a local nursery that grew poinsettias to sell each year around Christmas. I did some checking. It turns out this was not new. This was a family farm that had been in business in our area for decades. In fact, this was the 26th-consecutive year they planned to do a drive-thru poinsettia sale at Christmas time. It was an area tradition that seemed like it wasn't fresh enough to warrant a new story. I could have deleted the email and moved on. Something made me want to dig a little more. I'm so happy that I did.

Orban's Nursery is in the Christmas business. They have been family-owned since 1914. The company originally began as a tiny flower shop near Cleveland. Four generations later, Orban's Nursery is now a 20-acre farm that grows over 100,000 tropical poinsettias each year. I called the phone number listed on the nursery's website. I figured with all that tradition, it was at least worth a call. Marty Orban answered.

"Mr. Orban, I'd like to ask you a little bit about your nursery," I said. He seemed rushed. I bet he was, considering there was an annual drive-thru sale to plan and flowers to prep. This was a busy time of year for the Orbans.

As we chatted, I got a better feel for who the family was, but still wasn't sure if there was a story there. Then Marty, the third-generation Orban to run the farm, provided the answer.

"We just put up a little memorial for dad," said Marty. His tone of voice lowered. "He lived a great life."

Bingo. There was my story. Bill Orban, Marty's dad, passed away just three months prior to that phone call. He was the heart and soul of the nursery. He brought the business down from Ohio and introduced a passion for flowers to his son. They worked side-by-side for years and had many successful Christmases. Bill was dearly missed by his family and by many people not named Orban. This would be the first Christmas season he would not be around to share the joyful time of year with his many kids and grandkids. I had a story.

I arranged a time to come and meet Marty and his son, Tyler. I wanted to get there before the big drive-thru sale. If I could get the story done before their event, maybe it would drum up some business for them. We agreed to meet at the poinsettia patch around midday when the petals were soaking up the December sun.

I pulled into the long driveway and immediately noticed there was red everywhere. Huge patios filled with flowers lined both sides of the road as I slowly rolled up the concrete entrance to the farm. I had been a little skeptical of the plant total I'd read about online. It said the Orbans grew 100,000 poinsettias per year. By the looks of all that red, there was no doubt that figure was accurate. I parked the car outside a long trailer that housed Marty's office. A towering barn with a Christmas wreath shaded my car.

Marty emerged from the trailer with a grin on his face. We shook hands and he invited me inside. Despite it being just a few days shy of Christmas, Marty was dressed in shorts and a t-shirt. Sweat was beading up on his brow already. He introduced me to his wife, Becky. She was a lovely woman but had no interest in being on camera. I assured her I wouldn't ask too many tough questions. She wouldn't budge.

The inside of the trailer looked a lot like a bowling alley. There was a lot of wood paneling and it smelled musty. It was a bit of a mess but that's to be expected for a business that makes most of its money during the Christmas season. My eyes were immediately drawn to a framed newspaper clipping on the wall.

"He had a great memory," said Marty.

Bill Orban was named Manatee Country Agriculturist of the Year in 2013. The local newspaper article announcing the honor hung on the wall of the nursery office. Next to it hung a photo of Bill. His presence was still felt just a few weeks after his passing. On the opposite wall, Marty glanced at order forms hanging on clipboards. There was a lot of work to be done.

We walked outside and Marty led me to the nearest patio where thousands of poinsettias sat blooming. I gave him a microphone and set up two cameras. One of the biggest hurdles to working on your own is making the production feel bigger than it really is. I try to accomplish that by simply adding a second angle to my conversations. I positioned the cameras at the edge of the patio and got a very wide shot of all the flowers. It was far enough away that Marty eventually forgot it was there. The shot was gorgeous. It looked like Marty and I were standing in a field of fire. We chatted about his love for the farm and how each year he and his customers became new friends. This was a special place to him. When I asked about his son, Tyler, Marty's answers became a bit more sentimental.

"What kind of a flower man is Tyler going to be?" I asked.

"Better than his dad," smiled Marty. I wonder if Bill would have had a similar answer about Marty a few decades ago.

As we wrapped up our conversation, and carefully stepped around the poinsettias to avoid crushing the delicate petals, a car pulled up behind a rusty shed. It was one of those new friends Marty mentioned. They were there to pick up a beautiful bunch of poinsettias. Tyler beat Marty to the car with both arms full of flowers. The colorful plants filled the entire back seat of the sedan. The couple in the car exchanged pleasantries with the Orban men and offered their condolences over Bill's passing. It was a sweet moment to witness.

After the car pulled away, I introduced myself to Tyler. He was a sturdy mid-20s guy with a short, bristly beard and dimpled grin. He was a business student at a nearby college and enjoyed spending time with his dad at the nursery. We walked over to the barn for a few questions. It was filled with empty shipping boxes ready for holiday orders. A giant green tractor sat in the shadows ready to haul the boxes to the patios. Tyler sat down and I arranged my cameras. My first question was kind of a joke but it ended up being one of his best answers.

"Your favorite color is…?" I asked, purposefully trailing off my voice, fully expecting him to say 'red'.

"The color of the cement after the flowers are gone," he said with a chuckle.

It was a hilarious moment. The young guy growing up in the family business had every reason to be sick of the color red. It was everywhere. There were 100,000 flowers with ten or so petals each. That's one million red petals blanketing his 20-acre property. I'd be sick of red, too! We joked a bit and I mixed in a serious question here or there. It was fun and light-hearted. I've found when you keep your interactions conversational and don't ask too many pointed interview-style prompts, you get more genuine responses. Genuine was an adjective that could be applied to all the Orbans.

I thanked Tyler for his time and he sped off on the tractor. With one fewer Orban than last Christmas, there was a lot more work to be done. There was no time to sit and dwell on who was or wasn't around to help carry the load. Yes, Bill was gone. But, his memory was the reason why Marty and Tyler were working so hard. They had to push past the grief. There was no time to waste if the tradition Bill started was going to continue this season. They had to persevere through this emotional time to honor their loved one in the best way possible.

As the two guys went back to their flowers, Becky and I chatted near the car. "He was a character," she said of her father-in-law. "We just loved him. He was just a great person."

I have lost a grandfather. It was a weird experience. I lived in Oklahoma when my grandfather succumbed to cancer. It was a death we all expected but it was a death nobody wanted to admit was coming. I remember getting the phone call from my brother when "GP" died. It was the middle of the night in Tulsa. I was as sad as I was tired. I got up the next day and went to work. That's what you have to do. The pain is still real, but reality still calls.

Moving on doesn't mean forgetting. Moving on means working towards peace. My grandfather was a teacher and a musician. At least I didn't have to go back to a classroom the morning after he went to Heaven. Marty and Tyler are reminded of Bill's impact on their lives every time they look at a poinsettia. In some way, I think that is accelerating the perseverance process. The Orban men can either smile or bawl in the presence of those bright red flowers. After meeting them it was clear. The lessons they learned from Bill are going to help guide them down the road and every Christmas season ahead.

I have kept an eye on Orban's Nursery from afar since the first year we met. More troubles have hit them. A hurricane sliced across the state of Florida not long after our story aired. It caused hundreds of thousands of dollars in damages. It's just one more thing to overcome. They made it past that setback, too. The Orbans are a strong family.

Perseverance isn't easy. It also isn't impossible.

Romans 5:3-4 (NLT)
"We can rejoice, too, when we run into problems and trials, for we know that they help us develop endurance. And endurance develops strength of character, and character strengthens our confident hope of salvation."

BECOMING MR. UNIVERSE

Nobody is ever going to confuse me with Hulk Hogan. I've met him once. Nobody is going to confuse him with me, either. He's, well, hulking. I'm, well, not. I wish I could tell you I'm hiding incredible muscles under all these dress shirts and neckties. Truth is, I don't even like strong coffee.

The weight room was never my friend. I remember being mandated to spend hours there during my high school basketball days. During a shirts-and-skins game my freshman year, my coach singled me out in front of the whole team as an example of what he didn't want his players to look like. I believe the term "bird chest" was used. My skinny genes leave me more suited for skinny jeans. I went through a ridiculous phase during my first year of college where I started drinking protein shakes between classes to bulk up. Society tells young men that women want dudes with fast cars and big muscles. My first car was a station wagon and I don't even like to eat mussels.

Strength comes in many forms. I met a man for an *On The Road* story who exemplifies incredible physical and spiritual strength. He is a man who didn't quit when the headlines got ugly.

I don't think it would be fair to categorize Al Vaughan as a cocky individual, but he certainly is confident. I would be too if I looked like this guy! The bright green letters on his license plate tell you all you need to know about the mountain of a man:

"MR UNVRS"

Call it his rolling resumé. Call it his warning to all tailgaters. You don't want to rear end Al Vaughan. I never asked him for his height and weight, but let's suffice to say the answers are 6-foot-ish and BIG. This man knows his way around a weight room. It is the arena where Al feels most comfortable. I could practically hear the weights snickering at me as I set up my tripod.

It was early 2016 and Al had agreed to give me a demonstration of what a typical workout looked like for a man who was the reigning 'Mr. Universe' in his age division. I expected him to start hoisting 100-pound dumbbells over his head with his pinky finger or something mind-boggling. Instead, he showed me how proper, controlled weightlifting technique is the secret to sculpting a world-class body. It was all very good advice that I have yet to put into practice in my personal life. Maybe next year.

"I take pride in my physical fitness," he said, bending over to pick up some free weights. From across the room, his back looked like a cobra with its neck fanned out, ready to strike.

"You don't say?" I thought.

Every story has what call a "money shot". It is the image that leaves viewers with a lasting memory. Sometimes it's a close-up of tears. Sometimes it involves a perfect pop of sound. It can vary depending on the environment. Al's "money shot" came during his first set of chest presses. I was zoomed in on his arms. Heavy breaths escaped his lungs as he pushed the 35-pound dumbbells skyward. It sounded painful. Out of the corner of my eye, I noticed his huge smile. He wasn't in pain at all! He was enjoying this! I quickly whipped the camera around to capture that wide grin before his last rep ended.

"Eight, nine, ten," he said as he sat up and dropped the weights down to his feet.

Wasn't this supposed to be difficult? For me, it would have been taxing. But Al? He was just happy to be back in the gym after nearly having his love for weightlifting taken away by an opponent he never saw coming.

The gym was no more than 300 yards from Al's apartment, which looked more like a weightlifting museum than a residence. Dozens of trophies are displayed all over his home. There are trophies from his early days and tons of ribbons. He has framed photos of himself at competitions, compete with the spray tan and baby oil that makes those competitors look so greasy. They're displayed prominently near his front door. There was memorabilia stacked everywhere! It was like Cooperstown with a couch. Imagine what it must have been like to be surrounded by reminders of past successes while shriveling away in your armchair.

"I said, 'Doc, what's going on?' She says, 'You have throat cancer',"
explained Al. "Hit me like a rock. I never saw it coming."

The diagnosis was near-crippling: Stage 4 throat cancer.

"I don't have a problem telling you that I got in the car driving home
and tears started coming down my face," he continued. "I thought, this is
how it ends."

Within the first 18 months of my dating relationship with my wife, she lost
three grandparents to cancer. My grandfather lost his life because of the deadly
disease. My dad has dealt with it. So has my wife's aunt. Cancer has impacted
everyone in some way. Al knew all the deadly possibilities. They fogged his
brain. They clouded his hope. They could have suffocated his chances.

Imagine being as physically strong as someone like Al and feel the
strength flooding out of your body with each new chemo treatment. Imagine
how scared he must have felt sitting in hospital beds as he watched his once
bulging muscles melt into pudding. Al joked that he never lost his hair
because he had always shaved his head. It was the only thing about the
experience he could joke about.

Chemo shaved 51 pounds off Al's muscular frame. It took over four
decades of amateur weightlifting for Al to sculpt the body he had become
so proud of. Now he was losing it. On Jan. 29, 2015, Al had a biopsy done.
He endured radiation five times per week for seven weeks and needed
chemotherapy once per week for 2-3 hours each time.

"It was rough," he said, back at the gym, seated in a folding chair next
to the weight rack. I sensed that he was giving me an understated answer.
Just "rough"?! Maybe his competitive spirit wouldn't allow himself to give
any credit to the disease. Al told me he never even looked at himself in a
mirror for weeks. He was afraid he would be scared by the reflection. He
wanted to remember himself as a championship bodybuilder, not a scrawny
shell of a man.

One of the most popular collections of verses in the Bible is found in
Psalm 23. The chapter is read at funerals, recited in locker rooms before big
games, and taught in Sunday school classrooms.

Psalm 23:1-4 (NIV)

"*1 The LORD is my shepherd, I lack nothing. 2 He makes me
lie down in green pastures, he leads me beside quiet waters,*

³ *he refreshes my soul. He guides me along the right paths for his name's sake.* ⁴ *Even though I walk through the darkest valley, I will fear no evil, for you are with me; our rod and your staff, they comfort me."*

I especially love verse four. It's a picture of perseverance that offers us comfort in tough times.

"Even though I walk through the darkest valley, I will fear no evil, for **you are with me**; our rod and your staff, they comfort me."

You are with me is a promise. King David writes these words. He was a guy who understood troubles. As a boy, he had to kill lions and bears while working as a shepherd. As a teen, he killed a gnarly Philistine giant named Goliath. As a king-in-waiting, he fled for his life because the current king wanted him dead. Yet, David wrote that he was not afraid of evil because **"you are with me"**.

It's a wonderful reminder that God is there when we are facing our own giants. God is there when we are hearing news reports that only tell of terror. God is there when your relationship with your child is deteriorating. God is there when the diagnosis isn't encouraging.

It's hard to stay thankful in situations like Al's. bet it's hard to keep the faith! I bet it's hard to persevere! During moments of uncertainty, your attitude will dictate who wins that battle. For Al, it was either him or cancer. Al knew a fighter's mentality would renew his strength.

"Second place was not an option," he said.

Cancer zapped Al's muscles, but it couldn't steal his inner strength. Al's final treatment was April 30. On August 19, he was pronounced cancer-free. He resumed weightlifting immediately and in November, at the age of 60, earned the title of 'Mr. Universe'.

Al's humility was my major observation. If I had just stomped cancer, I'd want to shout it to the world. He, instead, took the stance of thankfulness and appreciation for having survived the storm. Life experience builds credibility. In Al's case, he is now able to preach about two different kinds of strength. He always had physical power. After defeating cancer, and outlasting a disease that's practically undefeated, he showed that he has an inner strength that's stronger than any muscle he's ever flexed.

Al Vaughan flexes in a bodybuilding competition

The photo in his home he is most proud of is the one of him holding the 'Mr. Universe' trophy. He doesn't love it because of the trophy itself. He loves it because he's posing with his doctor, who helped him conquer his disease and his fears. It's a picture of triumph that not everyone achieves.

Cancer competed but it's hard to be 'Mr. Universe'.

Romans 15:5 (NIV)
"May the God who gives endurance and encouragement give you the same attitude of mind toward each other that Christ Jesus had."

ERIC LOVES VANNA

Channel surf tonight around 5 p.m. and you are bound to hear the story of someone who is hurting. The headlines introduce us to a world full of people facing obstacles that feel insurmountable. Not enough money. Not enough help. No direction. No fertility. No hope. If you missed those stories at 5 p.m., don't worry. You'll get a fresh set at 6. All of them require perseverance.

As long as the devil is loose in our realm, we'll hear headlines we don't like. They can be depressing, but they are not the only things worth reporting. God did some incredible things today. Were you looking for them? We don't have to surrender to something other than God's triumphant plan. Yes, sour stories will pop up. But, trusting in God to offer us a detour away from pain will always pay off. Faith inverts the script. Perseverance powers patience.

There is always something trying to block us from where God wants us to be. There is always a hindrance. Some are big. Some are small. The good news is that most problems are not permanent. Most of us see our problems as gaping trenches. We need to start looking at them as puny divots. God is able to help you out of your situation. Perseverance is possible, and I love hearing about people who choose to persevere when things got severe.

Of all the people I've met in my time in television news, nobody has more greatly impacted my life in a positive way than the little boy who was not supposed to be here. Eric Piburn has defied both logical and medical expectations in his 11 years on this earth. After 38 weeks in the womb, Eric was born a fragile mess on December 30, 2006. He was bigger than doctors expected him to be at 6 pounds one ounce. He spent ten of the first 12 months of his life in the hospital, with tubes in every orifice, surrounded by the constant beeping of machines. The longest stretch in his own house was two weeks. The shortest time home before having to return to the hospital was just 12 hours.

Before I sat down to retell Eric's story for this book, I texted his mother and requested a list of the proper medical names for his many diagnoses. I know Eric's history, but I guess I'd forgotten just how much he's dealt with in his young life. The text I got back was 202 lines long. It probably would have been easier to snail mail me a scroll than to thumb that all out in a text message. It contained his ailments and all the necessary medicines Eric takes each day to combat them.

Unlike most of my *On The Road* stories, I did not seek out this one. My meeting with Eric was scheduled for me. I got an email from my TV station's promotions department. It said I needed to go meet an excitable little boy who loved the *Wheel of Fortune* game show. I packed up the car and made the hour-long drive to see a kid that would change my outlook on life.

If I had known what was waiting for me on the other side of the front door, I would have done some better mental preparation. Ever seen the old Tasmanian devil cartoons? That is Eric Piburn, only Eric wears glasses. The boy is a red-headed tornado in shoes. He had so much energy! His mother, Randi, greeted me. She was considerably calmer than her son. I immediately noticed that Eric was wearing a backpack. It contained clear tubes that carried oxygen to his nose from giant tanks in the Piburn's foyer. They didn't seem to bother him as he hopped up and down, showing off his favorite toy cars. His smile was infectious. I'd only known Eric for a few moments, but it was like we were best friends.

"Let's go play my favorite game," he said, leading me over to the bookshelf.

We wandered across the living room to a white bookshelf containing a ton of colorful board games. There was Sorry!, Checkers, and a few others that I recognized. The red box in the middle caught my eye.

"That one," Eric said, tapping the large box labeled *Wheel of Fortune*.

Randi unpacked the box and the three of us sat on the carpet to play. It was a board game version of the television game show that meant so much to the Piburn family. Eric went first. He flicked the spinner and called out letters. The board game included a plastic wall of letters like the one Vanna White manipulates on the TV show. Answer cards slid into place behind sliding tiles that would eventually reveal the winning phrase. Eric picked an 'N' and a few vowels. He spun again and guessed a 'P'. He was very good at this game! I could see the phrase coming together with each passing consonant, but it didn't matter. I wouldn't get a turn to choose a letter. Eric was in the zone.

After picking a 'V', he had figured out the answer.

"I got it! Pat Sajak and Vanna White!"

Randi slid back the remaining plastic tiles to reveal the correct answer. Eric was right! He smiled a gigantic smile and slapped a high-five with his mother. The joy on his face was pure. It was the most fun I'd had playing a board game in a while and I didn't even get to take a turn! His giggle continued for a couple of seconds before Eric asked if we could play again. Of course, we did. Telling local TV stories is a bit of a juggling act. In order to get the video on the air at night, you can't spend too much time playing board games during the day. But, being a caring person is more important to me than being a prompt journalist. Sometimes, you've just gotta play one more round. The camera can wait.

Eric won the next game, too. He had so much fun. He had forgotten about his oxygen tubes. He had forgotten about the physical therapy from earlier that morning. The endless needles, the doctor visits, and everything else a little boy should never have to deal with had all vanished away. He had so much heart. That was a little surprising, considering his doctors never expected Eric's heart to last this long.

Remember that 202-line text message Randi sent me? I can't pronounce most of the words she typed. It reads like a medical encyclopedia and a parent's worst nightmare. My brain started hurting as I attempted to decipher what she had sent. Eric has two major problems and both are considered terminal. In layman's terms, he needs a new heart and new pair of lungs. The highly dangerous transplants will have to be performed at the same time and come from the same donor. Even though he's 11, his body is the size of most six-year-olds. The donated organs will have to come from a younger child, who was healthy, and died in a way that did not harm his or her heart or lungs. Even if a match can be found, surgeons estimate that the procedure would have less than one-percent chance of succeeding and, possibly, an even slimmer chance of lasting more than a few days. Eric has received so many infusions already that it's assumed his body will reject any new organ almost immediately. That's just the major stuff. He deals with intestinal and kidney issues daily. Up until the day that I met him, Eric had never eaten a solid bite of food. Every ounce of nourishment that kept his brittle body alive came from either a port in his chest or a tube down his throat.

Not long after he took his first breaths, doctors told the Piburn family to take Eric home and enjoy every moment of their first year together. Medical professionals didn't see any reason to believe Eric would need a first birthday cake. As Randi explained all of this to me in her living room, out of earshot of her son, she uttered another phase that stung me.

"We know we're living on borrowed time," she said, taking a very long pause. "I just want more borrowed time."

It hit me like a cannonball to the gut. Those words had weight. They made me want to cry and scream and spit at the same time. I have no idea what it feels like to wake up every morning hoping your sick kid wakes up, too. I don't know what it's like to spend more money on medical bills than food each month. I don't know what it's like to live in a day-to-day fog of nervous energy.

If any kid has learned to persevere, it's Eric. After we'd finished our game, he flipped on his television to show me his loaded DVR. He and his mom had every recent episode of *Wheel of Fortune* saved. The show had become a huge part of their lives. Since Eric was so sick, he couldn't attend regular public school like the other kids his age. He learned letters and numbers by watching the game show. Randi, Pat, and Vanna would teach Eric math and spelling. They embraced the game show as part entertainment, part education. It was a connection to the outside world that made Eric feel good inside. When Pat and Vanna were on TV, it was easier to forget all his diagnoses.

After a few hours in his home, I thanked Eric for letting me hang out with him that day. He asked me to stay longer. I told him that I was very busy and needed to get back to work. I invited him to come see me at the TV station one day. He jumped and agreed. Little did he know that he'd only have to wait a few hours.

I do my very best to leave work at work. Most reporters don't do that. Most journalists are go, go, go, 24 hours per day, staying on top of the world around them. Me? I am too busy for all the world's busyness. I put in my time at the office before returning to my full-time jobs as a husband and dad. That's my mission field. I don't have time to get depressed by headlines. I can't be worried about who is getting shot and who is lying, stealing, and cheating out there. As much as I enjoy my TV career, I consider it my part-time job. I am a husband first, father second, and employee third. That order will not change no matter who signs my paychecks. But, on this occasion, I didn't mind fielding a few extra work-related phone calls from home. I chatted on the phone with a television producer in Los Angeles. Her job was to coordinate all the details for *Wheel of Fortune*. Our promotions department helped arrange a live satellite interview with Pat and Vanna. The two hosts agreed to "meet" Eric screen-to-face and spend some time chatting with him. We lined up everyone's schedules so that we could provide a surprise that Eric would never forget.

I was pumped up for this one. Eric viewed Pat and Vanna as royalty! I could tell after spending the day with him that meeting the game show legends was going to be a huge highlight. I was hopeful it would encourage him to keep winning his health battles.

Randi was in on the surprise from the beginning. I texted her the detailed plan. Eric needed to be at our TV station by noon the next day so we could coordinate the satellite shot. Before Eric went to bed, she told her son that they were going to get to take a special tour of my TV station the next day. I was eager to head off to work in the morning. It's not every day that you get a chance to change the life of a sick child.

Everyone's life has a purpose. Last year, I decided it was time to start executing mine. I want to use the platform that God has given me to make a positive change in the people around me. I don't care if they're strangers. I need, and God wants, my *On The Road* segment to produce kingdom connections. I want to use *my* career for *His* cause. He wants you to use your life in the same way.

Matthew 5:14-16 (NIV)

[14] *"You are the light of the world. A town built on a hill cannot be hidden.* [15] *Neither do people light a lamp and put it under a bowl. Instead they put it on its stand, and it gives light to everyone in the house.* [16] *In the same way, let your light shine before others, that they may see your good deeds and glorify your Father in heaven."*

A positive attitude means nothing without positive action. That means we need to help make kingdom connections happen. That means we must seek out those in need and fill a gap where we can. The hungry? The lonely? The scared? God cares for them all and wants us to care for them, too. Headlines throw a lot of Hell at us. The headlines in Eric Piburn's life are not uplifting. If we have the chance to change that, even for a day, shouldn't we?

I waited anxiously in the TV station lobby. I was pacing a bit. I knew what was coming. Randi knew what was coming. Eric had no clue what surprise was waiting for him. Behind me, in the main news studio, a team of engineers was working the phones with Los Angeles to make sure all the proper satellite connections were made. The microphones waited on the anchor desk. I was going to tell Eric that the studio was the first stop on his tour. He was actually going to get hooked up so Pat and Vanna could hear him. I was downright giddy.

Randi and Eric were accompanied by David, Eric's father, and Alex, his older sister. Nobody wanted to miss this. The Piburn family made its way up to the double doors. Eric rode in his wheelchair, attached to portable oxygen tanks. A thin paper mask covered his mouth. Even the slightest germ could cause major damage to his susceptible lungs. I welcomed everyone to our TV station and shook David's hand. I had not gotten to meet him the day before. He looked as excited as Eric. I asked the Piburns to follow me to the studio. Randi maneuvered Eric around corners and through hallways as we made our way to the scene of the surprise. It was hard for me to keep from smiling too big. I could not wait to see the look on Eric's face when he saw Pat and Vanna.

At least two dozen people were waiting for us. Word had gotten out about Eric's visit. It seems like everyone decided to take a long lunch break to witness this moment. Randi and David helped Eric out of his wheelchair and into a seat behind the anchor desk. Our head engineer hooked up Eric with a microphone and Randi took a few photos of her son. Not very many people get to sit at the news desk. Even fewer get to sit there and talk to their favorite game show hosts. I got the nod of approval from our behind-the-scenes folks. Los Angeles was ready to go. The lights were on. The cameras were set. The computer was recording it all.

Bobby prepares Eric for a big surprise

It was finally time. I waded through the growing crowd. About 30 people were now jammed into the studio. I crouched down beside Eric.

"This is pretty cool, huh?" I asked. Eric looked up at me from his seat with the same joyful look in eyes he'd had in his living room the day before. His blue-rimmed glasses were fogging up a bit on one side.

"Yep!" he gleefully shrieked.

I smiled back at him, knowing what was coming. "Well, it's about to get cooler. We have a surprise for you. Look over there."

Eric's eyes followed my outstretched arm to a large monitor in the middle of the room. An engineer yanked off a black sheet that covered the screen to reveal the big surprise. Randi gasped and covered her mouth as Eric shouted.

"HOLY MOLY! WOW!"

Staring back at him were his two favorite TV stars in the whole world.

"Hey Eric," said Pat Sajak.

For the first time in the 36-hours that I'd known Eric Piburn, he didn't have anything to say. All eyes in the room were on the little boy with the oxygen tubes in his nose. The cell phone cameras were snapping away. Tears started to flow from Randi's eyes. Even Eric's big, tough dad was getting misty-eyed behind the crowd. After about ten seconds, Eric's brain clicked. He realized this was all for him. There he was, 10-feet away from a screen with the image of the famous *Wheel of Fortune* duo.

"Hi Vanna White!" he yelled, waving his tiny hand frantically.

Their conversation only lasted a few minutes. They talked about Eric's love for the game show. They made a few jokes about how Pat's fingers could never get the puzzle board to work like Vanna's. Eric laughed and laughed. For a kid who spent most of his days struggling, this was a welcomed escape. Vanna and Pat instructed Eric to pay close attention to the screen because they had a special puzzle they needed him to solve. Vanna touched the corner of the puzzle and letters started to pop into view. The show's iconic music played as words formed on the screen. The reflection of the glowing TV shined in Eric's glasses as his vision narrowed. One by one, vowels and consonants appeared. He was trying to figure out the answer, but the letters were moving a little too quickly for him to solve the puzzle before the final letter animated. Once the message was complete, he beamed and shouted again.

"WHEEL OF FORTUNE!"

The puzzle read: "Wheel of Fortune loves Eric Piburn".

It was a magical few minutes. The two big-time TV stars said their goodbyes. Eric told Vanna he loved her. "I love you, too!" she replied. As the TV monitor went dark, I sat down in the open seat next to Eric.

"That was SOOOOO AMAZING!" he said. It really was.

Later that day, my news director called me into his office. It's kind of like being summoned to the principal's office in school. It can either mean really bad news or really good news. On this occasion, it was great. He told me that in his 35 years of local television, he'd only cried twice on the job. Watching Eric meet his heroes was one of those moments. That meant a lot to me. It filled me with pride. Not pride in myself. I was filled with a feeling of satisfaction for a child who needed a positive memory. We had all come together to make a little boy's day. Eric left that TV station with a smile on his face and an afternoon to cherish. He still had Pulmonary Hypertension. He still had Tetralogy of Fallot, Chronic Obstructive Pulmonary Disease, Gastroparesis, and Pulmonary Artesia. He will still need open heart surgery every six months to widen his clogged arteries. Those things are not going away. But, he also had a break from all that junk. He had an experience that few others will ever have.

I got to know the head football coach at my alma mater fairly well during the three years I covered his teams. A framed photo hung on the wall of his office. I have not forgotten it. It read, "It's easier climbing than hanging on". Perseverance is not something we want to do. It's something we are called to do. It's our way of trusting God with our circumstances and knowing the outcome will be alright. Persevering is not for the faint of heart, either. Some would say Eric's heart is weak. I could argue his is stronger than anyone's I've met. He's not just a boy. He's a climber. Even from his wheelchair. Doctors told Eric's parents he'd be dead a decade ago. He's still climbing. The ability to persevere when things get tough is a true sign of strength. It's easier to climb than hold on.

Eric poses with his shiny new Emmy award

Eric Piburn is the single biggest inspiration I've had in my career. He has taught me more about life than any other person I've interviewed. Stories like his are what make me excited to wake up and execute God's plan. *MY* career for *HIS* cause. I've been blessed in so many ways. God's influence makes me want to reach out and lend a hand to those still hanging. I want to help them climb.

You can do it, too. Persevering is hard, but the burden gets lighter the more we share the weight.

2 Corinthians 12:10 (NLT)

"That's why I take pleasure in my weaknesses, and in the insults, hardships, and persecutions, and the troubles that I suffer for Christ. For when I am weak, then I am strong."

CLOSING THOUGHTS ON PERSEVERANCE

I met a 41-year-old father of nine named Jason one morning. We spent about an hour in his backyard shooting a story. He was exercising on homemade jungle gym equipment and I was simply hitting the record button on a camera. The story was about his dream of opening his own family-friendly gym where he could teach people how to be healthier. After I was done shooting, we stood in his front yard for a few minutes chatting about his dream. His old, brown van was parked a few feet away. He told me how he, his wife, and a few of their now-grown kids made the 14-hour drive to North Carolina that past summer in that beat-up van. About mid-trip, the air conditioning blew out. Oscillating fans from a roadside Walmart provided the only cool air for 75 percent of the trip. It was stiflingly hot and miserable in that cramped "greenhouse" of a van, but Jason was all smiles as he described the vacation. He shared his family motto with me:

"When something goes wrong, call it adventure".

What a way to look at life. I know my kids. They would not be calling a 14-hour road trip with busted A/C an adventure. Not in the summer. Not in the winter. Not ever! But, life can be an exciting adventure during times of trouble, if you ask God to be your tour guide.

We focus too much on the detours and not enough on the destination. I focus should be on Heaven, not our problems. God finds us when we get off-course and reroutes us back towards His pathway.

How do you persevere? If your answer is anything besides, 'Trust in God', you're not going to have much success. You can't fix a God-sized problem with a human-sized solution. If God is the architect of our destinies, don't you think He knew we'd need an escape route from troubles? He's the Creator of the world, who breathed 100 billion galaxies into existence. He can handle our problems when we can't. Trying to sidestep problems on our own means choosing to under-utilize the greatest resource in the universe. This is no time to be stubborn. God wants to help you overcome. He wants to get you to the other side of your problems. It's His chance to show off His power. God is the galaxy's original handyman! Put Him on speed dial. He's ready to help us persevere, even if we think we don't need his help.

News headlines can put us on our heels. They can force us to play defense. God plays offense. He proved it in scripture many times. The Israelites were enslaved in Egypt for 400 years. God promised to set them free if they preserved through Pharaoh's torturous reign. God raised up a leader named Moses, who led God's people away from slavery and through the parted waters of the Red Sea to safety. Pharaoh's army pursued them but was destroyed when the walls of water crashed back into place. That's just one example! God's people persevere when we stay true to His word.

Singer and songwriter Bill Withers probably said it best in the lyrics of his well-known 1972 R&B single, *Lean On Me*:

> *"You just call on me brother*
> *When you need a hand*
> *We all need somebody to lean on*
> *I just might have a problem*
> *That you'll understand*
> *We all need somebody to lean on*

Nobody is going to confuse those lyrics with the gospel, but the overall theme of the song is the same as God's message to both believers and spiritual skeptics. Read the lyrics again. Now, pretend that God is signing them. He's begging us to lean on Him, not ourselves. That "somebody" to call on is God. There is no problem He won't help you overcome. You can lean on Him.

Jordan Raynor, best-selling author of *Called to Create*, has a great view on perseverance in his daily devotional, *Gospel Driven Ambition*. He wrote, "It is one thing to keep going no matter what; it is something far more beautiful to do so *cheerfully* and *hopefully*". How true. He also points out that in the original Greek translation of James 1:3, the word that is translated as *perseverance* means "cheerful, or hopeful endurance; constancy". It's not always easy to navigate the harsh waves of life with a cheerful and hopeful attitude. The key is to worry about the boat, not the water. Keep your boat intact and trust in your Heavenly captain to guide you.

There are only three positions in life: Entering a storm, in a storm, or exiting a storm. When I visualize these three life stations, I picture two incredible stories of Jesus. In Matthew 14, Jesus, after feeding over 5,000 people with just five loaves of bread and two small fish, instructs his disciples to head out ahead of him in a boat and cross over to the other side of the Sea of Galilee. After praying for a while, Jesus joins the 12 disciples by walking to them – on the water. A strong wind was blowing and waves were crashing against the boat. This was a crazy storm! Yet, Jesus calmly walked on top of the turmoil. The sight terrified the disciples. I think I would have been a little bug-eyed, too. Men don't walk on water. We sink. But, this was no ordinary man.

What strikes me the most about this is the reaction of both parties. The men, distracted by the chaos around them, screamed and cried out. They thought Jesus was a ghost. They were trapped in the middle of a howler. Juxtapose their emotions with those of Jesus. He strode up to the boat and coolly called out, "Take courage! It is I. Don't be afraid (Matthew 14:27 NIV)." Despite the scene, Jesus was serene.

Another passage I visualize when thinking about the storms of life is found in Mark 4:35-41. Imagine this scene: A hurricane is raging and Jesus and his disciples are stuck on the water in a little wooden boat. The oars are useless. The boat is probably half-sunk because it's so full of water. A dozen seasick men are scared for their lives and the Son of God is napping on a pillow in the corner. How could Jesus sleep through that chaos? I have been in hurricanes before. I've stood outside in tropical storms. It's part of working in local TV. We are, for better or worse, targets for nature's fury during natural disasters. I have felt the energy of an enormous storm and I did it from the "safety" of land. I can't imagine what it would be like to experience a storm that size from a 20-foot boat. Yet, Jesus snoozed right through it on a cushion in the stern.

The disciples woke Jesus up and basically screamed in his face. "Do you even care that we are going to drown!?" The miraculous part of the story comes in Mark 4:39 (NIV), when Jesus stands up in the rocky boat and commands, "Quiet! Be still!" The storm instantly stops. The verse says the "wind died down and was completely calm". Not a ripple. Not a wave.

It was total stillness. Snap your fingers. That's how long it took for the turbulent world around the disciples to experience 180-degrees of change. The difference between disaster and delivery was separated by three little words from the mouth of Jesus.

How do you handle times of worry? In both instances, Jesus' power delivers the men from their boat battle. In the story where Jesus walks on the water, the storm ended the moment He stepped in the boat. In the story where Jesus calmed the storm, the weather changed the moment He spoke. There will be upheaval in your life. There will be seasons that require perseverance. Your rescue could be closer than you think. Invite Jesus into your boat and let Him speak upon arrival. He is an anchor for worries. He'll pilot your perseverance.

In both of those gospel accounts, ordinary men needed extraordinary help to overcome something they couldn't handle on their own. Too often we try to ignore the help of others during stormy seasons. Worse yet, many of us try to navigate rough seas without the Captain in our lives. Believing Jesus *can* help is one thing. Relying on Him to guide you through storms is another. He was IN the boat during the squall! He was with the disciples the whole time, but the group only found relief from the waves after asking for Jesus' help. You're either entering a storm, in a storm, or exiting a storm. Will you try to ride it out alone?

Think of the waves in these Bible stories as headlines in our lives. There is always another one breaking. You can be paralyzed by them, and what they have the power to do, or trust that God has a handle on things. Tonight, the lead story will likely be something traumatic, or disheartening, or disruptive to peace in the world. Remember that God is authoring good news each day. He is ready to step into a boat. He's ready to calm the waves. He's ready to remind us all that help is just around the corner, if we're willing to look for it.

Persevering isn't easy. I'm not suggesting that the waves outside your boat aren't scary. They probably are very unsettling. I've lived through plenty of scares that required me to drop my faith anchor. I understand that not everyone who reads this book is going to be a Christian. Not everyone is going to believe that these boat stories actually happened. That's fine. All I know is that I have been in plenty of storms. Guiding myself out of them without the aid of a Heavenly compass is a lot harder than doing it with one. The same can be said for the people you read about in this chapter.

Brian and Holly Festa went through something they would not wish upon anyone else on earth. Losing two children is an unbearable thought. They made it through to the other side and have a loving family of four now. After losing Addie, their second baby, Holly and Brian found comfort in a church home. Community helps make perseverance possible.

Marty Orban lost his dad. Tyler Orban lost his grandfather. In both cases, the poinsettia men lost the rudder that had guided them through their industry for decades. Bill Orban left this earth a more colorful place. Working with bright red flowers without Bill by their sides required perseverance. On top of that, a tornado hit their nursery the following summer and caused $500,000 in damages. The community raised money to help with the cleanup efforts to get Orban's Nursery back up and running. This family is a model for persevering in the face of difficulty.

Cancer was supposed to kill Al Vaughn. His competitive spirit wouldn't accept his diagnosis. 'Mr. Universe' doesn't give up so easily. The only way for dumbbells to work is if you lift them and put them back down. Carrying weights around doesn't build muscle. It brings fatigue. Al chose to persevere by fighting. He never lost faith that he would beat his disease.

If anyone exemplifies the definition of perseverance, it's Eric Piburn. His little body looks like a roadmap full of scars left behind by countless surgeries. Yet, today, as I write these words, he's celebrating at his 11th birthday party. Medical experts predicted his funeral would come more than a decade ago. Instead, the kid who loves *Wheel of Fortune* is still fighting to watch more episodes. He's still persevering through every needle, scalpel, and medication. He hasn't accepted the destiny that doctors laid out for him. Instead, he cheerfully and hopefully battled and is providing the world with more joy than any other kid I know.

If you've been trying to handle your problems on your own, ask God for help today. Try to persevere with a running mate that knows how to finish the race ahead. Marathoners don't run 26.2 miles on Day 1. They start small. They tackle the challenge in increments and never stop moving. Eventually, the finish all 26 miles. Perseverance is a lot like a marathon. The finish line gets closer the longer you pursue it. You can't avoid storms forever. You're either entering a storm, in a storm, or exiting a storm. The next time your boat starts shaking, remember to "call it adventure" and let God be your tour guide.

VERSES ON PERSEVERANCE

Revelation 3:10 (NLT)
"Because you have obeyed my command to persevere, I will protect you from the great time of testing that will come upon the whole world to test those who belong to this world."

James 1: 2-4 (NLT)
"Consider it all joy, my brethren, when you encounter various trials, knowing that the testing of your faith produces endurance. And let endurance have its perfect result, so that you may be perfect and complete, lacking in nothing."

1 Timothy 6:11 (NLT)
"But you, Timothy, are a man of God; so run from all these evil things. Pursue righteousness and a godly life, along with faith, love, perseverance, and gentleness."

Psalm 18:29 (NLT)
"In your strength I can crush an army; with my God I can scale any wall."

Philippians 1:6 (NIV)
"Being confident of this, that he who began a good work in your will carry it on to completion until the day for Christ Jesus."

CHOOSE JOY OVER HEADLINES

*B*ad news can bruise our souls. Unexpected bad news can cripple us. In 1 Samuel 4, we read the terrible story of the Philistine army fighting and killing 30,000 cocky Israelites. During the victory, the Philistines captured the Ark of the Covenant from Israel, a sacred box which contained the Ten Commandments. One of Israel's leaders, Eli, lost two sons in the battle. When he heard the news of the lost Ark, it was too much for him to handle. He fell off his chair, broke his neck, and died. When Eli's pregnant daughter-in-law got the report that the Ark was stolen, and learned her husband and Eli had both died, it sent her into premature labor. She died during childbirth. Her son was named Ichabod, which means "Where is the glory?".

Bad news can lead to bad results. Creatively announcing bad news is an effective tool that the devil uses to crush our spirits. Depressing headlines show up when we can least afford to hear them, and digesting it all can be difficult. That's because we naturally have an intolerance to bad news. God didn't design us to be compatible with it. He made humans in His image, and His image is pure and holy. Bad news doesn't sit well in our guts because God doesn't like bad news.

That doesn't mean we won't see a steady diet of it in our lives. Fortunately, there is an antidote: *Finding Joy Beyond The Headlines*.

The Bible teaches us that only God is righteous. We are all just a bunch of sinners walking around on this earth wasting time before our next mistake. Because we have sin woven into our DNA, sinful actions are inevitable. Those actions lead to the horrible headlines and news reports we detest. There is no escaping the pattern. There is no way to keep from messing up. Sin has programmed us to fail and leaves us destined to fall short. You are not a perfect person and neither am I. Yet, even while swimming in a sinful reality, there is good news. We are awarded a daily chance to leave a positive impact on this world. We accomplish it through the way we reflect God's love to the other 7.5 billion imperfect people on this earth. Our paths cross with hundreds of new people each year. Don't you want them to see some goodness in you? Maybe your past keeps you feeling like you're not good enough. But, if God is in you, there is goodness in you. God gave you an amazing story to share. Are you willing to shout it from a mountain?

1 Chronicles 16:23-24 (NLT)

"*23Let the whole earth sing to the Lord! Each day proclaim the good news that He saves. 24Publish His glorious deeds among the nations. Tell everyone about the amazing things he does.*"

Notice the final phrase. It's my favorite part of those verses: "*...the amazing things He DOES*". Notice it doesn't say what God has DONE. It's what He is DOING right now that is worthy of our praise and attention! My job has helped me find and share the goodness God has implanted in people.

Tonight's headlines will be filled with death and anguish. I can say that with confidence because I know that evil doesn't take a day off. Dense fog led to a plane crash that killed five people near my house this year on Christmas Eve. It's heartbreaking. Families lost children that day. We can't escape sad news – even on holidays. What we can do is embrace the good things that God is doing all around us and use them to hoist the spirits of those who are hurting and seeking joy. To find joy, you must chase joy. It won't be beamed to your cell phone every hour. It lives beyond the headlines, but it's worth pursuing.

When I was little, my family constantly moved. I lived in seven different homes before my ninth birthday. Change was normal for me. I expected the unexpected. I remember the names of most of my teachers but very few of my friends. I never got too attached to them since I was only in the same school for a year or so. In my first decade of life, I lived through starts, re-starts, and even a divorce. But, joy was coming. When we finally planted roots in Clearwater, Florida, we moved to a street with another boy my age.

Kyle lived at the end of the block and was just a few weeks younger than me. We became instant buddies and grew to have a lot of common interests. We'd play board games all spring and roller skate all summer. We played basketball in the driveway year around. We'd dribble and shoot for hours. It was serious competition. The trouble for me came at nightfall when I had to make the long walk back home.

When I was younger, I was afraid of the dark. More accurately, I was situationally scared. I didn't fear the shadows in my bedroom nor the monsters under my bed. I never worried about the possibility of the Boogeyman lurking in my closet. But, I was nervous to be outdoors in the dark. It wasn't a paralyzing fear, but it was enough to make the journey home from Kyle's house plenty terrifying after sunset. I'd shoot hoops until dusk and then run the spooky marathon home. To a ten-year-old, traveling a distance that covers six house lots in the dark may as well be a cross-country flight with Freddy Krueger. A smarter kid would have come home when the sun was still up. I never learned that lesson.

I vividly remember the trip back home. I look back on it now and I chuckle but, at the time, it seemed like it took hours to get from Kyle's driveway to my front door. It was scary but there was hope. Every time I stepped off his curb and into the dark street, my only focus was the tiny glimmer emitted by the pedestal light in my yard. My dad installed that thing shortly after we first moved to that house. I hated it initially because it required me to maneuver the lawn mower awkwardly during my weekend chores. It was just difficult and clunky. It also became my life-saver once the moon came out.

The first few steps were the hardest. I think it's because I knew there was no turning back once I started. I remember huffing and puffing as my Nikes pounded the pavement. My over-active imagination kicked into hyperdrive with each step and my brain cycled through all the possibilities. The tree branches cast eerie shadows on the ground beneath my feet and I envisioned them coming to life to grab me. I half-expected a bear or wolf to appear out of nowhere. Surely monsters were lurking behind parked cars. My mind ran faster than my feet. The only thing I had to hope in was that lamp post at my house. My eyes never left it. I wasn't a fast runner but I felt like an Olympian on those retreats home. As I picked up speed, the light grew larger and brighter. Panic settled. My fears faded as I drew closer and closer. My gaze never left the faint filaments.

After what seemed like days, I finally made it. I always made it. All those things I feared were purely imagined and unnecessary distractions. I remember the feeling of security as I left the darkness of the street behind and entered the familiarity of the well-lit driveway. In my mind, I outraced all the evils of the world to get there. I made it. I was home. I was safe.

I think about our journey through life that same way. I also see it as an apples-to-apples comparison to our journey through the news cycle. Evil is a joy-snuffer. There is a lot of evil out there. Some of it is imagined. Some of it is real. Some of it makes a newscast and some does not. I consider much of it a distraction from what's really going on around us. From the moment we wake up to the moment our heads hit the pillows again, our days will be lined with reports that cast eerie shadows on our paths. Flip on any newscast. Turn on any computer. Pick up any newspaper. All will feature terrible headlines vying for your attention. Some of those headlines will take root and our imaginations will start to churn. They will hold our brains hostage. They will start to influence us. The key to finding joy beyond the headlines is to keep your eyes fixed on the light. Good news and uplifting stories live in your neighborhood. They live at your office. They are happening at your schools. There will be darkness along the way. Expect it! But, there is goodness waiting for you. Seek it! Your worldview will largely be dictated by how much light you consume and darkness you ignore.

When I think of ambitious people, I think of people chasing after a goal God has set in their hearts. I think of people unafraid of the negativity around them. I think of people who are launching themselves at a dream and not settling for second-best. There is no silver medal. There is no woulda, shoulda, coulda. There is only a desire fueled by faith that the One who gave you the mission will help you to complete it. I think of people like Madison Harrison, Mike Abramowitz, Sy Schimberg, and Donald Nutting.

When I think of joyous people, I think of people willing to look beyond the headlines that so easily cause us to stumble. I think of people who actively look for uplifting moments and bask in them. They find happiness in the world around them and overcome darkness with light. I think of people who are not easily influenced by headlines, but actively search for God's impact on our lives. I think of people like Peter Garino, Henry Witherwax, Davis Harkey, and Abby Vega.

When I think of thankful people, I think of people who are pleased through the pain. There are a lot of snares in this world designed to trap us in our sin. Thankful people tip-toe around the traps and keep their attention on what is most important. We have more to smile about than we have to frown about. It's easy to forget that with headlines like ours. Thankful people find ways to seek God's goodness in all situations. I think of people like Adam Smyk, Willie Reese, Noel Stafford, and Vicky Smith.

When I think of blessed people, I think of people doing the right things for the right reasons. Blessed doesn't mean you drive a Cadillac. It means you are taken care of today and trusting God to take care of you tomorrow. Blessed people are confident in their hope and excited to have the chance to make a difference. I think of people like Debi Shackowsky, Molly DuPont Schaffer, John Joyce, and Delwyn Collins.

When I think of giving people, I think of selfless servants. I think of people who put themselves last and others first. I think of people who make it their mission to do as much good as possible before their last breath on this earth. I think of people who want to see others happy. They are sacrificial and sweet. I think of people like Lee Hardy, Scott Hand, Becky Gama, and Noel Keesling and Joel Clement.

When I think of a loving person, I think of someone who isn't concerned with themselves. I think of someone dedicated to making other's lives better in any way possible. I think of someone who goes above and beyond. Lovers are givers with a little extra vigor. They care more because they know true love can provide much more than a shallow, surface-level connection. I think of people like Julie Clarke, Ken Deka, Dick and Fran Stanton, and Brent Kraus.

When I think of perseverant people, I think of warriors. I think of people who don't back down from a fight. I think of people willing to go all-in on their dream to accomplish what isn't likely. I see people who stare "no" in the face and scream "Yes!" right back. I think of people who never lose hope, faith, or internal fire. I think of people like Brian and Holly Festa, Marty and Tyler Orban, Al Vaughan, and Eric Piburn.

Psalm 27:13 (NLT)
"Yet I am still confident I will see the Lord's goodness while I am here in the land of the living."

This is a Psalm written by King David during a rough time in his life. I think we are a lot like David. He was looking for help when the news of the day seemed overwhelmingly negative. We get this way. We get crushed by the weight of the headlines and need help finding God's goodness through the messiness of life. Every night it's another story of a dead child, a crooked world leader, or a preventable injustice. The constant bombardment of damaging reports makes it difficult to stay positive, but God is not a bad news God. He is a good news God with so much to offer us. Despite the evil in the world, and despite the way it's repetitively spoon-fed to us, are you confident that you'll see the Lord's goodness around you?

There is more ambition, joy, thankfulness, blessing, giving, love, and perseverance happening right now in the world than the headlines convey. The problem is, too often, we seek the headlines first. They are hard to avoid, but it doesn't help that we tend to invite them in. We should not get into the practice of allowing destructive stories to trickle into our minds before we ever consider pursuing joy.

Who has this habit? You wake up, wipe your eyes, and reach for your cell phone. You're greeted by the news alerts from overnight. You check a few emails. You like a Facebook post. Pretty soon, you've wasted the first 25 minutes of your day. You're still in your pajamas, but all caught up on the disasters that took place while you slept. It's a terrible way to greet a morning. You wake up in an emotional ditch and spend the rest of the day trying to find a ladder. Seeking joy means putting the cell phone down and putting God in its place. Seeking joy is the first step to finding it.

Here is the typical week of lead stories in TV news:

Monday: *Caregiver Arrested After Abandoning 80-year-old*
Tuesday: *Athlete Apologizes For Saying 'Little Boys Don't Wear Princess Dresses'*
Wednesday: *Speeding Train Crashes On Snowy Track, Kills 20*
Thursday: *Earthquake Causes Millions in Damage In California*
Friday: *Bakery Sued After Refusing to Bake Cake For Gay Wedding*

No wonder we think the world is messed up. We're told the world is crumbling every night at 5 p.m., so we believe it. It's easy to let the lead story lead us to an untrue conclusion. The news is true. The outlook it suggests isn't always. There is joy out there. God didn't create us to be fearful. If what you're consuming leads you to a fearful place, then you are consuming something outside of God's design.

I believe good news ought to be in the news!

During the 11 p.m. news, you'll hear about the breeder mistreating dozens of her dogs. You may not hear about the woman across town who is committing her life to rescuing strays. You'll read about the politician who cheated to win the latest election. You may not read about his predecessor's mission to raise money for orphans. The newspaper will run a frontpage story about deceits within the local police department. I wish they'd spent more time writing about the officer who helped talk a distraught woman off the ledge of a bridge. The headlines are catchy but there is joy beyond them.

Now that I am old enough to reflect on the times I sprinted home in the dark as a kid, I'm glad I never left Kyle's house before sunset. I'm glad the darkness scared me. I'm glad my house felt like a million miles away. Almost 30 years later, those memories have led me to a beautiful conclusion: Keeping our eyes from getting distracted by darkness, and fixing them on the hope found in the light, will lead us to a place of safety. I needed faith over fear. Fears can overtake us if we let them. Imaginations don't come with off switches. Staying focused on a light source will give us something to sprint towards. Likewise, staying focused on ambition, joy, thankfulness, blessing, love, giving, and perseverance will lead us away from the depression of the headlines and straight towards God's good news.

I hope you keep consuming news. It's important to know what's happening around us. I just hope that in doing so, you remember to seek God's goodness first. Be encouraged by the joy around you. Don't be weakened by the bad news.

It is possible to Find Joy Beyond The Headlines.

Isaiah 52:7 (ESV)

How beautiful upon the mountains are the feet of him who brings **good news**, who publishes peace, who brings **good news** of happiness, who publishes salvation, who says to Zion, "Your God reigns."

Printed in the United States
By Bookmasters